MW01289143

But The Heavens Never Cried

by

Cindy E. Barg

This book is a work of non-fiction. Names of people and places have been changed to protect their privacy.

© 2004 by Cindy E. Barg. All rights reserved.

No part of this book may be reproduced, stored in a retrieval system, or transmitted by any means, electronic, mechanical, photocopying, recording, or otherwise, without written permission from the author.

First published by AuthorHouse 04/23/04

ISBN: 1-4140-9071-4 (e-book)
ISBN: 1-4184-4749-8 (Paperback)

Printed in the United States of America
Bloomington, IN

This book is printed on acid free paper.

DEDICATION:

Michael Scott Barg
a very gentle soul who is loved "Infinity"

"....death is but the limitation of our sight...."

=PROLOGUE =

On a brisk, October autumn in 1995, my telephone rang three times. A voice so distraught, screaming in horror resounded in my ears. After infinite minutes passed, I could barely make out the words being yelled at me, when they finally registered in my mind, "Your brother was murdered."

This is the true story about Michael Barg, a beloved son and brother whose death rocked the world of a close-knit family. It is about how a horrific tragedy can put your world into a tailspin, paralyzing your emotions and your soul. It is about how death of the most unthinkable kind can bring you down to such a level of perpetual resignation, you no longer believe you will ever put one foot in front of the other again. It is about confronting isolation, depression and extreme loss of the utmost variety simply because there are no answers to justify death. It is about all the other pains and tragedies that occurred in your life and now come to fruition because they have to.

Jerry Cooper despised Michael Barg from the moment he had laid eyes on him. Michael was a handsome, single, savvy, 39-year-old account executive, impeccably dressed, with piercing blue eyes and gray hair cropped close to his temples. Jerry Cooper, married with no children, was the head bartender at the infamous Cheers Bar in Logan Airport, Boston, where he swooned customers with an affable charm and a winning smile. Yet, behind that smile, something very ominous lurked. Big in stature, with thick, black hair piled on top of his head, he offered patrons an empathetic ear to listen to, flirted with the opposite sex and made fancy salt-rimmed margaritas. Jerry Cooper was the center of attention. That was his life. He thrived on the mindfulness his customers bestowed upon him.

Cooper also had begun a relationship two years prior, with one of the waitresses, Diedra Forte, a very attractive, single young woman, in her early thirties. Jerry Cooper showered Diedra with gifts, lavished her with large sums of money in times of need and fell in love with her imultaneously. Diedra was flattered by Jerry's affections, but she also felt suppressed by his controlling nature. Though their relationship had blossomed into an intimate one, Diedra was becoming more and more fearful of Jerry Cooper. His obsession with her was unappeasable and suffocating. Concurrently, Michael Barg, Jerry Cooper and Diedra Forte all met during a sales transaction. Innocently, Michael commented to Jerry Cooper how attractive Diedra was. Such an irreparable comment would prove one of the most deadly mistakes for Michael.

This personal narrative comes from an abyss of agonizing pain. It is estimated that over 20,000 people are murdered each year, leaving the survivors of their murdered loved ones to pick up the pieces. I never would have been privy to understanding how such a life-changing event could make my life go into a downward spiral, haunting me for years to come, forcing me to stop surviving and to live life again. This is a story of hope, of unrelenting tragedy that opens the heart to loving again. It is a story of transcending the grief through the art of love, no matter how long it may take. It is for all siblings and all individuals who continue to suffer. It is my personal gift to humanity; in recognition that you are never alone, that you are okay as you are, and that there is hope beyond the grief. Over and beyond anything else, this story is a validation that it is okay to grieve in whatever capacity you need to grieve.

Chapter 1

It was a brisk, autumn day, Saturday October 14, 1995. A walk with my children seemed most appropriate. We delighted in devouring scrambled eggs, homemade muffins and generous portions of fruit. The kitchen table overflowed with watermelon seeds, cantaloupe rinds, crumpled napkins and splattered orange juice. Demonstrative artwork of pressed cranberries and blueberries found their way onto the wooden table. My youngest daughter Emily, five, delighted in making masterful creations using food as her perfect medium. Kailee, eight, and her friend Colette, chit-chatted behind closed doors securing a privacy only known to them, while they readily dressed for our walk. As we opened the front door, the timer on the stove went off. The scent of baking bread and brownies filled the air. The teapot gently spewed aromas of peppermint.

I loved Cape Cod. Sandwich was the most historical town on this lovely island. Home was here. Tremendous serenity filled my soul. In a second I became distracted. I could hear the old creak in that rod. My favorite rocking chair sat dignified on my porch. I first saw it an auction. Though it needed to be tended to, I'd fallen in love with it. It was my favorite piece of furniture, lovingly crafted and painted green. The thin, embroidered comforter embracing itself on the rickety railing, was a reminder that winter was not far away. A delightful morning had been in the making, one filled with exploration, laughter and idle conversation.

Grabbing Emily's hand, I felt her soft, little palm, marveling in her innocence. My oldest daughter though, would not let on that she still enjoyed holding hands with me. A sigh bellowed quietly from my insides. I understood. She had protected her own space. I smiled, but I also felt wistful. She did not need me as much now.

When Kailee was first born, her head was perfectly round. She had jet-black hair framed delicately to her very tiny features. She was exceptionally petite. I was thoroughly ecstatic about her arrival. She slept so peacefully in my arms, never resisting my offerings of love. Today was different. Even at eight, she was independent. Emily on the other hand, came into this universe with a powerful struggle. She was a fighter. She adored when I would voraciously nudge up to her. Still, Emily loved being smothered with affection. It is not that Kailee did not desire this endearment; she merely chose her moments. For me, it was a very important lesson in letting go.

Chapter 2

Leaves were strewn in the air, floating aimlessly. They landed on our heads as we strolled through the neighborhood. A profound nostalgia swept through me. It was bittersweet. I was divorced a year ago in May. I had established a very successful practice in psychotherapy and I was well respected in the area. My friends were generous, kind and very real. For a split second I ached emotionally. The feeling was so overwhelming, tears came to my eyes. Something about the Cape air moved me to a level of heart-felt reflection. Emotions stirred within me that I thought were already accounted for years ago.

A yellow finch occupied itself on the oak next to my neighbor's house. He was subtlety eyeing me. It was an instant flashback to when I was twelve years old. Looking at my father, happily cutting the lawn, I remembered the smell of the green grass permeating throughout. He winked at me. A year later we were hit head on at one hundred miles an hour. My whole family and I were going on vacation to Maine. My dad was pronounced dead in the ambulance on the way to a hospital. Our beloved boxer, Beezee, who was in tremendous pain, was shot by a state trooper. I awoke in Massachusetts General Hospital being told that I would never walk again and I would not be able to have children. That was twenty-four years ago. I was flooded with sadness, but grateful for the memory of my father. My children pranced without suspect in front of me, caught up in their own playfulness. A gust of sea salt air raced up my nostrils. I snapped back to reality, remembering why I so loved the Cape.

It was good to be alive. The walk was slow and deliberate. We were captivated in our own private spaces. I looked at my watch. I had promised Colette's mother that I would return her early in the morning. She had plans with her family. The rest of us could leisure around. I stopped. I gently yelled out to the girls that we must turn around. There were mild protests, but to no avail, we arrived back at the house, got in the car, dropping Colette off at her home.

Colette thanked us about twenty-five times. Giggles were audible and warm hugs were given. We found our way back in our driveway. As we were climbing out of the car, Emily scrambled to unlatch her seat belt, throwing her body over the back seat, heartily laughing until someone would open the back door. The only way that door could be opened was for another person to get out, releasing it from the outside. Kailee looked back, pleading with her sister to open the side door. Emily, in her spirited way gleamed without budging. Emily was immovable. Kailee was impatient. I did not want to have to diffuse anything that was seemingly so miniscule. I got out and opened the back door. Emily gave out a mischievous snicker almost as if she were rejoicing in a great accomplishment.

We entered the front door, only to savor delightful smells saturating the house. I dropped my keys down on the table, contentedly entering the kitchen. I immediately went for the unscathed pan of brownies, preparing to cut them, when, all of a sudden the phone rang. It was but 9:00 in the morning. Kailee and Emily were hovering over the brownie pan when I picked up the receiver and said, "Hello?" I could hardly understand the person on the other end when I once again, repeated, "Hello?" The voice was so discomforting my heart started to race. It appeared as though infinite minutes had passed by. I tried desperately to make out an extremely distraught voice on the other end. Without warning, a primordial scream resounded so intensely I nearly dropped the phone. As if the voice had reverberated in my head a thousand times, garbled words shrieked distinctly, "Are you sitting down?" In between sobs of uncontrollable variety, I was barely able to hear the rest of what was being said to me, but I finally registered these words, "Your brother was *murdered*." I was completely and utterly thrown off balance. I felt as if I was going to pass out. An enormous wave of nausea came over me so violently I could barely stand up. My right hand clenched so tightly around the crease in the wall my knuckles had actually turned white. At that precise moment, I realized my mother was choking for air. I screamed back, "Who did it?" My hysteria broke loose.

I knew instantly it was my older brother who had been killed. My mother was shattered. Her yells were shockingly agonizing as I hung up. My heart was vibrating so acutely I placed my left hand over my heart as if to stop the pain. Kailee started to sob, running to her room. Emily stood still, in the middle of the kitchen, immobilized with fear from watching me. Her mouth gaped open. She was unable to speak. I began to amble down the hallway, back and forth. Everything appeared to be nothing. My pace quickened. I was walking nowhere, confused, hindered by my shock. Up and down, walking as if a force was pressing me forward but totally and completely lost, simultaneously. I became utterly oblivious to my once responsibilities. I was thoroughly lost in a space I did not comprehend. It was as though I was watching myself from a distance, yet I could not jolt myself back. My pace quickened to the point where

I could literally feel the pounding of my heart once again protruding out onto my chest. In that split second, I could hear sobbing coming from the back of the house. I remembered my children. I ran to my daughters' room, finding them both huddled together on one bed. Their pain and their fear became foremost. Weeping, we held tightly around each other. We rocked back and forth for what seemed like an eternity.

Chapter 3

I felt disconnected from myself. In my mind's eye, everything appeared surreal and unimaginable to the reality that just occurred. Concurrently, thoughts flooded my brain. I was the closest next of kin residing in the Boston area. My brother was murdered in Lynn, Massachusetts, a town, approximately thirty minutes east of the city. The nicer section, known as Diamond City, was surrounded by heaping, oversized homes snuggled closely together with wrap-a-around porches with panoramic views of the east coast. Oversized walls surrounded these mansions from torrential flooding. The not-so-nice section was cluttered with tenement buildings, sprawled one on top of another, broken doors, with cracks in windows and drifters sleeping against trash bins. A stark line between wealth and poverty was distinctly visible in Lynn. My brain deviated to a new thought. I would have to identify my brother. Feeling weak and ill, I became terrified. I knew nothing of how he was murdered. I absolutely had no experience with murder. I was mortified by my thoughts. Letting go of Kailee and Emily, I bolted upright. I had to make calls to relatives and to the police station in Lynn. I was now motivated by my trepidation as a cold sweat clouded itself onto me.

Despite the fact that I was in my own space, I felt totally disoriented. I was completely unable to take care of my children. Pausing, I called my friend Bette who lived down the block. On the third ring, Bette's husband answered. I was stammering. Bette's husband repeated hello. Answering back in a most distressed voice, I said my name. Bette's husband exclaimed to Bette that I was extremely distraught. Bette came on the phone immediately. I relayed the little information I knew to Bette. Hesitantly, Bette said, *"What?"* In less than five seconds, she regained her composure. She said she would be right over to get Kailee and Emily. No other questions were asked. I then proceeded to call my mother's side of the family in Philadelphia. I barely had any connection to that side of the family, except for the fact that I was my mother's daughter. I simply never had the chance to get to know them. Yet, I knew in my one minute of clarity if I notified Tami, she could complete the rest of the calling for me.

I fumbled for my shabby, red book filled with phone numbers and addresses of yesteryear, tucked and buried beneath papers, old lists of unwanted stuff and accumulated cookbooks. It fell off the counter, spilling out the contents of more collected lost phone numbers and addresses. Harried and befuddled, I picked up the book, all of its contents, scrambling to find my cousin's number. Grabbing the same phone I slammed down on my mother, I began to dial the number. One ring, two rings, finally. Tami picked up the phone and said "Hello?" I said, "Tami, this is cousin Cindy, Marilyn's daughter." Pause. "Cindy?" "Yes, Tami, cousin Cindy." "How are you dear?" Pause. More pause. "Michael was just murdered." I was a mess. There was a complete silence on the other end. Tami startled, said, "Who…what?" More silence. "Oh my God," she said. "All right dear, I will make calls for you." She hung up. I then dialed my very best friends. Deana and Gregg lived but minutes away. They would be there for me without question. Deana picked up immediately. In my half sobbing cries, I sputtered out an account of the phone call I recently received from my mother. She was completely and utterly supportive telling me she would be there right away. For some unknown reason, I again picked up the phone attempting to call my ex-husband, who lived approximately an hour away in his parent's house in Quarry. More rings. On the fourth ring my former father-in law picked up the phone. My speech was distorted. I managed to blurt out that my brother was just murdered. There was a slight delay. More stillness. "Is this a prank call?" Years ago, Aiden had been a newspaper reporter. Seemingly he was skeptical about anyone who would make such a call as I had. A week prior, my former in-laws were told by a doctor that one of their daughters had inoperable brain cancer. This news certainly added no relief. It was very apparent that I was extremely agitated. I began to cry. Aiden fumbled, handing the phone to his daughter who happened to be at her parents' house that morning. She took the phone from her father, "Is that you Cindy? Don't get off the line." Maggie, very slowly and very deliberately assured me she was going to call one of her siblings. They would be at my house as soon as possible. I was grateful for her intervention. Yet, I wanted to talk to my ex-husband. He was someone I was familiar with. No one knew where he was. This brought up a flood of memories from my marriage. My ex-husband was barely ever present emotionally. I never knew where he was when he was out and when I did need him, he simply was unavailable. I was too exhausted to feel anything, even disappointment. I thanked Maggie and hung up.

I started to pace around the house walking absolutely nowhere. My doorbell rang. Bette, half dressed, her hair still wet, gave me a long, endearing hug. She gathered my children, some of their clothes and told me that she would keep Kailee and Emily for as long as I needed. I thanked her. She walked out. I was completely alone in my home. I was so overwhelmed with what to do next, I completely forgot to call my younger brother Jacob, twenty-three, who was living and working in Manhattan.

Chapter 4

Approximately one and a half hours had transpired from the time I received the phone call from my mother. I knew my brother was either sleeping, at his office or simply somewhere unavailable to my knowledge. I called his apartment in Manhattan letting the phone ring twelve times. I then called his work phone. One of his co-workers, also a good buddy picked up. I asked if Jacob was working today. He had said no. I called his apartment again. No answer. I was becoming frantic. Jacob had to know. He had to know from me. I had no idea how to find him. I dialed his phone again. I continued dialing until I was exacerbated. I suspected Jacob might have been with his girlfriend Kara. I knew she was living with her parents outside of the city. Combing my mind for answers, I desperately tried to recollect where she lived. More time passed, as I agonized over not being able to locate Jacob. All of a sudden, I recalled the town. Picking up the phone, I made another pleading attempt to locate my brother. I prayed Kara's mother knew where Jacob was. I dialed. Kara's mother answered the phone. In a very polite, but trembling voice I asked if she had any idea where Jacob was. She said she did not. She could sense that something was terribly wrong. She had asked me if everything was all right. In my furor, I cried, telling her what little I knew. She gasped. She said she would find Kara, who would hopefully be able to locate Jacob. We both hung up.

I again rang Jacob's office in Manhattan. He was a stockbroker and he oftentimes worked on Saturday mornings. His same buddy answered. I had asked if Jacob was coming into work that day. He had no idea. We hung up. I called ten minutes later in desperation rekindling a hope that my brother had just walked through the door to his office. His buddy reiterated to me that he simply did not know where Jacob was. Finally and out of curiosity he asked me if something was wrong. I hesitated. I did not want my brother to hear such horrific news from someone else. Hesitating some more, I finally burst out uncontrollably that our older brother was just murdered in Boston. His friend screamed, "*Oh my God!*" Then he caught his breath. I begged him not to tell Jacob anything. He replied, "If I hear from him, I will tell him to call you immediately." I hysterically thanked him. We hung up.

Another forty-five minutes passed. My doorbell was ringing profusely. Deana was at my front step along with seven of my very close friends. She apologized for being so late. She could not find her husband and her children who happened to be taking a walk together. She became frantic in her search to find her family members. I could see her embarrassed frustration. There was no need for any explanation. I was terribly grateful and relieved to see her. There were silences, welled up eyes and simply hugs exchanged.

We all congregated in my bedroom not knowing what to do. I was oddly clear. My friends were unconditionally supportive. Another ring sounded on the doorbell. Deana ran to the front door. My former sister-in-law, Jenna appeared. She had driven over an hour. When I saw her, I collapsed in her arms crying. She cried too. Within seconds of my friends arriving, the phone rang. My bedroom was full of the most gracious and loving people I knew. The phone rang again. I picked up the receiver intuitively sensing that my younger brother was on the other end of the receiver. What if it was him? I played innumerable scenarios in my mind. Very apprehensively, I heard my younger brother's voice say, "Cin, my buddy at work told me to call you. Is everything all right?" I was overwrought with emotion. There was no plan. I was not able to locate Jacob for what appeared endless time. He was a family member I so loved and adored. He was very close to Michael. The minute I heard his voice, I was overcome. I spurted out, "Michael was murdered." "*What,*" he said? Then I literally screamed, in between reckless sobs of pain, "Michael was *murdered.*" He shrieked, "*What! Oh my God! Oh my God!*" Then I heard a huge noise in the background. I later found out that my brother punched a hole in his apartment wall. It was at that precise moment his roommate jolted out of his sleep, sitting upright. I also found out that Jacob and his roommate had shut their phone off that morning.

I was completely taken aback by own emotion. I handed the telephone to Deana. She very calmly took the phone and talked to Jacob, verifying that Michael had indeed been murdered. They hung up.

Chapter 5

I collapsed on my bed, tears drenching my face. Another thought. I knew I had to call the police station in Lynn. I forced myself back up out of bed. I walked to the kitchen and toward the phone. I so dreaded this moment. However, before I could dial, the phone rang. I was exceedingly shaken by the shrill of the ring I jumped. Picking up the receiver, I heard a man's voice saying, "This is the so-and-so precinct in Lynn, Massachusetts. Are you the next of kin to a Michael Barg?" I said, "What?" ""I am officer so-and-so. I am calling from the police station in Lynn, can you hear me?" I never got his name but I replied, "Yes." I told the officer I would be there as soon as possible. He told me he would be waiting for me. I was completely submerged in emotion at this point. I had to go, identify my brother, identify his belongings and sign a statement that I was his next of kin. Jenna walked into the kitchen. She offered to take me to the police station in Lynn and wait with me. She called other family members who would meet us there. The rest of my friends migrated back into the kitchen area, designating who would do what for my dogs, my children, who would keep the refrigerator stocked, etc. Food was the farthest thing from my mind. My friends found their continuity by maintaining some order in my home. It was the only thing that made sense to everyone. Nothing else did. Jenna and I left making the one hour and twenty-five minute trip to Lynn.

Chapter 6

There was so much going on in my brain, I felt restless. I was plotting in my mind's eye what I would do when I walked into the police station. I had this vision that I would be led to a morgue. A sheet would be pulled down over my brother who would be lifelessly lying there. It reminded me of when my father had died years ago, in 1971.

I awoke to a flood of doctors pouring over me in an emergency room. Hoards of lights were staring back at me. My mother was six months pregnant with Jacob. I had no idea where I was at that time, except for the fact that I was near death, in pain, and totally unaware of where my father, my mother and my brother were. One doctor held my head up as I asked where my father was. He told me that my father had died in the car accident. He told me I would be with my brother and my mother shortly. In my barely cognizant state, I assumed my father was lying somewhere in one of those refrigerators, after they were pronounced dead and then tagged. I was the first one conscious after our car accident. I thought I may be able to see my father. I slipped into unconsciousness. I awoke later in the intensive pediatric ward, a room adjacent to where my brother Michael was sleeping.

My brother was in a coma for two weeks, quietly in a world no one could break into. When he awoke, he would walk into my room, sitting quietly next to my bed for hours. He never made one sound. He would perpetually stare at me simply because I was someone tangible. I was not able to walk. Michael did my walking for me. He would plan secret trips with his hospital roommates who were confined to wheelchairs racing three chairs at once down the corridor late at night, in the hopes of raiding the nurse's refrigerator. Then he would bring me goodies I was not allowed to eat. He would find secret hiding places that only he knew existed. He would come back, gaze over at me, never stirring.

One day, he finally asked where Dad was. He did not understand why our father never came to see us. When Michael came out of his coma no one explained to Michael that our father had been killed in the accident. Sadly, I glanced at him. I told him that Dad had died. Michael looked back at me. He got up. As he was walking back to his room, I noticed his lip was trembling. There he lay on his stomach for ten days, not a spoken word out of him. The only visible evidence of sorrow I was allowed to see was one dried up tear-stain down his cheek. We never spoke about that day until years later. Michael and I never got to say goodbye to our father. I never got to say goodbye to Michael.

For years I had myself convinced that my Dad would come walking back into our lives because he had this secret mission he had to undertake. Planning a car accident was the best for all concerned. One day, simply he would appear on our doorstep thrilled to see us. Years later, when Michael and I were in our thirties, sitting on my living room floor in Boston we both talked about those events in that hospital room that day. Michael too fantasized about Dad having to hide out somewhere. He believed that Dad would re-appear back in our lives. That never happened. I was relieved to know I was not the only one who contrived such a scheme. Michael and I had to believe in something. We were young kids desperately missing our father. Nothing sufficed for the reality of what actually did take place. Despairingly, I attempted to believe I was again in a bad dream and that I would awaken to find Michael standing next to me. I could not understand how my brother could be murdered. You hear about murder in the newspaper, on the radio, on the television. The making of yet another ingenious plot was formulated in my mind. Yet, this would be a terribly cruel joke to embrace on loved ones. A murder in our family was unexplainable to me. I had this appalling dread filling me up. Michael was not coming back.

Chapter 7

Jenna pulled out from my house. She sped to the highway that led to the Sagamore Bridge. There were only two access bridges to get off the Cape. We were closest to the Sagamore Bridge. Although the season was nearing its end on Cape Cod, traffic could be horrendous. I was silently praying we would be overwhelmed with traffic. My panic at identifying my brother was taking over. No traffic. Jenna propelled on the highway and over the bridge without any glitches. I chattered aimlessly with Jenna as if we had not a care in the world. I remember telling a joke. We both laughed intensely. In retrospect, I understood why we participated in useless conversation. At that precise moment while a passenger in my sister-in-law's car, I felt reprehensible for even allowing myself to laugh. My brother was somewhere on a cold slab, alone, tangibly gone forever.

Chapter 8

Usually the ride to Lynn from the Cape is a long, tedious one. Despite what day you leave on, you will undoubtedly come into deadlock traffic once you encounter the throes of downtown Boston. The only way to travel east is either to elect to go onto another bridge or through a tunnel that submerges out on the other side to the infamous Logan Airport. Jenna opted for the tunnel. Amazingly, traffic was light and unaffected. Jenna breezed through. Eventually we arrived in the town of Lynn. Our conversation had abruptly stopped when we arrived in front of the police station. Transients were leaning against one side of the building while trash bins overflowed with potential treasures. Row after row of police cars were compartmentalized in tiny spaces, the bigger spaces designated for the upper echelon superiors. The vehicles looked like diminutive match car boxes, all in neat edifices, lining the building. I was ill. My heart was quivering uncomfortably. I closed my eyes praying I would make it through.

Jenna and I got out of the car, shutting our doors. We proceeded to enter the front of the station. A man dressed in police garb was sitting at a small, metal table near the door. He had asked what our business was. I quietly replied that my brother was murdered. I then stated my name. We had to pass through a metal detector. We were led up stairs to a locked room. It was visible that windows were present, but you could not see through any of them. I was already twice as uncomfortable. Upon entrance of the room, I was met by three detectives. Jenna's sister, Samantha, had already arrived with her boyfriend, Jason. They each gave me a loving embrace. I remembered Samantha's eyes being moist. Jess, Jenna's boyfriend had also come. He tenderly held me. No words were exchanged. All of us walked into the room. The door was then closed where we were introduced to two more detectives. It was very apparent to me that Jess, Samantha and Jason already had information that I was not going to be privy to. I remember watching my hands shudder as I began to ask the detectives how Michael was killed. I was given a very ambiguous answer. I once again repeated myself. Everyone glanced down. I could feel myself getting angry and equally as confused. Pleadingly, I asked the detective to tell me what had happened. He acquiesced, disclosing without emotion that Michael was slashed to death with a samurai sword. I put my hands up, screaming in horror. Jess looked at me, lowering his brow. Nothing anyone could say or do would take away the intensity of what I was feeling. I desperately wanted to see my brother. I wanted to identify him, make sure it was he who was killed and say goodbye to him. That was the least I could do for Michael; offer some dignity to him. I wanted to make sure he was clothed properly, washed, not exposed.

In the Jewish religion, the deceased is to be buried the day after their death. My brother had to be buried tomorrow. This was Jewish law. I had no access in making that happen. This was a murder. This was official business. I was silently furious. I also realized I had no control over anything.

I got up asking the detective to please let me go and see my brother. They informed me that Michael was in a hospital morgue lying on a metal table, approximately forty-minutes north of where we were. I could passionately feel my blood raging throughout my body. I demanded to be allowed to see my brother. I was refused. The detective, in a more compassionate tone told me that this was the worst atrocity they had seen in thirty years. Michael was so desecrated I would not recognize him. I collapsed. My body gave over. I slipped onto another metal table crying helplessly. Reality set in. I did not want to identify my brother. I was terribly frightened by the whole notion of identifying a dead body, especially one that I may very well be familiar with.

Momentarily, I understood deep within my heart that my brother would not want me to see him this way. I also knew that his soul had left his body long ago. I had to take comfort in that. I was fixated however, on wanting his body to be properly cared for and loved. I was never given that chance, nor could I bring myself to offer to do as such. For years there after, I was tormented by my thought of not being able to see him. Saying goodbye was essential for me.

In less than a minute I thought of all the ways I wanted to tell Michael how much I loved him, despite our differences. We shared a bond of a birth family that loved us dearly. Countless moves to new places, new schools, given my father's job, Sunday outings with our parents, summer excursions to the ocean, Broadway Shows, Yankee games, Knick games, cotton candy, candy apples, arrivals and losses of beloved pets, teenage issues, loyalties and disagreements, a devastating car accident, the death of our father, the birth of our youngest brother, high school graduations, the birth of my second child and my divorce.

Michael watched the entire birthing process of Emily. He had driven me to the hospital when I went into labor with such an intensity of speed I had to hold on to the side of the seat. Beth Israel Hospital was but seconds from where I was living at that time. Michael disclosed to me that he was afraid I would give birth in the car. He was nervous. I remember laughing, but I also was concerned I might. My history was to go fast, hard and to deliver quickly. I never let my brother know this, however. I was in sharp, acute labor. I knew Michael could not bear to see anyone in pain, let alone his sister. As we diligently raced to the hospital, memories deluged my mind of his sensitivity. When Michael was a youngster, he used to pick up caterpillars from baseball diamonds. He never wanted to see them stepped on. Clearly, he had not changed. Tenderness and susceptibility seized my brother's soul. Michael kept so much inside, it was often difficult to know what was going on. He appeared to be a master at hiding his innermost fears and feelings. He would never burden anyone with his concerns. Yet I knew. I knew when he lost our father, he had lost his best friend. Michael would not talk about how devastating the affect of losing our father was to him.

I could feel the next labor pain coming on. We immediately pulled right up to the hospital's main entrance. We got out. My husband, Michael and I were brought up to the birthing room. Michael seemed relieved to hand me over to capable hands. He then told me that he was going home to change. He was staying with me for a few months after just relocating back to the Boston area. The previous evening he had come home to my apartment at three in the morning. He was out with friends. I awoke him at five in the morning to let him know I was in labor. Our car had been at the shop for two days. By the grace of God, my brother offered to take me in whenever it was time. Unfortunately, Michael only received about two hours of sleep. He drove in his shorts and a tee shirt. Once in the hospital, he went back home, showered and came back, ready to support me.

Michael was meticulous about his dress at all times. I was breathing strongly when he came into the birthing room. Contrary to me being in pain, I noticed how funny it appeared to me when Michael walked inside in his three-piece suit. I smiled with a wince. I was ingratiated for my brother's presence honoring my child's birth. He was dressed to the hilt. I certainly wasn't. It took everything I had to birth this child. I was sweating profusely, I was in excruciating pain and I was completely naked. My brother looked at me, a bit reserved, then he stopped. He came over to me, whispering in my ear, "You can do this. Remember what we went through in the car accident?" I told him that I could not. He smiled and said, "Yes you can." Complications were arising. This child could not make it through to entry. The baby was transverse, posterior and it was losing enormous amounts of oxygen. My doctor told me I would have to have an emergency C-section immediately. Otherwise, I might lose my baby. I had this remarkable trust with Dr. Nadia. I told her to please do whatever it takes. The birthing room was cleared immediately. My husband shouted, "I love you." My brother put his hand on my husband's shoulder. Michael moved aside to let the gurney pass through. He was all too familiar with the medical paraphernalia. I was too. I was rushed down the hall. He looked at me lovingly. The doors slammed shut.

More flashbacks to my car accident appeared in front of me. Yet, this time, I was giving birth. There were so many doctors attending over me: An anesthiologist preparing me for my sleep; an intern prepping my arm for an intravenous IV; another doctor adjusting my head and so forth and so on. Everyone was talking quickly. It all was happening so fast. I was transported from a serene birthing room to a very sterile emergency room in less than fifteen seconds flat. I remember glancing out onto a clock affixed to an exit door in the corridor. I also saw a woman watching me with frightened eyes as I was frantically being wheeled down the hall. I was hoisted off the gurney onto a cold bed covered with only a thin layer of white bedding. I was freezing. I could feel an extremely painful contraction coming on. I told one of the doctors that I had to move. She responded, "Sorry, not now, we are putting you under. Please do not move." I would have bargained any which way to alleviate the searing pain I was enduring. The contraction riveted up my stomach all the way to my breasts. Prayer seemed the only alternative. I could feel the effects of the anesthesia working, but not soon enough. I once again clenched my teeth. My eyes immediately closed. Thank God.

I awoke to a baby crying in the distance. I was dazed, still bearing the affects of the medicine. I looked off to my left. I could foggily make out my husband whispering, "Emily, Emily, Emily." Then my head simply sagged to the other side of the bed, my eyes closing. I thought I imagined having a girl. I could not make out if I had been dreaming it or if I actually heard someone saying Emily. I floundered with attempts to stay awake. I finally mustered up the strength to ask, "What did I have?" Allen said, "A little girl." I knew. I always knew I would have another daughter. I fell into a deep sleep. I was told that my beautiful baby Emily was passed around to all the family members who had come to support my birth. My brother was the second person to hold her, minutes after she was born.

Too many unresolved goodbyes swarmed my life, my father's death, my grandparents' deaths, my friend Laura who died of cancer at twenty-six and now my brother's death and probably in about six months, my former sister-in-law's. I was handed papers to sign. I left that building with Jenna feeling depleted, cold and numb. I slept the entire ride back to Jenna's parent's house in Quarry.

Chapter 9

I awoke from a dead sleep, exhausted in Jenna's car, in the middle of Jane and Aiden's driveway. Every fiber in my body ached. I did not want to move, nor did I want to get out of the car. I was in no shape of mind to see anyone. I slowly lifted my body around noticing my ex-husband's car was parked out front. He was there. I was torn between enormous feelings of vulnerability and sheer frustration. Jenna was equally as frustrated. No one could locate her brother. Jenna appeared somewhat relieved to see he had arrived back at the house. Again, we got out of her car simultaneously, shut the doors and slowly walked up the stairs to the front of the house. The door was unlocked. We walked inside through the living room, only to witness Allen, my ex, reading a note that was left on the kitchen counter. He shouted, "Oh my God!" He immediately saw me, ran to me, putting his arms around me. I allowed myself to fall into his embrace. I sobbed. He did not move. He simply held me for as long as I needed to be held. Jenna broke down.

I released myself from his arms. I told him what I knew. I also told him I tried for hours to locate him. He said he was at a poetry reading in Cambridge. He had asked me where Kailee and Emily were. I responded they were being taken care of by Bette. All that mattered was that he was there now. I had no intention of confronting him about why he never left a note to where he might be. After all, we were divorced.

There were still so many calls to be made. I hopelessly wanted to hold my girls. Whenever I grasped my children, I would imbibe their sweet smells, sniffing their skin and their heads, feeling utterly contented. I needed them more than ever. Perhaps this was a selfish thought. Yet, I knew they would add a touch of innocence to this deplorable, blemished day. I called Bette to let her know where I was. She and her husband offered to bring the girls up to Quarry whenever I wanted. I thanked her profusely. I would see Kailee and Emily in less than two hours. I put the phone down, walked to the living room couch, and sat down staring out into nowhere. I had difficulty keeping my eyes open. I resisted. So did my eyes. I fell asleep for three minutes when the front door shot open. Jess and Jason had handfuls of cold cuts, salads and rolls heaping from a paper bag. They were preparing for my family to arrive. They were so terribly generous. I was nauseated from the smells, but not unappreciative. I had no appetite whatsoever. My hunger was completely gone. I had not eaten anything except a nibble on a muffin I had baked earlier in the day. Absolutely nothing appealed to me. I did not want to walk into the kitchen for fear of vomiting. I stayed as close to the front door as I could. It was now wide open. I watched people riding bicycles, neighbors exchanging conversation with one another and merely being. I observed the carefree manner of everyone else's lives. I wept. I knew my life would be forever changed again.

Aiden and Jane were at Katie's home at this precise time. Most of my ex's family was sitting vigil with her at her home, attempting to make sense of her recent diagnosis of inoperable brain cancer. I had to redirect my focus, concentrating on my brother's funeral. I was waiting patiently for my mother and Jacob to arrive at the Quarry house. We all decided this would be an appropriate meeting spot for all concerned, though I felt I was somehow invading a space I was no longer a part of. The home in Quarry was strangely quiet. Nonetheless, we could all decide what steps needed to be taken to arrange a funeral outside of New York City.

My dad was buried in Staten Island. This is where my brother was going to be laid to rest. I reminded myself that Michael was supposed to be buried tomorrow. He still lay in a morgue an hour and a half away. We had yet to locate a Rabbi in Brooklyn to officiate the burial. Unfortunately, we knew no one there.

I was somewhat fearful of seeing my mother. She and Michael were extremely close. Presently, I could not handle her emotion. It was her first-born child. Everyday, no matter where Michael was living, he would call my mother to tell her he loved her. My mother would never have that again with him. I also knew how fragile Michael was in this lifetime. Though incredibly bright, successful at work, admired by many women and well respected by peers, Michael endured an unspoken pain only visible to Jacob, myself and my mother. I am not sure if he could have survived the loss of my mother if circumstances were reversed. To die the way he did was unspeakable though, and my mother would most likely bear the burden of his death for the rest of her life.

Michael wanted my mother to move near him when he relocated down to Florida. This was ongoing for years, yet, my mother just could not take the leap. Michael dies and the shoulds, the oughts, the coulds and all the woulds escalate in her mind now. Unnecessary, useless thoughts, except to a parent who wanted so much to have that opportunity and who was devoted to her child.

In the natural course of events as a parent, it is incomprehensible to make sense of losing a child before you leave this earth. I could not fathom such an occurrence. The universe always has a plan, but it is often one that is without due justice to explanation. Despite the reason, a parent never gets over the loss of a child. Rather they attempt to go on with their life, clinging to a private faith that they will one day be reunited with their loved ones. What other rational is there?

Moments later, Kailee and Emily walked in the front door of my ex in-laws' house. I could not believe one and a half hours had already passed. Bette said goodbye. I whispered thank you. I ran to my children, stroking their faces, hugging them fiercely. I was so glad they were alive. I was also aware within a split second's time, anything could be eternally altered

Chapter 10

Kailee and Emily darted for the kitchen counter nibbling on pieces of sliced turkey, sliced bread, cream cheese and pickles. They thoroughly immersed themselves in eating. I watched them, despite the agony I was experiencing. They were oblivious to our pain and our grief, still to come. That was what was so remarkable about who they were, free-spirited, not waiting for clues to be who they thought they should be. They were in the absolute moment of whatever was going on. Observing them eat brought me down to an earthly reality I was accustomed to. Emily, relished her every bite, chewing contentedly with a serious vigor. I was forced to smile. Kailee, picked at her food with such a preciseness and calm, devouring it all the same instantly, I was momentarily flooded with a tickle of joy. One would never suspect the stream of events that recently occurred.

Soon after, Kailee and Emily began inventing games in the living room enabling them to experience a flood of innocent laughter, emanating from their bodies. Their range of play was free, pure and untainted. How could they possibly understand death in the scheme of things? It was their right as a child to simply be. The house in Quarry once again became alive.

Allen got on the phone. He began placing calls to the nearest funeral home in Milton, approximately fifteen minutes from Quarry. He was arranging to have Michael brought there before sundown. We could then arrange his arrival to another funeral home outside of Manhattan. I remember watching how many calls he placed, one after another to and from the morgue, back to the funeral home and so forth and so on. Allen tried desperately to locate a Rabbi outside of New York City. To my chagrin, I remembered it was Saturday. Most Rabbis will not even pick up the phone on a Saturday. Saturday was our Sabbath, a day for rest and atonement. Saturday was completely out of the question for inquiries as it concerned a Jewish talisman. We also discovered that tomorrow was a Jewish holiday. No Rabbi in this universe would be performing any type of service, whether it was a wedding, a funeral, a bris, a confirmation, nothing. It did not even matter the extent of the circumstances. This was a holiday, so minutely small, but in the scriptures it was stated, no one shall work on this day. I never even heard of this holiday. Though a Jew by birth and somewhat a practicing one, I was naïve to all the Jewish holidays that actually existed. The major ones I knew. Once again humility set in. This would also be a tremendous setback for my mother who desperately wanted Michael properly buried. It really was not a lot to ask, considering what my mother was going through. I reminded Allen that we would most likely have to wait until sundown.

I lost my ability to function. I was exhausted from all the underlying emotion I had yet to allow surface, let alone all the sentiments I had already withstood. Watching my children play was enough. I could barely focus on either of them.

Chapter 11

I was anxiously anticipating the arrival of my mother and Jacob. I had no idea who would appear first. I was hoping Jacob. I knew my mother would be horribly distraught. Jacob nor I could single-handedly handle her amount of grief, alone. More time passed. The sky was growing darker. I was immobilized on the couch. Kailee and Emily went about their business, simplistically and quite ardently. I heard a car. I ran to the front door, realizing my mother had arrived. My breathing became rapid. Kailee and Emily decided to nestle on the small sofa in the den watching television. Allen was making more phone calls. Samantha, Jenna, Jess and Jason respectfully stayed in the house, waiting for my mother to enter. I stayed at the front door until the car that was carrying my mother came to a stop on the opposite side of the street. My mother's friend and partner Mark, was visible sitting in the back of the car, while Mark's daughter and husband were in the front seat. I harbored tremendous anxiety. I opened the front door, running across the street to my mother. She got out of the car, terribly distressed. No amount of comfort was enough to soothe her. Her emotion ignited mine a thousand fold. We sobbed. Mark got out of the car. In his intermittent weeping, he begged for me to please take care of my mother. I understood intellectually what he wanted me to do, yet, I was at a complete lost with how to deal with my own emotions. I looked at him, simply nodding. I had no words. He and his children walked us into the Quarry home. They said goodbye, hugged us and got back into their car, making the four-hour trip back to upstate New York.

My mother was inconsolable. She sat on the couch staring into nowhere, but simultaneously and oddly, she was overly pleasant to Samantha, Jenna and the rest of the people congregating in the living room. Everyone was on overdrive, not anticipating what to do next or how to comfortably make small talk. My mother kept repeating over and over that she could not understand how

Michael was killed. She was offered a plate of food. She nibbled but could nor forgive herself for eating. "How can I be hungry?" she stated. "This is so silly." Yet, what else was there to do? Cold cuts were placed graciously on oversized platters in the kitchen, decorated quite attractively. They had been sitting out for quite some time. The logical thing to do was eat. No one had any appetites. No one had any notion of how to handle the situation at large. Eating sufficed.

I got up off the couch. Repeatedly, I paced in the living room. Another hour, perhaps two passed on. Although terribly exhausted, I could not sit still, otherwise I would succumb to excruciating anxiety. There was still much to do, so little time and a tremendous amount of confusion present. I had no notion of how my family and I were going to transport my brother from the morgue to Milton. Saturday was nearing its end. None of us had access to anything, even details about my brother's death. As I debilitated myself with countless thoughts of what if, a car appeared in the driveway. It was nightfall. Jacob's girlfriend Kara, pulled right up to the front of the garage with Jacob sitting in the front seat. I wanted to leap into my brother's arms to comfort him, but my body did not move. I was able to get to the front door and open it. Jacob bolted inside looking shockingly bewildered and angry, all at the same time. He walked straight to where my mother was, sat down, putting his hands in his face. For a moment, my mother became a parent again. She looked at Jacob stroking his hair. She was terribly sorrowful for what Jacob just lost, a brother, a mentor, a father figure and a human being who adoringly always called Jacob champ, from the day he was born.

Michael was fifteen years older than Jacob. After Jacob was born, Michael doted on him like an adoring father. I could see in my mother's eyes the pain she felt for Jacob, forgetting her own for an instant. She gently looked at him. Then quickly, she slipped right back on the back of the sofa, appearing far away. Jacob was seemingly agitated. He wanted to know what happened, why and how Michael was killed. I was the only one in our immediate family who had some information on his death. I still did not relay this information to my mother. I was afraid she would have a heart attack from hearing the grimness of his death. I needed to share it with my brother, but he was so angry, I was haunted by the fact that he would go out and do irreversible damage to the killer. I could feel my brother's rage and his woefulness.

Jacob got up, introduced Kara to Samantha, Jenna and Jason. He then proceeded to head for the back room. I took my cue. I followed him inconspicuously into the den. Jacob begged me to tell him what I knew. The difficulty was the fact I knew so little, barely enough to share in clarity what actually happened. I told him to sit down, pleading with him not to share anything with Mom. Surprisingly, he remained calm before I progressed. As I relayed that Michael was slashed to death with a samurai sword, I could detect

Jacob's disbelief and anguish for what Michael had endured. He recoiled. I could detect that Jacob was quietly tortured. He bluntly said, "I am going to kill that son of a bitch." I said nothing. We both walked back into the living room and sat numbly on the couch. My mother was still in her oblivion.

Allen came in the living room relaying information about a funeral director who would arrange for Michael to be transferred to Milton tomorrow. We could be closer to him now. My mother, despite her state of mind was persistent about having Michael in Milton tonight. She was not going to have it any other way. It was late. Everyone had subsequently left their prospective positions at the funeral home. There were no other options. Tomorrow was the next best choice. Mom wept, Jacob paced. I caught myself looking outside the window, muddled, lost and without any comforting words. One twenty-one am. Quietly, everyone in the house slipped away to separate bedrooms, doors closing. It was pitch black.

I was terrified. Staring up at the ceiling in total darkness overwhelmed me. As exhausted as I felt, I did not dare to shut my eyes. I was afraid of seeing my brother. I was not fearful of Michael, I was simply not able to get dreadful visions out of my mind of how he was brutally murdered. Slash. Hack. Slash. Hack. That is all I saw. I flinched at every blow. Michael never stood a chance. I kept thinking he would come back as this ghost, half mutilated and unrecognizable. I had no idea how such visions would terrorize me for months.

I was embarrassed at myself for allowing myself to harbor such thoughts. My work and my inner beliefs passionately stressed strong metaphysical approaches to healing such that the soul continues to live on, but in a capacity that stresses absolute love. I also have come to understand that when a life passes on, it simply crosses over into another dimension that is but a blink away from our earthly existence. I could rationalize that Michael was in a much better place. Yet, I also believed that because his crossing was so violent he was terribly confused when he passed. I was highly disturbed by this. I could not tangibly tell him what happened to him nor could I ever come to grips with how or what he must have felt when he was being brutally attacked. I desperately justified to myself that when he was brought to unconsciousness, blow after blow, his soul had already left his body, thus, causing him little time to experience physical pain. I wanted to believe this. My innermost core did believe this to an extent. I knew he had to suffer, even if it was out of sheer fear. Yet, my secular existence struggled unmercifully with the inhumanity of how he was killed.

I was instantly reminded of the myriad of vivid recollections I have had, that life does go on. I remember sitting in my father's favorite chair after we arrived home from our hospital experience in 1971. I was merely engaging in a relaxed state, when I distinctly smelled my father's cigar smoke. I glanced around and called out, "Dad?" I knew he was there and I knew his presence was very much alive. I was overwhelmingly peaceful. After his death I have had dreams of my father coming to me, smiling and telling me that everything was going to be okay, relating to whatever was going on in my life at that time. I have also seen some of the most profound experiences of loss and pain. I have known people who have tragically passed on. They have come back in personal visions to talk with me. I knew there was absolutely nothing to fear. I felt highly blessed that I could attune myself to a realm of life that brought me supreme comfort. Trusting that everything works out for the highest good was a good place to heal from. Even though such knowledge afforded me a humanly solace, I was equally as isolated in the world. Despite my budding and lucrative practice, despite the countless people who sought out my work, despite the knowledge I took with me, it was difficult to explain to others what I had come to know and what I had experienced. Many thought I had a thousand heads.

I fought with undeniable fear about Michael coming me to me in a form I would not recognize while I was equally savaged with ill perceptions about his death. Intellectually, I knew this would never happen. Michael's soul was indeed in a place that spoke only of unconditional love and tranquillity. He would only appear to me as I remembered him, exceptionally handsome and impeccably well dressed. Yet, I feared going to sleep. My potential night's rested was tainted by continual, horrific visions of his barbarous death.

I stared up at the ceiling for what appeared an endless amount of time. Kailee and Emily were blissfully asleep in the next room. Jacob and Kara were in the den on a fold out couch. My mother was adjacent to the room I was occupying. My ex-husband was upstairs in a room that was once inhabited by his siblings. No matter how much my body craved sleep, I refused to allow myself the luxury of it. I was consumed with dread. I could not believe I was allowing myself to be so overcome. There were no explanations. There was nothing to make sense of, except for the fact that Michael was dead, at least physically in this existence. I got up out of my bed, climbed up the stairs where I found my ex-husband still awake. I asked politely if I could please sleep in his bed with him. Nothing was questioned. I fell asleep, only to be awakened two hours later with a stream of sunlight bursting its way into the window. Morning broke through.

Chapter 12

6 a.m. The smell of coffee brewing was evident. I looked over the other side of the bed. Allen was already up. Unusual. Normally he slept in. However, given the fact that we shared a single bed with very little space, he most likely acquired little sleep. Coffee was his alarm clock. The coffee's aroma was filling up the house. Somehow, I felt temporarily comforted. I decided I would be gracious for that moment, given the dire day we all had to look forward to. I quickly showered, ran a towel through my hair, threw on the same clothes I had on the day before and sat on the edge of the bed anticipating anxiety of the worst proportions. I had no idea what I would face or what was in store for any of my family members. Michael would be driven to Milton. Jacob and I would have to, at some point, go to the police station, be escorted by a police official to Michael's apartment to gather his belongings. I had no idea how I would confront a murder scene. All I could imagine was blood everywhere and remnants of Michael's things strewn about. I was fully blown back into my fear. I also knew that Jacob, despite the fact that he was a young man would be equally as terrified. Gender had no consequential meaning. We were all brought down to such a level of unremitting resignation. Everything I had experienced in my life seemed minuscule compared to what Michael went through. Yet, on the flip side, this tragic occurrence would unleash a thousand-fold, pain of the most unmistakable variety for me.

I went downstairs. Jacob and Kara were still asleep. My mother's door was slightly ajar. I could see my mother was up, looking far away, off into a distance I could not see. However, I attempted to understand the feeling behind the look. I, too, was a parent. I could not ever fathom losing my children before I died. I looked away, allowing my mother her grief. It was all I could do not to invade her most private and intimate thoughts. I felt horrible and deeply saddened for her. I could never bring her son back, nor could I do anything to abolish her suffering.

I gathered my composure and turned toward the living room when I heard Jacob rustling in bed. He went immediately into the bathroom, showering without saying a word. Soon after, he reappeared with only a towel around his waist, looking bewildered as he attempted to find his belongings. Kara got up. She showered quickly, dressed and put the couch back together. Good mornings were not appropriate. Eyes touching eyes with grimaces of shock and disbelief were very much visible and felt. Jacob looked terribly hurt. His anger was not as prevalent, at least momentarily. It was much too soon to see how Michael's death would impact Jacob's life.

Michael was Jacob's best friend. A week prior, Michael and Jacob were at Yankee Stadium in New York City, enjoying the best of baseball. Going to a Yankee's game was a highlight for both of them. They were passionate about the Yankees. Each knew beyond a shadow of a doubt the Yankees would make it into the World Series that year, despite whatever odds may have been present. Michael had purchased the tickets earlier. When they had both approached the gate to enter the stadium, Michael explained to Jacob that he gave Jacob the tickets. Jacob appeared a bit perplexed. Jacob responded that he did not remember having the tickets. Thus, the search began. Jacob emptied all of his pockets, went through everything he had on. Still, no tickets. Jacob was beside himself. Indefinite minutes passed, intensifying Jacob's bewildered state. Michael, a pure tease, affectionately called out, "Hey, Champ, guess what I have?" Jacob turned, momentarily humbled, while Michael was laughing, heartily swinging the tickets between his fingers. Jacob reciprocated with a laugh. They playfully jabbed each other while Jacob quietly concocted thoughts of payback in the very near future. The day was light, but loving as these two brothers held an unspoken respect for one another. It would be the last time Jacob would ever see his brother alive.

7:00 a.m. Another batch of coffee was steeping. Allen had already consumed three cups. I could sense he would devour much more, in efforts to stay awake. My mother had not come out of her room. The motivation to do anything was small. In her distressed state, there seemed to be little reason for her to live. In 1971, her husband and love of seventeen years had died in a violent car accident. Now her first-born child was savagely taken through murder. If I could have gone back in time, at least for one gigantic moment, I would have played the scenario of my father gingerly, playfully and lovingly sweeping my mother across the sidewalk in mischievous arms, swaying her to one side and then another. They were always laughing together. Michael and I had the benefit of seeing this happen quite often. Jacob only through words and distant pictures got a glimpse of their happiness. Yet, the tape played through.

No more husband to laugh with. No more son to celebrate his life with. The reel was empty, as was my mother's heart. Jacob's was angry. Mine was numb. The pieces of our lives were like a broken puzzle. Nothing fit.

8 a.m. The phone rang. It was Jenna's boyfriend. He wanted to know how he could assist our attempts in solidifying details for funeral arrangements. Jacob and I had no answers. My mother was in her own domain, unreachable. Allen took the phone from me, exchanging words with Jason. He hung up. Samantha made a phone call to her boyfriend, Jess, where they quietly discussed details of accelerating Michael's arrival to Milton. She hung up. Allen called a synagogue in Quarry to find a referral for a Rabbi in Brooklyn. He hung up. I called my friend, mentor and spiritualist minister, Ida, on the Cape to reveal to her the events that had taken place in our lives. She listened with utmost compassion, telling me she would pray for my family. I hung up. The phone rang. Allen picked up the phone. It was a call from a Rabbi in Boston. He recommended a Rabbi in Brooklyn who may be able to officiate the funeral for my brother. Words of gratitude were spoken. He hung up. Once more the phone rang. Again, Allen picked up the phone. It was Aiden inquiring about the happenings of our day, who also relayed information to Allen about his sister Katie. He hung up. The phone rang another time. Allen picked up the phone. It was the funeral director in Milton, sharing news about Michael's arrival. Michael would be in Milton by noon. Allen said goodbye and hung up.

9 a.m. Three more hours and Michael would be resting at the funeral home in Milton. The house was very still, agonizingly quiet. No more rings. No more calls. No one talked. No one exchanged glances. Silenced prevailed. No one did anything. I could feel a loitering, crawling palpitation building up in my chest. The anticipation of Michael being returned to us heightened. "The worst atrocity they have ever seen in years, the worst atrocity" and so forth and so on. These words replayed over and over in my mind like a broken record. On one hand, I felt somewhat relieved that we would have Michael closer to us. On the other hand, I dreaded the possibility that we might actually be able to tangibly say goodbye to him. I could not recollect if I had told Jacob what the detectives had said to me about how desecrated Michael looked after his attack. I knew Jacob would want to see his brother. I decided not to say anything. I knew I had no control of whatever Jacob elected. I simply closed my eyes, praying and asking that everything please work out for the highest good. In the moment I could trust. Two seconds later, my palpitations were building. I was forced to sit down, while enormous tears streamed down my face.

Jacob walked into the living room. He saw my face, but none of us could comfort the other. It was not expected. He glanced over at me again, then blankly stared out the window. I could feel him welling up. Kara then came in.

She began to pace. Anyone could feel the pain permeating throughout the room. We all felt it. We were all equally aware of not knowing what to do with it.

I was seemingly a veteran at pain. I saw so many kids dying at Massachusetts General Hospital in 1971. I would turn my head while I lay in the pediatric intensive care ward and watch, while doctors tried to resuscitate a child's heart. This was a daily practice on my floor. I never knew who would be the next person to die. Sometimes I would not want to go to sleep. I was afraid that I would be that next child. This became so routine for me, I anticipated at least three children dying a week, though I still held a quiet fear about it happening to me. When I was finally released from the hospital, I was equally ecstatic and frightened. I could not believe I was walking out of the hospital with minimal help. I was concerned however, if something was to go wrong, I did not have access to having immediate aid when I arrived back home.

A few years later in high school, I was selected as an American Field Service Exchange Student to India. I found the people, the culture and the way of life drastically different from that of the United States, yet amazingly challenging and wonderfully enlightening. I also experienced accumulations of dying people at my feet when I walked through the streets, many of them children. To my disbelief, so many were already dead as I was walking over them. I remember their eyes still being open after they passed, pleading for help in a way I could not offer any hope whatsoever. They were gone. Everyday in my life while I was living in India, I had to make my way over and around them. That became a habitual practice. I promised myself I would never become indifferent. Dying was commonplace. Unfortunately, in order for me to survive, I often had to look the other way.

After graduating from college I eventually moved to Boston where I would meet one of my closest and dearest friends, Laura. This young woman was a gifted artist who painted the most brilliant canvasses. I knew Laura about a year when I was awakened one morning by a phone call from her. In brief conversation, she matter-of-factly said she had just found out that she had cancer. My heart sunk. Laura was twenty-five. I had no words. She sounded upbeat. She had Hodgkin's disease. She reiterated to me that it was curable. More hope.

Within three months, Laura's health was failing greatly. It was later discovered she was misdiagnosed. She had lymphoma of her chest. Eight months passed. I found myself walking into Dana Farber Cancer Institute everyday talking to Laura about everything that meant something. I brought her a single flower each and every time I saw her. That is all she wanted.

Two more months passed. I continued my daily visits to the hospital. I walked into Laura's room one afternoon, dismayed not to find her there. I looked around thinking the inevitable. No Laura. I then heard a faint knocking on the inside of the bathroom door. Momentarily, Laura was having trouble coming out of the bathroom. The door was completely shut. I was oblivious to her being inside. She could barely walk. Her hair had already fallen out months ago. Within an overnight period, Laura was shriveled up like a very old person, unable to stand up. I helped her to her bed. We talked. She told me she knew she was going to die soon. She finally accepted the fact that she had to accept her fate. She said that the one party she would miss the most would be her memorial service. We laughed. Yet inside, I ached.

Hours passing, I said I would come by tomorrow to help bathe her. I would also bring her a single rose. Extremely early the next morning, I received a phone call. Laura had died in her sleep. She was twenty-six years old. I was beside myself. I had already picked up the rose the night before. It had fully blossomed on my nightstand that morning. I cried hysterically.

My connection to animals, especially canines, is extraordinary. We have this uncanny ability to find each other under the most adverse conditions. After putting many to sleep over time, I told myself I would never get another one. The pain is too much to bear. Yet, I am convinced the universe brings them to me. The very first beloved dog I had on my own, when I left home and ventured into the world was a beautiful, German-Shepherd mix, named Shanghai. I found her in a garbage can in Virginia, about the size of my hand. She was my everything, my buddy, my loyal friend and my most cherished companion. We shared rock climbing, canoeing, swimming in the river rapids, hiking expeditions, home-bound rainy nights, movies and popcorn on the couch, college experiences, moves and much more. She was an expert Frisbee-catcher, a superb swimmer. She had this remarkably, broad insight than most evolved humans. She understood everything. I often felt she would actually speak back to me. We had this unreserved trust that never could be broken. I wholly respected her essence. The day I brought her in to lay her to rest was devastating. All the moments I shared with this unconditionally loving friend was now coming to an end. Initially, I could not bring myself to do the inevitable. She had so much dignity, but she was in such pain. However, she never showed her discomfort. I had to let go. It was a prerequisite for respecting her. I stayed up with Shanghai all evening, telling her I was terribly sorry for making a decision that I was ill equip to make. Somehow she trusted. That was my signal. The following morning I carried her into the vet's office, weeping uncontrollably as I held her. She looked at me as the vet released the fluid from the needle and into her vein. I had her body wrapped around my arms. Despite her unmitigated pain, she managed to put her paw over my wrist as if to say we will see each other again one day. She was gone. I will never forget our bond. I will never forget her. It was but another death to add to my list of those humans and those creatures I deeply cherished. This was my M.O. I understood death. Yet, I continued to cry ludicrously like it was always the very first time.

Chapter 13

11:20 a.m. Forty more minutes, Michael would be at the funeral home in Milton. I was more distressed than I was previously. Jacob started to pace so much so, I followed in pursuit of distraction. Jess and Jason simultaneously walked into the Quarry home with Jenna and Samantha close to them. They were whispering. I had no desire to make an effort to strain. I was not sure if I wanted to know something that perhaps was not meant for me to know. I had this picture in my mind. Jacob and I would drive to the funeral home, walk in, talk to the funeral director, say our last goodbyes to our beloved brother securing the final details. This was something we had to do for Michael. I was so ill prepared for what I would experience next, I reached for the nearest wall in an effort to hold myself up. I ran outside, grasping for breath. I attempted a long walk around the block. I could not bring myself to go to the funeral home. I again became immobilized with dread while my breath became short and quick. I was dismayed by my thoughts of wanting to back out of this responsibility. I had always had this horrid dislike of funeral homes. I simply did not want to go. What would I tell my brother and the rest of the people waiting for me, endeavoring to solidify final decisions? I could not face going back to the house. Embarrassment filled my insides. I wept under a beautiful maple tree. I did not want to be discovered, nor did I want to reveal my tear-stained cheeks. Relatively quickly, I collected myself. Deliberately walking back around the block and up the driveway, I opened the back door, thinking I could sneak in without being noticed. However, Allen came through the kitchen and said, "Oh, there you are." I felt as though I was caught. He explained that it would be best if Jacob and he go to the funeral home while Jason and Jess go to the police station in Lynn to collect Michael's belongings. I was needed here to retrieve delayed phone calls, still coming in. I was silently relieved and incredibly thankful. I also felt spineless. I prayed Michael would forgive me.

My panic ceased as I entered the living room, where I again found my mother staring up out into a dimension that was all her own. Samantha and Jenna were making small talk in the kitchen preparing a light brunch. I migrated to the oversized chair near the front door. I sunk in as far as I could go. I did nothing but wait. The phone rang. Jenna picked up the receiver and said, "Hello." After endless minutes she appeared in the living room attempting to explain that Michael's body was not quite ready for transport. My mother gasped. I was jolted upward. Jacob and Allen turned abruptly and simply stopped. It was suggested by the funeral director that my mother, my brother and I meet with him as soon as possible before Michael's arrival. We were expected there in less than fifteen minutes.

Terror filled my eyes. My plan was hopelessly changed. As I experienced this terrible feeling coming over me, I thought I was going to pass out. I managed to stay afloat on the living room rug. When I was ready, I gathered my bag, my watch and proceeded to go out the front door in Allen's car, along with Jacob and my mother behind me. Allen offered to drive us there. Samantha and Jenna would watch Kailee and Emily who were playing together inside the bedroom.

The car ride was much too quick. Allen drove alongside the building until he found the driveway to the main entrance. The car was painstakingly quiet. We stopped. Automatically, the passenger door opened, then another and another until we were all congregated in front of the door leading into the funeral home. Allen held the glass door open for my mother, my brother and myself. We slowly walked in, all of our eyes darting everywhere but nowhere. It was dark. The ambiance was cold and unruffled. Very shortly thereafter a rather young man approached us reaching out his hands to us. He introduced himself as the funeral director. He then brought us to another office, fairly spacious with enough chairs to accommodate my mother, my brother, Allen and I. When we were all settled in as best as we could be, he went on to explain Michael's arrangements. I had a very difficult time with what the director was relaying. It sounded so calculating and abrupt. Although the funeral director was very gracious in his communication, this was a business and we were down to it. My mother then went on to ask innumerable questions as to how Michael would be taken to Staten Island. It was explained that once Michael was appropriately taken care of, he would then be transported by plane to Brooklyn to a funeral home of our choice.

There was one problem however. Michael's body was so malevolently attacked, in order for his body to be shipped, it had to be embalmed. Without that procedure there was absolutely no way his body could be shipped to New York. Every eye met. My mother looked at me, Jacob looked at my mother. I then looked up at the funeral director. I explained that in Jewish law, embalmment was out of the question. Unfortunately, at that moment, I could not explain why, but it simply was not acceptable according to Judaic law. The funeral director tried to explain why the procedure had to be done. It was very obvious to Jacob and I how difficult this was for the funeral director to expound on. We knew immediately that if Michael's body was not embalmed, there might be very little of it left by the time he flew to New York tomorrow. We told the funeral director to go ahead with it, despite my mother's objections. Perhaps some honor could be given to my brother, regardless of how little honor was given to him when he was being killed.

The next agenda was buying a casket for Michael. None of us had any experience with doing as such. We were all then led to a room that was filled with caskets of all sizes, colors and designs. Allen, out of respect to my family stayed behind. We followed the funeral director inside this extremely somber room. He told us to please take our time. He walked out. The door shut. We had no idea what to do. All of us were looking around, shockingly bewildered. We were so taken aback. As ill prepared as we were, this had to be done. It would be one thing picking out something for a wedding, a bar mitzvah or even a baby shower. This was way beyond what any of us could presently handle. I paced back and forth as did Jacob. My mother was concerned with burying Michael in a casket that was nice and comfortable. Jacob and I cared, but we were not focusing on how nice the casket was. Our brother was dead and to my knowledge, his soul was long gone from his body.

We all decided on this light colored coffin that was simple and refined. We walked out. I could feel the agitation building. When we met with the funeral director he attempted with compassion to soothe us. He explained that he would call us when Michael arrived. He also asked us to please have ready the attire we wanted Michael to be buried in. Finally, he went on to say how much the casket was. Money was exchanged. We shook hands. We walked out. No one talked during the ride back to Quarry.

Samantha and Janna looked at us quietly. There was no room for small talk. My mother, Jacob and I were too emotionally exhausted to reveal any new news. The couch looked inviting. We all progressively wound up there, unable to move. Kara came in from the kitchen. She sat next to Jacob on the couch. Silently, he pulled her closer to him.

2 p.m. The phone rang. Samantha picked up the phone, exchanging conversation. She then entered the living room explaining that Michael's body just arrived at the funeral home. We could go over there anytime. It was somehow a relief to know things were progressing. Jacob wanted to go by himself. He did not want my mother or myself to accompany him. I understood why. He needed his space now. It would enable Jacob to secure a private vigil for his thoughts and his devotion to the only brother he knew and whom he

loved. He needed this. There were no objections. Allen offered to drive Jacob as he was unaware of the area and how to get there. Jacob appreciatively accepted.

The night before Jess and Jason arrived at the police station in Lynn to retrieve some of Michael's clothes. Today, they were going to go to his apartment to collect the rest of his belongings. In the meanwhile, Jacob was directed to a closet where some of Michael's things were placed. Jacob pulled out a blue suit that was very familiar to all of us. It was Michael's favorite, one he looked quite handsome in. The decision was made. Jacob gently unwrapped the suit from its plastic bag. I distinctly remember feeling nauseated at that precise moment. I knew my brother too, was wrapped in a plastic bag. I dismissed my thoughts. Jacob then went into the room he had slept in. He retrieved a baseball from his night bag. Jacob came into the living room with the suit in one hand and the ball in the other hand. I understood that Jacob wanted Michael to have this ball with him when he was buried. I wept.

When Jacob was but a wee child, Michael initiated him to Yankee Stadium the same manner in which Michael was introduced by our father: Cracker-Jacks, cotton candy, Yankee banners, baseball caps and baseball cards with a flat stick of bubblegum wrapped in thin, white paper alongside. Despite whether they lost or won, every season we would all go cheering loyally for a team my father grew up with. Michael perpetuated that ritual with Jacob. One day when Jacob was perhaps five or six, Michael reached out, catching a foul ball the Yankees had driven into the field. Jacob lit up an enormously wide smile. It surely was a highlight for him that day. That baseball had so much meaning for Jacob. Firstly, the baseball was caught by Michael. Secondly, it was caught in Yankee Stadium and thirdly it was a baseball the Yankees used. Jacob kept that ball in his room all the years he was growing up as a momentum and a blessed reminder of the time they both spent together.

Today, this ball had other meaning for Jacob. It was a symbol that they would always be together, forever bound to a passion and a loyalty of brotherhood, friendship and a love of the game of baseball. Jacob held tightly to the ball, walked out of the house with Allen behind him. The car rumbled. They were gone.

Chapter 14

My mind was ticking away as questions were filling up. Questions I had no answers for and questions I wanted to have answers for. How was Jacob holding up? Was he able to see Michael? Was he too vulnerable to see his brother? Did Michael look as horrible as the police officers described? Could Jacob survive such a viewing? Did Jacob renege on seeing Michael? Was the funeral director sensitive to Jacob's state of mind? Shouldn't I be there too? Humility became familiar again as I realized some things I just did not have any control over. I learned that many years ago in my life some things have this miraculous way of progressing for the highest good, despite what I could or could not control. Yet, Michael's death posed so many new questions for me, setting off new fears. Letting go was now painful. Michael's life was cut way too short. There was still much we needed to tidy up in our brother-sister relationship. I was dumbfounded as to where and how to muddle through all that unsorted stuff. I was in much too much of a distressed state to ponder such questions, nor could I attempt to find any answers. I also was very distraught over how Jacob and my mother would get through all of this.

For years I have taken care of others, guiding individuals on a journey that afforded them unconditional support. I knew well, how to inherently help others to heal. I just did not know how to intrinsically heal myself with as much grace and devotion. I stopped asking questions. I found myself reverting back to when I was a young teen selling candy bars for Michael's little league team. I was great at it. Michael never liked selling door-to-door. I sold the whole box in less than twenty minutes. He then gave me another box. I was off. The irony was that Michael was a top account executive for major corporations in the television industry. He was very successful at what he did. Yet, I was always amazed he chose a profession in sales.

The living room couch was my survival bench. One hour had passed since Jacob and Allen departed. It was a low-key day for my children. Jenna and Samantha were gracious in their care taking of them. I knew I needed to eat, but nothing seemed to satiate my desire to sustain myself. My energy was depleted. My mind was too distracted thinking. The waiting and the anticipation of what would come next was overwhelming. I could not watch my mother's pain anymore. I could not tolerate my own, nor was I even aware of how much pain I was in. Well beyond exhaustion, my mental and physical faculties were on rote. I simply had to give it up to something much bigger than myself. There was nothing to control anymore. I was too empty inside to attempt to master what was out of my hands. The couch was available. I fell asleep for what appeared to be hours, but what turned out to be only twenty minutes. My body felt incredibly weighted down. I also had difficulty moving. I felt like I was in a dream. If only.

The front door opened gently. I could detect on both Jacob's and Allen's faces their meeting was agonizing. I did not have the heart to openly ask what went on. I waited. I knew when Jacob was ready to share what had happened, he simply would. Jacob was predictable that way as was I. We never made bones about letting our emotions hang out. We were both open and strong about our feelings. Neither of us had problems communicating them. Today was different. Events and happenings were felt before they were spoken about. The trauma over the last few days stunned and paralyzed us. Survival was the best we could ask for. Inside though, we were grossly damaged. Jacob looked at me. I knew instantly to follow him outside. It was apparent that he did not want my mother to know the previous occurrences. I also knew that Jacob needed to get off his chest whatever there was to get off. My survival mode was waning thin. I got up off the couch feeling as if some intangible force was carrying me off. I walked outside with my brother. We sat on the front step outside the door where Jacob relayed to me his experiences.

When he and Allen first arrived at the funeral home, the director embraced them. Immediately, Jacob asked if he could please see Michael. The director then replied that he had not yet seen Michael. Apparently, Michael was still in a body bag. Once he could view Michael he would let Jacob know the outcome. The funeral director in no uncertain terms wanted to be sure that Jacob was able to endure whatever Michael had been minimized to. He did not want Jacob to be dreadfully shocked. Jacob however, was certain he could handle whatever he had to face. The funeral director held to his position, again repeating that he would comply as long as he could view Michael first. Jacob nodded. He said he would wait. Within less than ten seconds the director came back with such a look of aghast and horror on his face, he simply shook his head. The funeral director had no words. His look alone was sufficient. Allen, who had his hand on Jacob's shoulder, glanced with anguish at Jacob. Jacob understood. He was beside himself. He had looked up at the funeral director and very sorrowfully he had asked if he could please place this baseball in the casket with his brother. There were no protests, just a simple gesture of a sympathetic nod. Devastated, Jacob walked out, crushed by what he previously experienced. Allen followed. Minutes into the car ride back to Quarry, Jacob began to sob. He questioned anything and everything there was to question in life. Allen listened, crying along with Jacob. Jacob could not find any answers. He was choking in his hurt. Jacob continued to sob.

Chapter 15

We sat on that front step for a long time. All I could do was listen. There was no need for anything else. It was unimaginable to us how Michael could be so assaulted and left for dead. Both Jacob and I could only surmise details we were unaware of, filling in the broken pieces. We were not even aware of why someone would even want to kill our brother. Also, Jacob was told by the funeral director that Michael's body was too savaged for the embalmment too take. These thoughts had a brilliant way of maneuvering their way inside of us, leaving us feeling even more helpless and ravaged. Judaic tradition would be observed. We got up, went inside the house and came back to reality. The burial had to be tomorrow. We had to make further arrangements.

Jason and Jess had yet to return from the police headquarters in Lynn. Jacob and I were merely biding our time. We wanted to gather as many of Michael's belongings as possible. He and his space had already been terribly violated. Jacob and I had this need to protect whatever was left. Jacob paced. I paced. I sat down. Jacob sat down. I looked out the window. Jacob looked out. Jacob paced again. I paced with him. Our thoughts were amazingly in sync, but we were still a far cry away from the true hurt and rage building slowly up inside.

Another hour passed. We could hear some commotion outside. Jess and Jason had returned with a pick-up truck filled with the rest of Michael's personal possessions. Jacob and I ran outside to help retrieve whatever was available to carry. As I reached out to be handed a box of books, I noticed there were bloodstains all over them. Without any warning, I wept convulsively, falling to the ground simultaneously. Jason caught my fall, helping me to my feet. He grabbed the box I was holding. Very tenderly he told me to go inside. I then saw Jacob begin to cry. The impact of gathering my brother's items was startling and terribly shocking. Jacob and I became immobilized with pain of the most intense and unmistakable variety. The items in the boxes were very tangible, very real to

Michael's life and what he lived. This was the closest we could get to him in the last two days. Yet, his death was a reality now. Every item in these boxes told a story about Michael. Each were filled with mementos of his life. Spackled spots of blood lined the boxes and the items in them. Some stains were bigger than others. Some seemed fresher than others. His murder finally sunk in. We were both deeply affected by our own visions of his struggle to save his life, his final breaths and the abhorrent visions of every slash he withstood unmercifully. I ran in the house, into the bathroom and locked myself in for as long as I needed to. I sobbed frenetically. The pain was so deep I collapsed on the floor allowing my eyes to simply shut. No one came after me. I needed to wail. I needed to hurt. I was grateful for the solitude.

I appeared back in the living room watching Jacob, still collecting boxes from the truck. The enormous agony Jacob carried was evident. His face bore it all. However, he bravely attempted to conceal what he could as he continued to carry all of Michael's life in his hands.

The three men walked quietly back into the house. Nothing was said. Jacob went to the counter in the kitchen and sat down. Kara was pacing behind him. In one sweeping motion, Jacob put his hands up to his face. He began wailing, saying over and over again, "How could this happen, how could this happen?" It was then that Kara paced faster. She started to cry. It was the first time Kara broke. Jacob's emotion triggered her feelings. The pain Kara carried for Jacob was visible, yet she was equally as helpless. I wept.

Nothing was getting easier. As far as I could see, nothing would. Despite what we just executed, there was so much more to be done. We were very naïve as to what lay ahead of us. For the thousandth time, I looked out the window because I did not know what else to do. Jacob stayed in the kitchen, unable to move. My mother was chatting needlessly to anyone who could hear her. I felt as though I was watching a scene from a movie, yet the track was painfully slow and tortuous. "Hi Mommy," my kids screamed joyfully. "We're hungry, mamma." The frame was interrupted. The movie shut off. I remembered I was a mother. I went into the kitchen to prepare a very late lunch for Kailee and Emily.

Chapter 16

Rings exploded through the silence. 7:00 p.m. Allen picked up the
phone. A member of a Jewish congregation in Brooklyn called to tell our family
that a Rabbi could officiate a funeral service on Monday. It was done. Pause.
No one said anything. Now we could leave. The pacing ceased. The adrenalin
in our veins came to a stop. Exhaustion prevailed. Heading down to Cape Cod
seemed to be the next best thing, as we could shower, pick up new clothes and
be in a familiar place. Allen offered to drive us down. I accepted. I also found
out he would be driving us out to my cousin's house in Rosedale, New Jersey
where we would stay for the next several days, commuting back from Brooklyn,
then Staten Island and then to Jersey. I had been informed that my cousin Denise
had already planned meals, alerted family members to be in attendance. She was
patiently awaiting our arrival.

My mother, Kailee, Emily and I were pressed into the back seat of
the car sitting quietly. Jacob sat up front with Allen. There was no need for
communication. I closed my eyes and fell into a deep, one-hour sleep.

Allen pulled his car into the driveway of my house. He too, had lived
in this home, where only a year ago, we divorced. A bittersweet expression was
visible on his face. Though depleted, I was glad to be home, at least temporarily.
I entered the house. My heart began to palpitate. I remembered yesterday,
being abruptly stopped in my kitchen from a hysterical phone call. I could not
bear to pick up the phone nor did I want to anticipate it ringing. As I walked
in the living room, I noticed friends had placed cards, flowers and platters of
food everywhere. The house was spotless. My refrigerator was stocked. Love
permeated throughout. The love was abundant and gracious. Tears came to
my eyes. I was very thankful for the wonderful friends I had. My beloved
canine buddies, Succi and Stella were there to greet me unconditionally. I
could not have felt more loved. They sensed something very grave, responding

accordingly, as if they knew what I was thinking. I blessed their absolute, free and perfect love.

We all congregated in the kitchen when a knock was heard. Deana was at the front step. Her familiar face comforted me. I opened the door, giving her a very long embrace. No words were exchanged. She put her arm around me. She then hugged my mother, my brother, Kailee and Emily. She also brought with her, trays of food, assembling them in the kitchen, informing us that more would soon arrive. In her mind Deana could not have done enough for us. She wanted so much to do more. Deana always had this remarkable ability to give graciously, without expectation and it was no different now. She said that she had to pick up Ashley and Elly, and they, along with, her husband Gregg, would be back later to spend the evening with us. I kissed her goodbye whispering thank you. As I watched her driving out onto the road I felt a terrible pang of emptiness. The feeling came over me so quickly, tears again flooded my already stained cheeks. I closed the door behind me while I desperately attempted to think about nothing, nothing and everything.

I had a flashback of ten days ago when Michael and I had last talked. He called me to see how the girls and I were doing, inquiring if we needed anything. Michael was never a big talker, thus, the conversation was sweet and short. We hung up and said, "Have a good day, I love you." The plan was to talk to each other in another week. I realized that week was today and that today would be never. I knew that it would not be until the day I died that I would actually see my brother again. That was my only source of comfort.

I needed to believe in something more tangible. I was becoming desperate. I just did not want to believe that Michael was gone, literally. I walked into my kitchen, away from earshot of my family. I picked up the phone. I then dialed my brother Michael, praying this was all a mistake, hoping he would cheerfully pick up and say, "Hello." One ring sounded, then two rings and then a third. His answering machine clicked on and said, "Hi. This is Michael. I am not here right now. Please leave a message and I will get back to you, beep." Desperately, I then pressed another number, listening to the messages that were left for Michael after he was murdered. Immediately I heard my mother's voice wailing, "Michael, it is Mom, I am here, please pick up. I am so sorry, so sorry, so sorry, so terribly sorry Michael. I love you." More sobbing. I then heard his girlfriend's voice, hysterically pleading for him to pick up. I put down the phone. I was beside myself. Tears burst through my eyes. My vision was blurred. He did not pick up. He was never going to pick up. I retreated to my bedroom, Succi and Stella following behind me. I closed the door quietly. I lay on my bed with each dog at my side, staring up at the ceiling. I could distinctly hear the rhythm of their breathing.

I remember reading in one of my spiritual texts that when someone is murdered, or when they are in an accident or they are taken abruptly, they appear lost, unclear as to what happened to them. They do they know where they are. My eyes welled up again. I thought about where Michael's soul was and how he was doing. The dogs' breathing remained serene and peaceful. I prayed Michael was at peace too. In fact I pleaded with God to make sure he was. I fell asleep.

I was awakened by playful laughter in the background. Emily was joyfully humming to herself and giggling with her sister Kailee, in their bedroom, adjacent to mine. I looked at the clock, realizing it was 9 o'clock in the evening. I bolted upright, startling Succi and Stella. I ran into the children's room. To my relief, Allen had them tucked away in their beds, bathed, deliciously smelling good. Kailee and Emily were chatting across their beds, slowly falling asleep simultaneously. I noticed Tweetie Bird dangling off of Kailee's fingers, soon to land on the rug below. I caught Tweetie, gently placing the stuffed animal next to Kailee's face. I kissed Kailee goodnight, whispering, "I love you." I walked over to Emily's bed, quietly pulling the covers up from around her legs. I stroked her face and whispered, "I love you," then I kissed her on her cheek. I thanked God for my children, only knowing all too well, they are simply borrowed.

I quietly walked out of the room and down the corridor into the living room. Allen was attempting to ignite a fire in the fireplace. My mother was in the bathroom.

Jacob and Kara were sitting on the couch opposite the fireplace. I sat down on the rocking chair affixed in my proverbial stare. I knew we had to leave early the next morning. There was still much to prepare: Packing my luggage, preparing lunches for the kids, packing their clothes, getting to my cousin's house, a good five hour trek, then the funeral service the next day for my brother. A day later, it would be another long haul back and another five hours. We would then sit Shiva in my home. This was a Jewish tradition that lasted for seven days. We would acknowledge Michael's death, grieving along with others who will come to share our loss. It was one tradition that emphasized the grief as well as the joyous memories. In our case, how Michael was killed would only exasperate the grief. I knew I would be grieving Michael's death for the rest of my life. In respect to my mother who would still be with me for at least another week, I had to allow for this time. Our lives came to such a drastic and abrupt halt, I wanted my children to resume some normalcy in their lives. As I had learned and I was continuing to learn, resistance only perpetuated more resistance. I got up, acknowledged my brother and Kara, excusing myself. I proceeded to pack, then I drew a very hot bath, steamed with essential oils and a lighted candle. I cried uncontrollably in the bathtub. It was easy to fall asleep. It was one of the few nights thereafter I would be able to sleep as easily.

51

Chapter 17

Chatter permeated through my walls. Kailee and Emily were awake. I looked over to the side of my bed, the clock, visible as ever. 7:32 a.m. Thank God they were up. They were my alarm for the morning, though they were oblivious to their unconscious responsibility of such a task. I was grateful to them. I was a perpetual early riser. I never needed an alarm clock. Today was different. October 16th would have been a beautiful day for baking breads and pies, traveling north to see the brilliance of the autumn colors, embracing the delectable smells of the season. I lay motionless in my bed. My house was filled with distraught people who tried in vain to make sense out of something that was impossible to do. My heart was hungry for joy and burdened with tortuous pain. Fall time was my favorite time of year. I could not remember when the tree in front of my house had changed colors.

I got up, patted Succi and Stella who were sitting next to me, unreservedly. I made my way to the slider in the kitchen to let them out. I could hear the shower winding down. Jacob was just getting out. Kara was dressing. Allen had coffee brewing. My mother was still behind closed doors. I watched Succi and Stella as they moved to the far side of the fence. They could roam freely and for as long as they chose. They appeared deliberate today, not as playful. I reopened up the slider. They both bolted inside, next to me. They knew. They knew everything. In their own way, they were sitting vigil. It was a reminder of what I would soon have to do.

The plan was to get dressed as quickly as possible, eat, and get on the road. Kara and Jacob would drive in Kara's car while Allen, myself, my mother, Kailee and Emily would drive together in one vehicle. Kara would then drop Jacob off at my cousin's house. She would go back to Long Island where she lived. She would meet Jacob tomorrow.

My mom got up, dressed quickly, saying very little. She grabbed a cup of coffee. My good friend and a devoted dog sitter, Sally called, verifying to me that she would graciously take care of my animals for as long as I needed. I turned to my very loyal comrades, patted their snouts and hugged them, telling them that I would be home soon. They did not budge from where they sat. They simply looked up at me, diligently watching my every move. The phone rang. I jumped. I reached for the phone, but Allen picked it up. He then handed the receiver over to me. It was Deana. She had told me that she was going to watch the house. She would see me in two days. I thanked her a multitude of times. We hung up. I left a few lights on, held the door open for the rest of my family. I locked the front door. Allen opened up the trunk of the car, piling bags one on top of one another. Kara and Jacob were waiting in their car, ready to follow us. We left.

The ride was uneventful, but seemingly long and very tiring, especially for Allen as he did all of the driving. We pulled into the driveway of my cousin's house. Before we got out of the car, my cousin, Liza was already out the front door. Denise, her mother, came after. Liza was overwhelmed with grief. She hugged us, crying. Denise went immediately to my mother, embracing her tenderly, wincing as if someone had just stabbed her. No words were exchanged. Denise led us in, showed us where our prospective rooms were. We all congregated back into the dining room. Jack, Denise's husband walked inside the house. Immediately he went to my mother, enclosing his arms around her. My mother started to cry.

Jack and my mother grew up together, laughed together and shared a childhood together. They spent summers together in Atlantic City, at family reunions and old-fashioned picnics, strolling on the boardwalk, conversing with a Bubba or a Sadie of the generation before. This was a sacred ritual. Today, they were sharing my mother's grief, a profound sorrow where no comfort was sufficient enough. Jack gave my mother a tender nod, letting go, sensing my mother needed to be alone. My mother retreated upstairs. The kids and I made our way into the kitchen to see if we could be of help to Denise. Allen and Jacob collected the remaining belongings from the vehicles. Jacob kissed Kara goodbye knowing he would see her tomorrow.

There was not an awkward silence, rather a respectful one, within the parameters of my cousin's house. Denise had been an intensive care nurse for years. Every fiber of her soul understood peoples' grief. She was a pro at making others comfortable. She did not intrude on people's personal thoughts. Rather, she took the necessary and practical steps to ensure ease for all concerned. Food was already prepared. Beds were made with new, crisp sheets. Towels were laid out with fresh soaps. Videos for my children were in place. Closets were emptied to supply ample space for other's possessions. Jack was warm and embracing. He was tender and soft-spoken, only using humor when appropriate, never undermining the suffering we all bore. I felt very comforted to be with family. Although I did not know my mother's side of the family well, I knew we were all connected by events, circumstances, and blood that perpetuated our lineage. Conversation was easy. Harrowing moments were respectfully supported.

Kailee and Emily found tremendous joy in being in someone else's home. They laughed, they chatted endlessly, creating their own space. They were extremely content, oblivious to the horror of what recently had occurred. I was not able to go into detail on how Michael died. I did not want them to be terrified to go to asleep, simply because Michael had died in his bed. I knew at some point or another, both children would ask more questions. I decided I would deal with whatever came up as it came up. I knew Kailee would be comfortable with not wanting any more information than was given. On the other hand, Emily would want every detail and for every detail to be explained precisely. She would be persistent until she understood everything. I dismissed the thought.

We were going to be eating shortly. I made my way into the bathroom, washed my hands, splashed water on my tired face, helped Kailee and Emily clean up, then followed my brother and my mother into the dining room. Denise had prepared a feast. Though none of us were terribly hungry, we were all very gracious, gathering around a loving space. Michael's death was not discussed. We merely talked about stuff that was inconsequential to anything that was going on presently. That was all that could be endured, at least momentarily. Jack spoke about particular moments he and my mother had shared as a child. Laughter was even audible at the table. My mother felt horribly guilty for emitting such expression, but it was a release she needed and one that was spontaneous and without justification. Time simply passed. The sunlight drifted into nightfall. Plates strewn with unwanted food, empty glasses and crumbs were still visible on the linen tablecloth. Nobody had any desire to get up. It appeared that bellies were satiated but hearts and souls were empty, filled with a heavy sadness.

I cleared the table. Jacob and I offered more help, but Denise refused. Everyone went to different places in the house. I walked into their den where I found Kailee, Emily and Allen sitting quietly on the floor resting and talking. The inevitable came up. Allen was gently sharing with Emily that Michael had been stabbed but very badly. Very innocently, Emily asked, "Was he sliced like a pizza?" My heart broke. Her question was so faultless, so genuine. I was completely taken aback. I looked at Emily very lovingly. Glancing at Allen, I merely wrapped my arms around Emily. I replied, "Not exactly." Emily again innocently inquired, "Was he sliced like a pizza?" I repeated that he was stabbed several times, but not sliced the way a pizza would be sliced. She stopped there.

Thank God. I had no more answers. She snuggled inside my hug. She then looked at Kailee, chatting playfully with her, never again asking me any more questions that evening. The purity of her question moved me profoundly. It was a logical question for a five year old. Kailee merely absorbed the silence. She resumed her play with Emily.

Time was passing all too quickly. When it was close to 11 p.m., I walked Kailee and Emily to their bedroom that was stuffed with an oversized bed. There was still ample room for more people to fit into it. Both girls lay close to one another. Kisses were exchanged as were goodnights. Within minutes the children were peacefully asleep.

Everyone went to their prospective bedrooms. Allen and I decided we would retire in the basement on a couch that opened up into a bed. My mother retreated into her room, Jack and Denise to theirs, Jacob to his. As I was making my way onto the couch, I shut off the lights. The minute I placed my head on the pillow, I panicked. It was unimaginably dark. The blackness suffocated me. Images of Michael being murdered overcame me. Again, slash, hack, slash hack, slash, hack. I could not get this dreadful image out of my mind. The darkness exacerbated these visions. I sprung from the couch, breaking into a cold sweat. My breathing was short and stifled. I was viciously groping for a light. I stumbled over items in the room, knocking them to the floor. The more I allowed the darkness to take over, the more terrorized I became. I screamed to Allen, "Find the light." I was completely consumed by the blackness of the room. I became paralyzed with fear. I could not help thinking that Michael would appear to me mangled and unrecognizable. My breathing became more foiled. I screamed, "Please find the light, please." Allen did. Without any words being uttered, we folded the couch back into its frame. We then proceeded to the den upstairs where we slept on the floor. Windows surrounded the room. I knew the light from the night sky would be visible. All of a sudden I heard a noise upstairs. I got up. I found Jacob scurrying into Kailee and Emily's bed. He lie on the edge of the bed stiffly, his eyes fixated up on the ceiling. I had asked him if something was the matter. He confided in me that he was terrified to fall asleep. He too was having dreadful nightmares of Michael's murder. He did not want to be alone. The girls provided a certain solace for him, though they were completely unaware of their function to do as such. Jacob was immobilized with terror. It was a dread that was unexplainable to anyone, except to Jacob and me. A quiet understanding was our bond. It was an unspoken silence that we both shared each and everytime haunting visions of Michael's death appeared to us. I whispered goodnight. I walked into the den, got into a make shift bed on the floor and spent hours drifting in and out of sleep, the ceiling being my canvass for support. Allen was in a deep sleep, snoring vigorously, only adding to my inability to fall asleep. Daylight was peering through the curtains. It was 6 a.m.

Chapter 18

     I forced myself to stay under the covers for a few more minutes. I was too exhausted to get up. Yet, I was equally as restless. My eyes simply would not shut. I dragged my body up, walked to a bathroom near the den, splashing water on my face. I looked at myself in the mirror. I began to cry. I appeared haggard, far away, almost as if I was looking through myself. I shivered. I started the shower, blasting the hot water with the hopes that the steam from the water would saturate the bathroom walls. I stepped inside the shower, allowing myself to be completely smothered by the vapor and the pounding water on my back. In some way, the water provided a cleansing to my already weary body. It also brought out my grief. The harder the shower beat against me, the harder I cried. I had no power over my emotions. They came when they wanted to, they left when they wanted to and they would reappear at the oddest moments, consuming me that much more. I shut the shower off, dried myself and got dressed.

     It was extremely quiet in the house. I was anxious to get started and finish the day. Today was Michael's service and Michael's burial. No one knew the Rabbi, nor did the Rabbi know anything about Michael and his life. I had difficulty comprehending what the Rabbi would say about Michael to honor his earthly days. I was also concerned about my mother being overwrought. The day had barely begun. It already seemed as though hours had passed, leaving me emotionally and physically depleted.

     6:45 a.m. I went upstairs to peek in on Kailee and Emily. They were still asleep, innocent in their slumber, peaceful in their pose. Jacob looked at me giving out a mild groan. It was apparent that he barely received any sleep. He was next to Emily who moved constantly in her unconscious state. He got up, stretched and headed toward the bathroom. I left the room, making my way downstairs.

I picked out the only dress I brought with me. Throwing it over my shoulder, in an attempt to find an iron, I couldn't help noticing the sun peeking through the curtain. The prior day's events were so full and so intense I packed haphazardly. I was missing my toothbrush and other basic necessities necessary for an overnight stay. Yet, I realized how minuscule these things became. I knew my cousin Denise would have ample supplies of what I needed. I simply waited, unpacked Kailee and Emily's dress, pulling out their shoes and their socks.

Time was passing too quickly. It was already well after 7. Jacob came downstairs, already showered, looking tired still. Conversation was sparse as the grimness of our day became apparent. We had to be in Brooklyn, at the synagogue before noon to meet with the Rabbi to give him some history about Michael and his life. My mother I knew, did not sleep. She never did. I sensed that she was already up, contemplating the grimness of what lie ahead as well. Jack and Denise were in their bedroom, running water was audible in their bathroom. Jack was on the phone making last minute details for the ride to Brooklyn. I could finally hear sounds emitting from Kailee and Emily's room. Allen could be heard in the background tossing and turning, resisting getting up. Again, the sun shone brilliantly with sheer, thin rays peering through Denise's curtains in the living room. It was a stark reality to the foreboding anguish felt in the house.

My mother came downstairs, ready to go, talking very little. Her eyes were red and drawn. It was easy to surmise that she spent most of the nighttime crying. Jacob was dressed. Jack and Denise walked in the kitchen, dressed as well. Coffee was already made. Bagels and cream cheese were out for anyone who wanted to eat. Allen had dragged himself into the shower, quickly preparing himself for departure to the synagogue. I went upstairs to help Kailee and Emily dress. When finished, they came downstairs, beautifully dressed with their hair in lovely ribbons. They were full of life, exuberant to be driving in a limousine. That was their highlight for the day, especially for Emily. She could not have been more thrilled to be picked up in a luxury car that may even be equipped with a television. Her innocence was genuine. Such innocence added a tender humanness to this very warped day. Emily was unaware however, that this big, beautiful, oversized car, with leathered, upholstered seats would be behind another oversized car carrying her Uncle Michael in a coffin.

Although death was very familiar for me, I could not possibly fathom a procession in which my brother was the main event for whom I was a part of. It was unthinkable and unreasonable. My eyes welled up. I quickly brushed away the tears before they fell down my cheeks. I had such a difficult time comprehending the fact that Michael would be tucked away in this box, cloistered by walls of wood, lifeless. I knew one day I would bury my mother in the natural course of events. I never, ever thought I would, at thirty-eight, have to bury my brother at thirty-nine. The sequence of events appeared terribly out of sync to me.

Jack called to all of us. The car service had arrived in front of the house. As my cousin held the front door ajar, quietly, we all filed outside. I was taken aback by the beauty of the day. The sun was luminous, warm and inviting. It was a moment of respite for my brokenness. I could distinctly feel my heart open, easing my pain. This was but a moment, a glimpse of what time might heal. I took a deep breath. I walked into the limousine, squeezed between my mother, my girls and my cousin Jack. Jacob and Allen sat in the front seat.

I looked out the windows cognizant of the fact that there were parts of New Jersey that were actually pretty. New Jersey is stereotyped as the state of toxic wastes, a land of industry. The old, brick homes shaded by manicured trees and shrubs seemed outstanding. Jack and Denise lived in suburbia with tailored streets and centers of villages that were cropped according to town protocol. A rather naked reality compared to Brooklyn. My view became shattered when we crossed over a bridge as we made our our way toward our destination. Slums were exposed, overcrowding apparent, with garbage filtered on the streets. Two blocks away a more affluent area was exposed. Quite obviously, people had more money to trim their streets with trees, potted flowers and expensive cars. It was hard to believe only a stone's throw away, poverty and wealth existed simultaneously. The city was renowned for this diversity, equally as mesmerizing and depressing.

We were slowing down, nearing a side road that led us all into the driveway of a synagogue. The car stopped. No one got out. Motivation was scarce. We all knew that somewhere in that sacred temple Michael quietly lay. It was time to say goodbye. It was time for closure. It was a reality no one wanted to bear. It was our brother and my mother's son in that box. Nothing in that single moment could suffice for the anxiety and the extreme pain we all silently sustained.

I got out of the car along with the rest of my family. Allen approached the front of the synagogue holding the door open for all of us. As Jacob and I walked in, the lights appeared dim. The ambiance was somber. Family members on my mother's side had already arrived. Many of Jacob's friends, personal and work were there offering respect to Jacob and our family. Jacob, my mother and I were met by the Rabbi who gently led us to a room far away from the sanctuary. This was to be a discreet meeting, where no one else could interfere. The Rabbi was kind and most attentive. He motioned for all of us to sit down. He then asked us to please share in any capacity Michael's life and how Michael died. As my mother relayed information on Michael's ruthless death, the Rabbi was shocked and in disbelief. Terribly overcome with Michael's death, the Rabbi could not possibly understand what would lead someone to viciously kill another human being. He said that he would do the very best to honor Michael. He was terribly sorry. He put his head down in his hands. Silence. We all got up. My mother walked over to her cousins. Jacob and I walked into the sanctuary. We were completely confronted by the view of Michael's coffin staring back at us. The sight was most distressing. This was the very first time since Michael was murdered, that any of us were tangibly close to him. Jacob asked me if he could please spend a few minutes alone. I obliged. Walking away into another room mistakenly, I found myself around the corner, again viewing Jacob from a different entrance. I did not mean to witness Jacob's final goodbye with Michael. I merely found myself there, staring at him. Jacob went over to where Michael was resting, placing his hands back and forth on the coffin. He was distraught, afflicted with the most intense sorrow. Very tenderly, as Jacob kissed Michael's coffin, he began to weep. It was at this moment I knew how fragile Jacob was. Tears poured down my face. My heart pounded harder. I attempted to catch my breath before I was heard. I looked over to the other entrance, noticing my cousin Howie viewing Jacob, his eyes too, welled up with tears. Quite by accident, Howie caught Jacob's vigil. As my glance caught Howie's gaze, we merely stood still, staring at one another. This was a shared moment among us all, though Jacob was not cognizant of having participated.

Many people were congregating into the sanctuary. It was a small synagogue, simple, but peaceful, a far cry from the step outside a world that was still plagued with violence and hatred. My mother, Jacob, Kailee and Emily and sat in the front row as instructed by the Rabbi. Others sat behind us. Everything again became surreal to me. Michael's coffin appeared so small. I could not imagine his body in there. I felt as though I was in a space only known to me. Closing my eyes momentarily, I realized all too well, that I was here, at a place that made absolutely no sense to me.

It was apparent that no one wanted to violate our space. I turned around, noticing my ex-father-in-law arrived. He sat in the last row. He drove five hours simply to pay his respects. I had no idea he would be coming. Smiling at him, I gestured thanks. He nodded. I was most appreciative. I knew he too, was suffering with the recent news of his dying daughter.

The service began. The Rabbi got up and wiped his face. He held on to the small podium in front of him, standing impeccably still. He very slowly, very deliberately offered words of comfort about Michael's gentle soul. The Rabbi suddenly stopped. He recomposed himself for a moment, then he wiped his eyes. Out of nowhere the Rabbi began to sob uncontrollably, catching his hands again on the podium in front of him. He attempted with deep compassion, a delivery about violence and the world in which we lived as it related to Michael's death. I was deeply moved. The Rabbi knew nothing about Michael, except for the fact that he was a human being slaughtered without cause. Again, the Rabbi stopped. He was barely composed. He placed both his hands solidly on the podium as if not to fall. Intermittently, between sobs, he finished his thoughts. I felt his genuine pain. Distraught beyond belief, tears saturated my face. Within a moment, silence predominating, the Rabbi turned to my mother, Jacob and me, asking if we would please all rise and stand in front of Michael's coffin.

I felt my knees wanting to buckle beneath me. I walked with Jacob in hand, my mother facing the Rabbi. Something overcame me. Without a moment to pass, I put my hands on the edge of the coffin, attempting to open the lid. Jacob looked at me as if I was losing my sanity. I let go of the wooden edges around where Michael lay. I looked up at Jacob, closing my eyes momentarily. I wanted to see if Michael was really inside the coffin. I snapped back to the here and now, holding tightly to Jacob's hand.

"Yit-ga-dal, ve-yit-ka-dash she-mea ra-ba, be-al-ma di-ve-ra chi-re-u-tei…….." "Let the glory of God be extolled, let His great name be hallowed…" began the Rabbi, as he sang the Mourner's Kaddish. The music was riveting, affecting everyone in the room. I looked over at Aiden who was holding his face in his hands, his head down. To my left, Allen, sitting quietly with tears streaming down his face stared at the Rabbi intensely. My mother, Jacob, and I still stood, weeping simultaneously. The Rabbi proceeded to finish the prayer, "O-she shalom, bi-me-ro-mav, hu ya-a-she, shalom a-lei-nu ve-al kol…" "May He who causes peace to reign in the high heavens, let peace descend on us, on all the world, and let us say, Amen." "May the Source of peace to all who mourn, and comfort to all who are bereaved. Amen." The Rabbi continued, "The light of life is a finite flame. Like the Sabbath candles, life is kindled, it burns, it glows, it is radiant with warmth and beauty. But soon it fades; its substance is consumed, and it is no more. Something of us can never die. We move in the eternal cycle of darkness and death, of light and love." Silence. It was done. The service was over. I sobbed.

I have always understood that within the ebb and flow of nature's cycle, God's eternal law still abides. I believe that God supports the struggles in our living state as much as he does in the hope in death. God cares for all souls of all the living and those that have passed and it is with his power that we can gather our strength. It has been said often that our best homage to our deceased ones is when we live our lives most fully, even in the shadows of our loss. Every bit of our lives is worth the life of the whole world where every one breath is the breath of our creator. As we affirm this oneness we too, affirm the worth of the person whose life has now ended. No one is ever alone and every life finds purpose. I felt so empty, so alone and so in pain. Michael often would say, "You have to dig deep." I could not imagine my well deep enough this time. I kissed my brother's coffin and walked back to my seat. The Rabbi then motioned for me to come up to the pulpit. My brother and my mother were too distraught to offer words.

I looked out at everyone, not prepared to say anything. I allowed my heart to speak. In a broken voice, tears flooding my cheeks, I spoke of death being just a fine line away in a dimension very close to earth. I asked that everyone please pray for Michael's transition, thanking everyone for being here. Eyes were wet. Souls wept. Dead silence prevailed.

Everyone assembled in the front room of the Synagogue. Only a few would go to the cemetery where Michael would be put to rest. The hearse was parked closest to the main entrance, the limousine behind it. Family members in various cars would be traveling behind. Jacob, Allen, my mother, Kailee and Emily entered into the limousine. Allen held the door open for me. As both of us approached the limo, we turned in unison, watching my cousins lift Michael's casket up on to their shoulders, placing him gently into the back of the hearse. Allen turned to me crying. Almost immediately and bizarrely, Allen looked at me and asked, "Michael never really liked me, didn't he?" I had no answer. The question was so out of the ordinary, I merely hugged him. I suppose in moments of great despair, we glance back at the past, overwhelming ourselves with what ifs. Allen and Michael were very different, neither of them ever establishing a brother-in-law relationship. Also, Michael could not tolerate how much emotional pain I was in during my marriage. This only accentuated Michael's dislike for my ex-husband, not necessarily making it a justification.

I got in the car glancing out into nowhere. The ride would be a good forty-five minutes. Michael would be buried in a Jewish Cemetery in Staten Island, where my father lay. The only plot available was my mother's. She and my father had planned on being buried near each other. Yet, no one planned on my father being killed at forty- two. Thus, my grandmother used her plot to bury her son. After my father died, my mother purchased a plot across the way from my dad's grave. There was no other ground available. Michael, thirty-nine and unmarried had no need to buy a plot, at least so he thought. Now my mother used her plot to bury her son. The irony of it all seemed terribly pitiless.

The procession began. I tried in vain to tune out anything associated with what would come next. Looking out of the window at the slums to my left did not suffice. Nor did looking out of the window at the prominent section to my right suffice. The resplendent sun offered little solace. I was beyond numb. I was dazed, I was shocked, stupefied, paralyzed and more. Perhaps it was the only way to survive this ordeal. This was simply too much. Yet, I recalled the times I reminded myself how God gives us only what we are able to handle. This seemed momentous.

We came to the Verrazano Bridge. It was enormous. I knew once we crossed over, the cemetery would be but minutes away. I had a flashback to when I was a very little girl driving to the city. We had to go over a bridge. I remember it being colossal and terrifying. I crouched down as low as I could go onto the back floor of the car, covering my head until we passed over the bridge. I never looked up. Ever since, I have never liked bridges. I put my head down as we entered the tollbooth, shutting my eyes until we made it to the other side of the bridge. I was grateful I was not driving. We were nearing the Richmond exit. We proceeded to bear into the right lane where the driver turned off the exit. I remembered vividly being on this route years ago.

One year after my father was buried, we had the unveiling, a sacramental tradition native to Judaism. The headstone is covered in cheesecloth for one year. It is believed that once the cloth is unveiled, the soul, once settled, will be lifted to a life of eternal peace. I remember my grandmother sobbing hysterically after my father's stone was unveiled. Neither Michael, nor my mother, pregnant with Jacob, nor I could attend the funeral. We were critically injured, desperately fighting for our lives. A year later when we were all at least physically well, we participated in the unveiling of my father's stone. Today, we would all attend Michael's burial. Physically we were fine. Mentally, our states were delicate.

We came to the entrance of the cemetery. We made our way to where Michael was to be put to rest. The cars in the procession quietly followed behind our car. Tami and Aaron, my mother's cousins got out. My mother's brother, his wife, my mother's aunt and her son also got out. Some of Jacob's friends pulled up. They too got out. Aiden arrived. He stood near the back. Others filed in gathering around the grave. I had so much difficulty accepting the fact that Michael would be put into this hole in the ground, smothered with dirt, his body atrophying. I hated myself for thinking this way. Yet, I simply could not get this image out of my mind.

On one hand, I knew Michael was already out of his body. I believed his soul was on the other side, his body was merely a vehicle that housed him. I also believed Michael was here, more concerned about our state of mind. Nonetheless, my earthly perceptions took over. I could not, momentarily get over the image of Michael's body rotting in the ground. It was a horrible description of what I felt, but it was real and very vivid.

As a youngster, I used to walk in graveyards, looking at historical sites of families, great grandparents, grandparents, parents, children, etc. I used to find great comfort and fascination walking around these burial grounds, imagining the times in which these individuals lived. Today, I could barely bring myself to be there. Everything seemed so final, so desolate.

I remarked how brilliant the sun was, a downright difference from our state of minds. My mother looked at Jacob, then at me. She pleadingly said, "I wanted the heavens to open up and cry for Michael today. It should have poured." With that, Jacob and I lowered our heads. The Rabbi began the service singing. Four family members then lifted Michael's casket up. Silence. Very deliberately, they lowered Michael into the ground until he was in place. I overheard my mother in a crying whisper, "Goodbye my love. I will see you again, one day." I was so overcome by my mother's words, I could barely stand up. I was immediately brought back to 1971. My mother, Michael and I walked into our house after spending months in Massachusetts General Hospital. It was an extremely somber day. I walked back to the den where I found my mother sobbing, rubbing my father's coat sleeves on her cheek. My mother never saw me. I was profoundly touched by that sorrowful moment.

Tears again inundated my eyes. My heart was tortured. This was it. We had laid Michael to rest, at least what was left of him. The Rabbi asked us to please pick up a bit of the earth and throw it onto Michael's casket. This ritual was symbolic of saying goodbye, sending Michael off to a better place. I watched while Kailee and Emily picked up heaps of dirt, throwing it over the coffin. They gingerly ran back, picking up wild flowers growing on the ground. They played. We wept. This was a remarkable, synchronistic balance of sheer innocence and insufferable pain. It was a moment I will never forget.

As I walked away from Michael's grave, I glanced back one more time. I quietly said, "I love you Michael." My heart felt heavy. I knew that Michael and I had unresolved stuff between us. I also knew I would be forced to let go and trust that the love we had was unspoken, despite our differences. Yet, my pain flooded that trust. I looked up and watched, while my brother Jacob walked over to our father's grave. Jacob just stood still, his head lowered. He placed a rock on my father's tombstone, another ritual, symbolic of letting the deceased one know that you were there. He walked away, never looking back. Everyone made their ways to their cars. Some of us exchanged words and hugs. Some of us remained silent. Some of us would never be the same. We entered the cars in which we came in and made the journey home to Jack and Denise's house, where we would stay for one more evening. Silence predominated the car ride. Tissues were sparse.

Chapter 19

Reality ceases to set in, especially when there are numbers of people around to distract you. The house was pouring with people who came to sit with us, eat with us and merely be with us. I was not abreast of the fact that I was exhausted. Greeting people at the door, talking with cousins, sharing memories about Michael was nonstop. Jacob was in high gear as well, conversing with family, shaking hands, crying and laughing concurrently and simply being. My mother sat at a chair, in the dining room, not moving. People came up to her. She simply sat, allowing conversation when appropriate. Food was plentiful, the energy flowing, both somber and heightened.

Considerable hours had passed. Food disappeared as did people. Nightfall crept in. Previous events began to run their course in my mind. Reality was here, hard and cruel. There were no more distractions. The one saving grace however, was that fatigue won me over. I was completely and utterly physically drained. Sleep seemed to be the answer. I walked into the den, sprawling myself out on the rug. My mind was not deluged with visions of Michael's murder. I thanked God for this little miracle.

I awoke to dinner being set out on the table. My stomach did not intend to devour anything more. I was overwhelmed by the notion of eating. It is known that food brings people together at gatherings. People have conversations around food. People celebrate around food. People lament around food. Food is a huge part of the Jewish culture. Despite the circumstances, food will always be present in abundance. It is in accordance then, that to share we must also eat.

I felt like puking. My insides felt weak. Although sleeping satisfied some of my depleted state, my belly was saturated with knots of discomfort. Michael was dead. He left this earth violently and so abruptly, no one in his immediate family could do anything to stop his very untimely death. I was tormented for not being able to sense that my brother was in trouble the night he died. I was even more tormented that I slept so peacefully that October 14th. Where was I? I have always had this sixth sense about things. I recanted that dreadful evening, torturing myself for not being able to help Michael. It turns out that Jacob was going to visit his brother that weekend, but plans changed. There could have been two burials this weekend. I shrank into a ball on the mattress, shivering frantically. "Mommy, okay?" I swung myself around and saw Emily climbing up next to me. I grabbed her, fervently hugging her. "Mommy is okay," I answered. I picked Emily up. We headed downstairs.

The dining room table was graciously set. Beautiful, handcrafted crystal decorated the table, along with heaping sizes of chicken, potatoes, challah, green beans and fresh salad. It was a feast. Family support was comforting, though few words were uttered. Emptiness also prevailed. One member of our family was missing. Michael's absence was strongly felt. It was odd, almost uncomfortable not to have Michael tangibly there while all of us could heartily eat. I could have never imagined the emptiness that would sit with me for years to come. That evening was a mere glimpse of how such affliction could crush one's soul. I grappled with some salad. I then excused myself. I walked outside breathing the air as if this was my last breath. I looked up at the stars, searching for the brightest one in the hopes to connect with Michael. I sobbed hysterically. I begged Michael to give me a sign that he was okay. No sign. I shook, turned around and I headed back into the house. Jacob's eyes met mine halfway up the stairs. He merely followed me with a sympathetic stare, saying nothing. That was all I needed. I recollected myself. Again, I sat down at the table. Conversation began about nothing and everything. Midnight. Dishes were cleared. Remnants of crumbs were splattered on the table, as was the profoundness of this day. When everyone left to get ready to sleep, I walked gently into the kitchen, gathered a plate, a fork, a napkin, and a glass. Michael had a place at the table. I did not want him to be forsaken. I walked upstairs, got under the covers with Kailee and Emily, falling asleep in my clothes.

Chapter 20

I thought I heard a bird chirping. I tossed in bed, viewing the clock sitting on the nightstand, grimacing. 6:02 a.m. I shoved the covers over my head, refusing to believe morning had arrived. Closing my eyes seemed but minutes ago. I could distinctly hear Emily breathing. Again, a bird's chirp was distinctly audible. Meandering to the nearest window, pulling back the curtains, I came nose-to-nose with a lovely bird, small in size, wearing a yellow belly. It sang. How ironic the circumstances, a beautiful creature should be singing at my window. Perhaps this was a sign from Michael. I did not know how to interpret such a sign, nor did I feel it necessary to do so. An intense peace filled me up. Within seconds, the bird flew away, out of my sight. Shutting the curtains, climbing back into bed, burying myself under the comforter, I closed my eyes.

Voices were faintly heard. I peeked out from under the covers, observing both Kailee and Emily chatting endlessly to one another. It was 9:30 a.m. I had no idea that I had fallen asleep for another three hours. I also realized that time did not matter, at least momentarily. Reaching over, I grabbed Kailee and Emily. They laughed as I tickled them, cuddling them tenderly. Pulling myself up, I stretched, making my way to the nearest bathroom. I could sense that someone was downstairs in the kitchen. I quickly showered, dressed, made the bed, offering Kailee and Emily help. All of us were ready to go. Our bags were packed and placed at the top staircase. As we came downstairs, I could smell eggs and a variety of other odors, permeating throughout. The table was freshly set from the night before. Allen had already showered. Jacob was also downstairs, ready for our trip back to Massachusetts. My mother had yet to appear. Passing time, all of us simply assembled in the kitchen conversing with each other. One of us even laughed. The shock had worn off. Yet, the uneasiness of emitting a happier emotion was still very much felt. The release to do so was sorely needed.

Mom appeared in the kitchen, ready for departure. All of us again went to our prospective seats at the dining room table, according to where we had sat, beginning two days ago. We ate, we talked, and we ate some more. Coffee was replenished. Danish was set out. Conversation was trickling as were our appetites. It was time to go. Everyone helped cleared dishes. Allen made a last look around the house, making sure all of our belongings were collected. Bags filled the front foyer. Jack and Denise gave everyone heartfelt hugs, saying little. We stood still, embracing the moment, thanking them for their generosity. Waving goodbye in the car, we quietly pulled away.

This very small automobile was packed. Jacob was in the car for the ride home. Kara would see him in New York the next day. I was crammed between my children and my mother with very little room to do anything but sit still. I was amazed we could all fit into such a tiny space. Five hours was a long duration to be pinned between people and the door handle. I had no choice. I put my head next to the car window, keeping it there the entire ride home. My mother fell asleep, as did Kailee and Emily. Although I was very close to nodding off, one of the children would move, knocking my arm by accident. I stayed awake. We were very close to the Massachusetts State line. Another two hours before we would make it to Cape Cod. I asked Allen if he wanted any help driving. He replied, "No."

The sun was lovely, trees were slightly bare and the smell of salt water could be detected. Another half hour had passed. The Sagamore Bridge was visible, connecting the Cape Cod side. I was glad to be home, but I also felt tremendous despair. There would be no more distractions to keep my adrenalin going. Though my friends were plenty and wonderful, I felt terribly isolated. Pain swelled in my heart. I could almost feel my heart breaking. I knew I had to sit Shiva soon. I knew Kailee and Emily would resume their school activities in a day or so. I knew Jacob would be leaving tomorrow. I knew my marriage was over years ago, though it literally ended the previous year. I also knew that I took on a tremendous amount of responsibility. People's delicate emotions were in my hands, as I soothed them, encouraged them, empowered them, offering them options either to commit to pain or to joy. For the most part, my clients were wonderful, teaching me lessons they were hardly aware of. Yet, they relied on my support and my knowledge. I was very good at what I did. Today, I felt as though I could be there for no one. Terror filled with me up. Yet, I was a brilliant survivor. I was hoping that I could reconnect with that compassionate fighter inside. There was no question about it. I had to. I had much to consider: Kailee and Emily, my dogs, my clients, my business, my home, my children's school events, an ex-husband who was troubling to me, my own life.

I had come to understand that pain could be a wonderful steppingstone toward spiritual growth. I often espoused this philosophy to many of my clients. Adversity can act as a catalyst, providing great gifts in the art of letting go. Yet, I have always known that I have the free will to either learn from my hurt or stay stuck in it. Everything I shared with my clients is exactly what I needed to master myself. It is no irony that I attracted in what I needed to learn. Yet, I was too disheveled in my thought to momentarily trust I could get through this terrible tragedy. I had to survive. Again, too much was at stake. My children needed me and I needed them. They also needed me to continue to be a grounded, reliable parent, someone they could count on. To be a single parent was hard enough. To be a single, responsible parent was even harder. To be a single, responsible, grieving parent was the hardest. I left that thought, dismissing it for another day.

We were in my driveway. The tree in front of my house was in full bloom, brilliant with color, sitting dignified, an amazing contrast to our previous events. I was anxious to go inside to reconnect with my devoted canines. I knew, they patiently awaited my arrival back home. As I entered, Succi and Stella passionately greeted me. They jumped, howled, licked me and vibrantly wagged their tails. It was such a needed welcome. I nudged my body wholeheartedly into theirs, relishing in their perfect love of me. Everyone else made their way into my home. Little was said. There was not much to do but to relax. However, in doing as such, our minds became completely filled with Michael's death, his brutal murder, his service and his burial, all we were still terribly confused about. Keeping busy was better. We simply did not know what to do. The telephone rang, startling me and everyone else in the room. I answered. To my relief, Deana was on the other end. She relayed to me that she, Gregg and the girls would be over soon.

The doorbell rang. Jacob went to answer, but Sally had already entered. She wanted me to know that the dogs were fine. If I needed anything more, I was to call her. I hugged her graciously, thanking her as well. It was time to settle back in the house, unpack and put some regularity back into Kailee and Emily's lives. Despite the fact that it was only one in the afternoon, it seemed like it should have been nightfall. Everyone was dragging, especially emotionally. So much happened at such an ungodly pace, none of us really were prepared for the after effects.

My telephone rang non-stop that afternoon. I answered call after call, talking to people and friends, accepting their sympathies, while expressing my gratitude to them. People stopped in, offering baked-goods, meals and little gifts for the girls. As it turned out my house became a blessed sanctuary for my family and my most loyal friends, who offered their unreserved support. Deana, Gregg, Ashley and Elly had already arrived. They immediately took care of the little details: setting the table, replenishing cold cuts, washing dishes, greeting people, etc. Within a half hour's time, everyone had made their way into my kitchen, approximately thirty people, talking, holding hands and embracing shoulders tenderly. Matter-of-factly Deana described a dream she had, just the evening before, concerning Michael. Everyone stopped talking, putting their attentions solely on her. She said: "Michael came to me yesterday in a dream, late last evening. He was wearing his blue suit. He looked very peaceful. He told me to please tell my mother, my sister and my brother that I am fine and that I am with my father. To make sure they understand, I am giving them the Queen of Hearts. Please let them know I love them very much." Deana finished. I looked at Deana and shouted, "Don't move!" I bolted over to a wooden drawer. Inside my mind's eye, flashed a deck of cards. The girls and I seldom played with them. They were in the same space I had put them when we first moved in five years ago. When I opened the drawer next to the telephone, I almost fell down. I pulled out the deck, all the cards being face down, except the very first card. It was face-up. It was also the Queen of Hearts. Jacob yelled, "Oh my God!" Everyone gasped in the room. I looked at Jacob, smiling joyously. "I told you Michael is very much alive. This is his sign to us!" The atmosphere in the room lightened. It was a miraculous moment. Although, I was unaware of the symbolism of what the Queen of Hearts stood for, I felt incredibly blessed to have been part of this sacred occurrence in my home. At least thirty people witnessed the event. No one could deny otherwise. Also, Michael was buried in his blue suit. Deana could not have known this.

I have always known that a fine line exists between our earthly dimension and the heavenly plane of life. Death is but a mere transition to the other side. An existence, I believe that is full of unconditional love, acceptance and a continual, evolving knowledge. Michael, a year before his death came to me. Very matter-of-factly he said that he was going to die very young. I sensed a calm about him. I also did not find this information to be disturbing. However, the information Michael shared came out of nowhere. I simply took in what Michael relayed to me, never feeling it necessary to discuss it further.

I have met many people in my travels, in my work place and in a myriad of situations that have shared similar thoughts about dying. I have also read in spiritual texts how individuals often know of their impending death, though they are unaware of how they are going to die. I would have never, ever suspected my brother could die such a vicious death. Nor can I possibly believe that he would know that he would die such a barbarous death. He knew that he would die. I believed him.

Everyone conversed, laughed and shared more. Tomorrow, I wanted to call my friend Jill, asking her about the Queen of Hearts. She was very involved with Tarot. Clearly, she would know what the Queen of Hearts stood for. The day progressed very quickly. Reminders of people's support were quite visible still. Unopened cards lay on my kitchen counter. Unwrapped flowers had not yet made their way into my vases. Homemade meals, sealed pies and breads covered my table. Cleanup was inevitable. Allen had already driven back to Quarry. Jacob was leaving early the next day to return to New York. Kailee and Emily would be going back to school tomorrow morning. My mother and I would sit Shiva in my home for the next seven days.

I felt I needed to establish more normalcy in our lives. I desperately wanted to resume living, though in less than a year, I was told my family and I would attend my brother's murder trial. How in the world would anything seem normal? Thus, we would sit Shiva, despite my inner protests. We would rehash, in less than a year's time again, Michael's murder.

Nightfall came. Kailee and Emily were peacefully tucked away in their cozy beds, big linen comforters draping their little bodies. Warm shadows embraced their walls as glow-in-the-dark stars and moons ricocheted light off from their ceiling. Their slumber was lovely to watch as they gently slept. Though Kailee and Emily were somewhat unaware of where Michael was killed, I wondered if now, they did have a care to worry about. I must have gone in their room checking them innumerable times that evening. Thankfully, both children slept right through. My mother was in another room, preparing for the evening's rest. Jacob had fallen asleep on the living room couch. I said goodnight to anyone who could potentially hear me. I let Succi and Stella out. I then prepared a very hot bath. I lit a candle, burned incense, drenching my body in this long-awaited pool of water. I allowed myself to stay in the tub for an undisclosed amount of time, cleansing out my pain, but feeling just as immersed in it.

All of the recent events of just the last two days appeared so anti-climactic to me. Whirlwind telephone calls, expedited arrangements and continual conversations with a host of individuals was overwhelming. Yet, everything happened so fast. Now it was done. It was over. I was amazed how much a human being can accomplish even in the worst of situations. Every crevice of my body, submerged in the steaminess of the vapor, opened each pore on my skin that much more, exposing my vulnerabilities. I was simply too tired to cry though. I wanted to sleep, but I was too awake thinking about yesterday, though there were no more calls to make or arrangements to schedule. It was very quiet. Everyone went home. There were no more distractions. Less than one second must have passed before I was overcome with the most profound isolation.

For a split second, time stopped. My friends had lives, commitments and responsibilities. My children had lives. Jacob had a life. Allen had a life. My mother had a life that she would resume soon. Everything would be appear normal but such appearances would be shadowed by an inexplicable, haunting grief. Grief, most likely, many would not want to ask about or even want to know about. Why would anyone? In an assumed day in a daily life of what is deemed normal, most people will ask "What do you do?" as opposed to "Who are you?" If there was an even slight chance to voice who I was, how timely is it to say, "I am a person who is in a terribly grievous state. My brother was murdered, slashed to death in his bed with a samurai sword by a raging madman." Such grief would have to be mounted in my soul, protected, away from the public view of how normal is perceived. No one could handle my response, nor could anyone appropriately comfort me.

Grief is like the seasons. It is always there, yet, it comes and goes, varying with degrees of pain. Just as the sun rises, it sets. Some days are less luminous than others. Just as it rains, it ceases, leaving a clouded view or a clearer one. However, it will either rain, or snow, or the sun will shine, the leaves will eventually change color. Grief is no different. It is simply there. Certain days are better. Certain days are gut wrenching. Certain days are simply that, days, where the gift of numbness wins over, clouding over the searing loss and emptiness that is ever present.

Michael's death was still incomprehensible to me. I knew I just buried him. Yet, everything appeared too real to be real. As I look back on my family's life, I am reminded how violently my father died: A car accident killing not only my father, but our dog, leaving the rest of us holding on by single threads of life. All because another man hit us head on at one hundred miles per hour. Even though this tragedy was not at all viciously premeditated, it still happened. Our car was like an accordion, so I was told years after the accident. We were pulled out by the jaws-of-life, horribly mangled, unconscious, not expected to live. Twenty-four years after our car accident, Michael is malevolently killed, left to die, soaking in his blood. Is there any rhyme or reason as to why certain people are subject to more tragedy than others? Is there any explanation that is reasonable for having loved ones leave this earth so violently and without any warning signs? I put my questions temporarily to rest. I opened the drain. I sat in the tub until the water ran out. I picked up the nearest towel, wrapping myself in its softness. I threw a long t-shirt on, walked out of the bathroom and into my bedroom. I lit a candle near my bed, shut my curtains, then I stared at my wilted flowers sitting on my dresser. Every week it was a ritual for me to buy myself fresh flowers. No motivation existed for me to throw them out. They simply sat there, dead, lifeless, brown and without any specific form. They look terribly sad. Their reflection depicted the ambiance in my home. I proceeded to get Succi and Stella, opening the slider in the kitchen. They peacefully accompanied me back to my bedroom. I nestled in my bed, staring up and out into nowhere. I fell fast asleep.

Two hours later, I bolted upright in the middle of my bed. My heart was wildly racing. My breathing was heavy and labored. I was frightened as hell. I looked around. I could not for the life of me make out where I was. I panicked. I flailed my arms around, grasping for anything familiar. Stella, startled, stood up on my bed and began to pace. I stopped. Finally I realized where I was. I took hold of Stella, patting her gently, calming her down, yet, I continued to feel the pounding of my heartbeat bursting through my chest. Succi, still on the floor, observed quietly, her eyes continually on me.

Tears poured out of my eyes. Sweat bathed my face and my neck. Michael's violent murder inundated my brain once again. I imagined him gasping for breath. I imagined him terrified, never really knowing what was going on. I imagined him being viciously stabbed over and over, grimacing in overwhelming pain. I imagined him struggling to breathe, only to be brutally hit until there was no more life inside of him. I shuddered frenziedly. How could anyone commit such a horrific crime? Though, I hardly knew the extent of Michael's attack, I imagined each blow. I winced at the stammering affects it had to have on Michael. I felt bludgeoned emotionally. I cannot really imagine what Michael must have felt. I could not fall asleep. That samurai sword became a visible fixture in my mind. I was immobilized with terror. Falling asleep was too great a risk. I stared up at the ceiling, tossing and turning at the same time. I begged God to help me think about something else, while simultaneously I reprimanded myself for being such a coward. I reached over my bed to my standing lamp. I put it on. The darkness was too much to bear. I just lay in bed, my eyes wide in horror as I repeated in my mind's eye Michael's last moments. I remained that way for the next five hours. "Mama!" Morning came. I was in no shape to move.

Chapter 21

"Mama!" I turned my head around to my dresser. My clock read 6:20 a.m. I could distinctly sense that Emily was in a very mischievous mood. "Mama, Mama, Mama!" I knew she wanted me to get out of bed. She wanted me to wait outside her bedroom door. She would stand precociously on the other side, immersed in playful giggles. Then, she would open the door. We would both say boo exactly at the same time. Emily loved this. I simply could not budge. Emily would persistently call out Mama until there was nothing left for me to do but to stand in front of her door. I gently yelled back that she must come in my room so as not to awaken her sister. Silence. With some hesitation, she frolicked spiritedly into my room, hopped onto my bed, hugging me. She smelled delicious. I was grateful for her joyous state. I attempted to explain to Emily that I needed a bit more time to wake up. She sat on my bed, chatting to her make believe friends, her stuffed animal and to me.

Today would be our first day of sitting Shiva. I reminded myself to contact my friend Jill about the Queen of Hearts. I also knew I had to get the children ready for school. I decided I would drive them as opposed to letting them take the bus. Sandwich is a very small town. I did not want Kailee and Emily to be initially bombarded with questions and awkward stares from others. The principal's office and guidance office were extremely empathetic to our family's tragedy. They kept a very low profile but they were available if Kailee and Emily needed them.

Emily had just begun first grade, Kailee fourth grade. I knew each child would be anxious to renew the school week, though they were starting on Tuesday. After eating breakfast and making lunch for the kids, Kailee and Emily packed into my car. Less than two miles away we arrived on the school grounds. I parked the car in front of the main entrance, got out, helping Kailee and Emily up the walk to the main entrance. Each of them gave me a hug. I waved to them in the hallway relaying that I would pick them up later.

Teachers, the principal and parents recognized me standing there. Many of them came up to me expressing their condolences. I did not have it in me to discuss anything about the previous days' events, nor did I suspect that anyone dared to ask me about it. I had not showered. I was wearing the same clothes I had slept in. I was not cognizant of the fact that I had lost ten pounds in the last week. My appetite was gone. My desire to nourish my body was nil. My tendency to withdraw and not eat during severe moments of stress was commonplace to me. I did not realize how much I retreated from myself during those days. People simply stared. I left the school and headed home.

When I arrived at my house, my mother was up, ready to sit Shiva. Though we were over the initial shock of my brother's death, we were still in a state of numbness. I needed my space from everyone and everything. I could not engage in conversation about Michael's brutal murder. Jacob did not stay, nor could he. I was the only one along with my mother who sat, passing the time away, waiting for people to come to pay their respects. A splattering of friends might visit today or during the week. Most of my mother's very good friends were living in upstate New York. Michael's friends did not even live in Boston. It seemed rather unproductive to sit around waiting for people to come who simply could not be here. I also needed to work because I had so many responsibilities that were recently neglected. I knew on some level that despite how I wanted to go on with my daily life, my mother needed to participate in this ritual. I needed to merely respect her wishes. No matter how many rituals I participated in, I would never be the same. I was desperate to reclaim back my life.

I made a call to Jill leaving a message for her to call me, describing my request. She called within a half an hour, relaying to me that the Queen of Hearts was symbolic of a love for family. The love never, ever dies. I was ecstatic about the information I had just received. I thoroughly believed Michael needed to come through to let us know that he was okay. His love for his family was foremost.

I have never doubted for a single minute that the soul indeed lives on. The grieving it seems is so much harder for the survivors on this earth plane. Intellectually, I was aware of how important it was for people to ritualize their grief and to mourn. On a much deeper level, I sensed our loved ones who have passed need to be encouraged to move on through the other side, attaining spiritual growth. Thus, in my mind's eye, sitting Shiva provided us with an avenue to mourn. However, I also felt it allowed Michael's soul to linger close to the earth plane. Michael would be terribly distraught over our grief. He would want to make sure we were fine. However, I did not want to prolong Michael's need to move to the light on the other side.

The day passed slowly and intentionally. When it was time to pick up Kailee and Emily, I was mentally empty. The night was long as were the next several days. Many of my friends visited. Some members of Allen's family came to pay their respects. It was a very difficult week. I was so thirsty to be alone. I looked to my dogs for comfort and sanity. Kailee and Emily's adjustment back to school went well. Sitting Shiva was coming to a close. My mother would be leaving the following day. I was grateful for some solitude. I was a master at maintaining seclusion. It was a needed reprieve.

I resumed my counseling practice but not with the vigor I once had. I loved my work, but I was so emotionally distracted, I did not think I could be of great help to my clients. I also had yet to come to terms with a very painful marriage. Grieving what I never had was an afterthought. I never felt as excruciatingly empty as I was presently feeling, yet, I was equally as restless. However, the emptiness I felt was but for a fleeting moment. I did not allow myself to really feel the depths of my grief. There was much too much to ponder over.

The girls and I so needed a change, but where too? I always loved my work but I needed to do something that would be light, without severe mental strain. Even though I worked for myself, I still found great satisfaction in helping others, despite the isolation in my job. After my divorce, I pulled my practice into my house. Thus, everything I did was centered in that space, away from much civilization.

I decided I would wait tables to free my soul and my brain for a while. I had waitressed in the past and throughout college to supplement my income. Cape Cod's season would be coming in months. Waiting tables would be a great way to earn fast cash. It would also be a job I would not have to take home with me. I decided to cut down on seeing clients. March would be my goal, working at a restaurant.

I would still face more challenges with my ex especially if I continued to live in close proximity to him. Our divorce was a year ago, May 1994. My ex had been full of such anger, he brought me into court nine times for contempt after our divorce. Some of the charges were vindictive and without cause. Looking back, it is always much easier to understand how anger can be a result of fear. However, while in it, the emotions trigger a thousand fold. Despite this horrific tragedy, I simply never knew what to expect. I was so mentally and physically haggard by my ex's ill will, I had thought for some time about leaving the state. I knew I would have to plead to the courts for permission to go however. The thought alone overwhelmed me. Yet, the seed was planted. The timing stunk.

Chapter 22

1996 and three months after Michael's death, we had a dreadfully long winter with torrential snowstorms that were relentless. Normally, the Cape escaped such vicious weather. Yet, day after day, for hours on end, I shoveled my driveway, tackling heaping, piles of accumulated snow. I could not believe how much had fallen each week. My arms were terribly sore lifting snow packed with ice. I was acquiring more and more of a strong dislike for the harsh weather. Despite my valiant efforts to clear my driveway, to my dismay, the town plows later, piled the snow right back up at the top of my driveway. That was it. My decision was made. As much as I loved the Cape, I was ready to see more sun, more warmth and more people smiling. It was February. I was determined to go somewhere south to make a new start for myself, Kailee and Emily. I would have my work cut out for me. My ex undoubtedly would make my attempts at leaving toilsome.

I reminded myself of how short and unpredictable life really is. If I had any fear, it would be superimposed by my undeniable belief to live life on purpose, with a burning passion. I had always lived my life like that. Yet, for the ten years I was married, I allowed myself to be overcome by a neglect that was so elusive to others, yet so horribly visible to me. It hurt like hell. I cried myself to sleep too often. My deepest sorrow was the fact that my ex-husband never noticed the suffering I bore. Despite the love I once had for my husband, despite the devoted mother and the caring human being I was, I lost me. My ex was so emotionally unavailable to me, I spent years walking on eggshells, attempting to be someone I was not. I not only lost respect for my ex, but I also lost respect for myself. Kailee, Emma and I needed a good change, in fact a great one. I was determined to make that happen for all of us, regardless of my ex's protests.

Furthermore and adding to my already discomforted state, I was terribly troubled by my former sister-in-law being afflicted with brain cancer. I had a very difficult time reasoning why a woman who so wanted children would be denied the opportunity to raise them. If she did succumb to her cancer, she would leave two little girls, four and one and a very devoted husband. My heart ached for Kelly. I knew my pain over Michael's death had yet to scratch the surface. After just saying goodbye to my brother in a coffin, I was not so sure I could handle more pain at this time. Yet, I had to see Kelly to let her know how much she meant to me. She was one of the most generous human beings I ever knew. Years back, she asked me to be a bridesmaid at her wedding. Some of her closest siblings were not even asked. I felt honored. Thus, kids in tow, five days after I lay my brother to rest, I drove to see Kelly. That would be the last time I would ever see her alive.

Chapter 23

It was March. The snow had slowly melted. Everything natural that could be thawed out was. It felt good to see more of the sun. I would begin to waitress at The Captain's Table in Sandwich, a mile from where I lived. The restaurant was on the water making this a huge bonus. Sid and Dot, the owners, were gracious people allowing my transition to be smooth. I decided to keep my feet somewhat wet in my practice. I continued to see clients I had had for a good while. I did not want to establish close relationships with new clients, only to tell them that I would be leaving them. I knew that Michael's murder trial would happen sometime in a year or so. No matter where Kailee, Emily and I were living we would have to come back to Massachusetts regardless. I wanted to move out of state by the end of August. That was my goal. I also began to research school systems, job prospects and educational programs within the southern regions. Much of my practice was based in a strong spiritual philosophy that emphasized an individual's inherently ability to heal themselves. There were a myriad of school curriculums stressing such philosophies. Also, living near the water was essential to me. The ocean was remarkably healing. As much as I sacrificed in a very disappointing union, I did not want to renounce even the slightest affection for what was important to me. I new my truth. I was determined to listen to it.

My mother, Jacob and I talked periodically. There was a huge brokenness in all of us. Michael was tangibly missing from our lives. This was a silent torture that bore its way into our souls. None of us truly knew how to manage this kind of pain, despite the tragedy we endured years ago. All we could do was acknowledge the pain. Ironically, accepting the hurt made us surrender to an even greater pain. It was a catch twenty-two. When Michael lost our father, he lost his best friend. When Jacob lost Michael, he lost his best friend. When my mother lost her husband and her son, she lost two individuals who were her best friends. When I lost my father and my brother, I lost a part of me.

Jacob decided to move to Atlanta. I was guided to Sarasota, Florida. My mother stayed in upstate New York. By the beginning of April, I had secured plane tickets to Sarasota for a later date. It was there that I would put together a very thorough book, including a job offer, letters from the principal of the best elementary school in Sarasota, an acceptance into an acupuncture school and the house Kailee, Emily and I were going to live in. The months I worked at The Captain's Table, I met scores of customers from Sarasota, Florida. No irony I thought. The universe had a most divine plan. I had a small notebook of potential professional people to contact when I arrived in Sarasota. I truly believe these individuals were brought to me. That impenetrable trust I had once had was as vivid as it could be. Leaving was now becoming a reality.

One glitch however. I still had to present my plea to leave the state. My heart sunk for a moment. My ex could be very resistant and extremely difficult. On a soul level, I understood his fear. On the surface, I could easily be triggered by his reactionary ways, leaving me feeling depleted and angered. His children would be moving over fifteen hundred miles away. In an instant, fear came over me, flooding that trust I had just experienced. I vowed I would never walk into a courtroom again after my divorce. I always told my clients that thoughts create reality. I needed to revamp mine quickly. Within a place deep inside of me, I trusted. I really did.

In the scheme of things called life, this was nothing. In 1971, I walked out of Massachusetts General Hospital, being told I would never walk again. I bore two incredible babies, being told I would never be able to have children. I got out of a very unhappy marriage to a man who severely neglected me emotionally. I recently buried my brother. In the scheme of things, this was a piece of cake. In the greater scheme of things, this was but another mini lesson in the art of letting go.

It was getting late. Kailee and Emily were already asleep. Again, I kissed them goodnight. I hugged Succi and Stella. I affirmed, "There is nothing for me to fear. God's spirit of good is at work and divine results are now coming forth." With that I fell asleep.

Chapter 24

Months had passed. The sun was brilliant, with a warm summer wind blowing. The Captain's table was filled to capacity as we were in the height of our tourist season. Though life was going quite smoothly, I knew in one more month I would be standing in front of a judge. Much was going through my mind. My divorce proceedings were horrendous. I found the court system to be far more abusive than I would have imagined. I understood how anger could bring out the worst in our personalities under dire stress. Somehow I understood my ex's need to attack me, but not as a mother. My intention was never to take his children away from him. I simply wanted all of us to have something he never provided for, a future. Inevitably, I knew if I asked my ex for a divorce there would be major consequences. There were. I went into the courts believing the truth would eventually come out. Ultimately it did, but not before endless months of ruthlessness and mercilessness ensued. I also found it incomprehensible that I had to plead to the courts to leave. I was raising my children, sacrificing everything for them, working three jobs just to stay afloat.

All my fears came up again. However, I would be more than prepared this time. It would be unjust for any judge in their right mind to deny me an opportunity that would better myself and my children. I planned on having over fifteen of my closest friends in the courtroom. I had complied a superb collection of all the information I needed to have to move to Sarasota. Three conditions in the state of Massachusetts apply for moving out of state: A new job, going back to school and getting married. Two of those criteria had been met. Yet, the courts were unpredictable. So were many of the judges. Justice did not always prevail.

It was easy to feed on my fear. I needed to nourish my deepest truth. Nothing and nobody was going to determine my future or my children's future. Only God. I was exceedingly gracious for the belief I had in him, despite the moments I allowed my fear to take over. A new customer walked in. My thoughts about court drifted for the time being.

Chapter 25

I worked round the clock attempting to put money away. Yet the more I worked, still money was sparse. I was up to my head in debt plowing myself out of the tremendous liabilities that were left from my marriage and my ex. My name was on joint accounts, regardless of the fact that my ex was to be responsible for specific bills. I had a big rent, utilities, a car loan and a host of other responsibilities. The child support I was given did not even cover my monthly house payment nor other expenses that accrue with raising children. There was never enough and barely enough.

While married, I finally found my niche with a wonderful counseling practice. Years of undo patience and the perseverance to pursue a Master Degree and the motivation to a establish a solid clientele became a dream for me. I wanted more time to be with my children, but I never had that wish gratified. Unfortunately, my ex was laid off more than he was in work, due to the nature of his work.

Although my children never wanted for anything, my exhaustion working fulltime and being a fulltime parent took over. Missing the simple moments with my children was my concern. I silently battled whether to pay the electric bill, buy food or buy new shoes for Kailee and Emily. This was an ongoing struggle. Nonetheless, I would do anything for them. Now, was no different. Although I was on my own with my children I was far more alone in my marriage and more lonely. That was unbearable. The girls and I had each other. Our space was full of warmth, peace and an unconditional love. Serenity filled our home. I made a sacred promise to myself that our home would never be violated with the kind of injurious anger that was ever present in our previous living situation.

I stuffed away my supreme frustration and my indignity for a man I thought I would spend the rest of my life with. The anger would only bind me to more suffering. I simply could not stay stuck in it. It was an insidious ache though. Surely, that was worth fighting for, at least for my salvation and for Kailee's and Emily's redemption.

Chapter 26

The inevitable came. Court day was here. I was a nervous wreck. I diligently worked hard on attempting to maintain the deep faith that helped me through other stressful moments. I was to meet my attorney along with many of my devoted friends. I dressed. I drove Kailee and Emily to their destination. Taking one of the most scenic routes on Cape Cod was a conscious choice. If I had to go to court this would be the only way I would travel today. Traversing this road would at least divert some of my anxiety.

Journeying on Route 6A provided any person with a deep sense of calm. Grand homes with breathtaking wrap-around porches, ocean views and brilliantly constructed antique stores covered this road from the beginning to the end of the Cape. Something was familiar. I could never pinpoint what it was though. A musing of sorts had continually stirred my soul each and every time I drove on this island. Deja vue occurred frequently for me. I simply accepted that my soul and this earthly place were bound together.

My fate would be determined shortly. I was strongly connected to Cape Cod and the people who inhabited it. I was looking elsewhere to change my life. A duality was definitely visible to me. Yet, in a matter of moments, such a duality would be broken. If the judge said no, I would somehow have to make my life change here. If the judge complied with my plea, then I was basically a free agent with my children to pursue our future elsewhere. Tears rolled down my eyes. I observed the bluest of skies and the greenest of rolling hills sweep before me. I was taken by the magnificence of this holy land, wistful of what I would be leaving behind. A welling in my heart was felt. So much had taken place for me here.

Arriving in Barnstable, familiarity had become customary. A good majority of my time was spent in this town. Inside, the court appeared cold and linear. Outside, the town was beautifully picturesque. For several years, sitting and waiting for a judge to call myself and my ex to his bench predominated all of my time. The longer I waited, the higher my attorney fees accrued. Eventually, the judge would decide our fate for us. My ex-husband was so unyielding, our meetings would be agonizingly disturbing. Fear verses love, fear verses love was all that swooshed in my head. That conflict was as present as ever in that courtroom. I could distinctly remember the panic that would set into my heart. Nothing could alleviate what I felt. I spent so much of my time waiting to be heard and not being heard, the anticipation of what would come next depleted my faith that whatever happened, would happen for the highest good.

Today as I made my way onto the paved lot and inside to the second floor, that dread cunningly excreted out of me. I was angry at myself for letting the fear control me as opposed to me controlling the fear. My heart was beating faster than I was walking. So many of my friends had arrived, embracing me with blessed prayers and warm encouragement. Only fifteen minutes had passed when I heard Barg versus Pratt. My friends looked up at me, smiled and entered into the courtroom accordingly. I looked around. There was absolutely no sign of my ex-husband present. My attorney said, "Let's get this over with and get you out of here." She and I walked up to the bench. Without further ado, my attorney presented my plea. The judge asked me about Sarasota. I presented him with a very thorough book filled with vital information. He barely looked at it. He then smiled and said, "Good luck Mom. Take good care of those babies. By the way, have a great time." That was it. I was stupefied. My attorney looked at me, thanking the judge. She then gave me a big smile and a warm hug. I turned around to see everyone of my friends, tears brushing their cheeks. It was over. It was incredibly easy, nothing like I had experienced previously in court. My ex never showed up because there was nothing left to fight over. We legitimately could leave. As I approached my friends, receiving a multitude of hugs, a decision was made to eat breakfast at a cozy nook across the street. I thanked my attorney. We all left.

When we made our way into the café and to our chairs, placing two tables together, chatter began. High energy was permeating among my friends. Yet, as I sat, I felt a definite exhaustion closing in around me. I became very quiet. My friend Vera looked up and had asked me if there was something wrong. My glance met everyone and with tear-filled eyes, I spoke very gently, "I can leave. I can actually leave." More silence. Then without anticipation I began to cry. After years of a grueling and painful marriage and judges making life sentences to me and my children, I was given my freedom back, without any conflict whatsoever. I could leave. I could take back my power. I could choose to finally live the life I wanted with Kailee and Emily. I closed my eyes. In a rather half-witted tone I said to my friends, "I am terrified, I really have to leave now." Everyone watched with tender eyes. Within minutes, subdued conversation began. My friends all knew that despite my innate ability to always take boundless leaps of faith with an unbreakable trust to back me up, fear was present within me. Their support was unconditional, despite my momentary doubt. I was going somewhere I did not know a blessed soul. All of us were extremely close. We knew what that meant. We would be saying goodbye. That was the most difficult part. Somehow, again in the scheme of things I knew this too was all part of my life journey. Our lives would always be linked together. In our hearts we knew that. Through this impassable bond, we would always be inseparable. Our lunch that afternoon lasted four hours.

Driving back to my home in Sandwich I reverted onto an old country road that took me to one of my favorite places near the water. It was magical, somewhat secluded, oftentimes affording me the luxury of being the only one there. I pulled up as far as I could go. I shut off the engine, got out, soaking in the most splendid sea salt air. Sanctity filled my insides. I began to weep like a baby, embracing at the same time, all I was grateful for. My time on the Cape was coming to a close. Moving on from here was symbolic of saying goodbye to my marriage. It was not the loss of my ex that I had to grieve, rather it was mourning the lost of all my hopes and dreams that never manifested in my marriage. Moving on was very symbolic of tangibly letting go. It was a catharsis of sorts. Moving on also meant starting over, taking a risk, creating a new beginning from scratch and never, ever looking back. I picked up the flattest stone I could find. With a gentle sweep, I skipped the stone across the ocean's surface. I glanced around one last time, simply taking in the moment.

In a hour or so, I would have to pick up Kailee and Emily. They both knew about our possible move down south. I could now tell them that we were about to embark on a new venture. Our goal: the very end of August. I had exactly two months to pack up my house, tie up loose ends with old clients, referring them elsewhere, getting together with my beloved friends, making sure Kailee and Emily were placed with appropriate teachers in Sarasota, securing a moving van, obtaining a rental car that would also fit two canines, myself, Kailee and Emily and mapping the twenty-nine hour trip down to Sarasota.

My motivation was clearly to move on. As much as the adrenalin was flowing in me, I was submerged in a multitude of mixed emotions: high anxiety, nervousness, excitement, everything that could be physically and emotionally felt. Yet, I was also overcome with intense fear. This fear provided me with as much motivation as it did immobilization. I had always done so much in my life and with a fearlessness that was insatiable. Almost a year ago, I lay my brother to rest. How could anything else be that hard? Yet, I was physically and emotionally gripped with an extreme trepidation that I never experienced before. I could not afford such an emotion.

Sitting back without quiet worries was uncommon to me. Knowing that so much responsibility lay on my shoulders was familiar. Raising children, maintaining my practice, my household, paying bills, concerned if my husband would have his job the next day and keeping myself afloat were about all I could sustain. The neglect became severe and very sorrowful, with very little support emotionally and financially. There was no doubt in my mind how much my ex loved his children. To love them however, is to also make sure they were well taken care of, emotionally, spiritually, financially and physically. I truly wanted a partner, someone I could make decisions with, someone who would take the initiative as well. I never wanted all of that responsibility by myself. A solid home, a base, a place where Kailee and Emily could feel safe was vitally important to me, as was a partner who was present.

Yet, nothing could satisfy the loneliness and the extreme despair I did feel in my marriage. I certainly did not want to live through Kailee and Emily. Ultimately, I knew one day the girls would leave, making a life of their own. The idea of being with my husband who was so emotionally inaccessible anyway, was intolerable. I could not imagine another ten years of neglect. I also knew that on some level my husband was terrified of emotional intimacy. Perhaps it was safer for him to disconnect for fear of exposing too much. I had that understanding. Yet, I so needed his sharing. The isolation I already experienced would have been multiplied a thousand fold years later. Who would I talk to when the kids left? I was alone so much in my marriage, doing all the necessities to manage a family, a household and a business. Doing it on my own seemed much easier than to remain with someone who chose resistance over responsibility. I did not want to hold onto any resentment. I had vested so much of my life and my heart into an individual who was so unaware of my presence and who simply did not know how to partner, I was silently tormented. My husband's potential was enormous. Holding on to what he could be, became a false servitude for me. Crying myself to sleep for years was debilitating my ability to move forward. Leaving and filing for divorce was the greatest gift I could have given to my husband. The only way to alleviate my pain was to forgive and to let go. I also knew my greatest empowerment to Kailee and Emily was to show them how to love themselves. That could not be done if they were living in a home that was embroiled with animosity. Thus, I asked for a divorce. I made the choice to leave. In doing so, however, I paid an even bigger price to be more emotionally mistreated. On some levels, I knew I would experience ill will from my ex. Yet, I simply could not love him anymore in the way he so needed to be loved. I was terribly drained. Rather than build up more and more anger, I sunk into an abyss of quiet desperation and disappointment. There simply was nothing left to give. Despite how tormented I felt by my husband's neglect of me, part of me felt sorry for him and terribly saddened equally. I simply did not know how to get out of my marriage. I agonized for months on end how to leave, avoiding ways to hurt my husband. Yet, despite how often I deluded myself into possibly believing that he would calmly and gracefully accept my resignation from our union, the more emotional pain I endured from him.

In my contemplation one evening, after I again ludicrously cried myself to sleep, I remember placing my hand on my chest. A real, physical ripping in my heart was detected. The more my body was breaking down, I knew that this was a clear indication for me to begin to look at what was going on for me emotionally. I have always credited the human body as being a vehicle to house emotional pain. For all the years I was espousing this to clients, going to retreat centers offering seminars on this very topic, I was facing the same issues. This was such a wake up call and a painful one at that.

After holding my hand heavily on my heart as if to stop the pain, and in my fitful sobbing, a very strong voice became audibly clear. It said, "He will never change." I felt as though someone literally knocked me over. Plainly, it was not my voice, not in the least. I looked up, took my hand off my heart. I stopped crying. I became very still. It was at that point I made my decision to leave. I would tell my ex-husband that evening. Despite what I knew I would face from him, despite the emotional anguish I might have to put up with, the time was now. I was not going to look back. I did not even know how I was going to do it all, but that became an afterthought. My emotional sanity was too much at stake. I could not viably be present or good for anyone if I did not listen to what I knew. A force so strong inside of me was pushing me forward. For the moment, I forgot about all the shoulds, all the coulds and all the woulds. Another leap of faith was intrinsic in my life.

My divorce was hard enough. Arranging a funeral and burying Michael was even harder. Leaving the Cape, a place I so loved and where I had built a life was very discomforting. Though I was letting go intentionally, I knew I was also taking with me a wealth of heartfelt love and memories that would stay with me for a lifetime. If my fear transcended my faith, I could always smell the sea air in my soul. In my heart, I could imbibe the closeness I had with friends. I was counting on this for my sustenance.

Chapter 27

Michael had been dead ten months. Hard to believe as so much had transpired prior. The end of August and my house was practically bare. I had managed to pack everything neatly in marked boxes, leaving only one mattress on the floor the girls could sleep on. Another box was left open for necessity. My pots, pans and some utensils were visible for me to utilize still. I also managed to scour the entire house, including the basement. Something I learned from my parents, especially my mother. Leave it clean. My poor dogs looked so bewildered. The house was in disarray simply because everything was taking out of its place, put away in containers with furniture broken down, resting against anything it could lean on. They knew something was up and they knew whatever was up was something of momentous change. I would be picking up the moving truck in less than four hours. I had no idea how I was going to load all that I had onto the truck the following day. Yet, somehow, I knew I would be okay. Jacob would be flying into Logan Airport from Atlanta. He would arrive in the afternoon. He would then drive a rental car down to Sandwich, drop it off the next day only to caravan the twenty five foot truck I rented to Florida with my car attached to it. I would drive the rental with Kailee and Emily, Succi and Stella and a packed trunk with ice boxes of food and goodies.

The children would start Sarasota schools a week late. I still had to tie up loose ends before we left. Kailee and Emily were excited and anxious concurrently. With all that I had left to accomplish, I did not have time to be apprehensive. Too much was happening at such a quickened pace, my mind and my body were going nonstop. I had to work at The Captain's Table the prior evening. At the end of my shift, all the waitresses presented me with a huge basket of gifts. They gave me a small party, blessing with me positive thoughts. I was utterly and completely taken aback. I cried. Everyone shared in with their own tears of encouragement. One more thing to let go of. I joked that there was nowhere to put this gift. We would be packed to the brim.

That evening, when the children were sleeping, I browsed through this lovely basket. With an unspoken indebtedness, I heedfully unwrapped all of the presents. I was touched beyond belief. Spiritual journals for me to write in, massage and bath oils, insightful prayer books, fun snacks to munch on, organic dog bones for the dogs and a beautiful carved inscription about letting go and moving on was framed delicately, cloaked in flowered tissue paper. These individuals whom I knew for only two months took the time to truly honor my essence. I took this as a very positive sign that my present life's change was for the highest good. I cried. I cried harder. I cried some more. I pulled out my sleeping bag, fell asleep next to Succi and Stella, only to be awaken by the nudge of Succi's very wet and very cold nose under my elbow.

Morning had arrived. Time to get up. Let the dogs out was the message. I checked in on Kailee and Emily. They were still sleeping. It was but 7:30 in the morning. I showered quickly, opened the slider one last time letting the dogs back into the house when knocks appeared at my front door. Seven of my very best friends' husbands appeared on my step. They said, "We are here to pack the truck up." With enormous smiles on their faces, I thanked each and every one of them a thousand times over. One of my friends must have tipped their husbands off, setting the plan in motion. I never asked anyone for the help. They were simply there. Another mini miracle I was terribly gracious to have received. Less than one and a half hours later, my truck was packed to the hilt, ready to go. Each man hugged me, wishing me well, asking me for nothing. I watched them disappear as quickly as they had arrived. Kailee and Emily woke up. They could not believe that the house they spent five years in was empty, except for the one mattress they had slept on.

It was all so bittersweet. Five years of walking on the Sandwich boardwalk every weekend, overlooking the most stupendous marsh. Sundays, eating at Marshland's, a low budget, cozy eatery with the most extraordinary food, especially breakfast. Climbing magnificent jetties on the rocky shore. Skipping stones in a body of water that continually provided you with an inner tranquillity. Frolicking in and around the duck pond, feeding the ducks with crumbled bread you were not suppose to feed them with. Wild geese aggressively chasing you for trespassing onto their terrain. Riding the antique carousel once a week located in the most brilliant of flower gardens. Munching on deliciously home-baked sweets in unique old shops, over filled with relics and history of the century before, decorated with lace and white linen. Mini trips to the ice-cream shop, sitting peacefully on the wooden chairs licking cones that were dripping in goodness. Excursions to the historic library, listening to story time of famous characters in famous children's books. Friday night was

Pizza By Evan night, extra cheese on the pizza. Ballet lessons, swim lessons, barbecues, starry nights with friends and children completed our life. Rich, warm memories. Memories to feed on. New memories to make. Hellos to be established, new experiences to create. Ten minutes later, Jacob pulled up at our house beeping his horn, smiles included and enormous hugs to be had.

Chapter 28

    This time it was good to see my brother under different circumstances. I offered him an overnight stay at a friend's home, but he opted for a motel room later that evening. My home was completely bare. Although Jacob was quite flexible, I could not even offer him comfort in my own home. Kailee, Emily, Jacob and I went out for a hearty lunch. We talked for hours about our trip and life in general. Conversation about Michael came and went. Cracked voices were distinct as were tears swelling up in our eyes. Too soon still. The wounds were very fresh, not even a year had passed. We both wanted to discuss how we missed Michael, but our hearts were far from being mended. We were both aware of a pending trial, but further details were not given to us or any other family members. The ride to Florida would be a supreme distraction. I was terribly grateful for Jacob's help. The more we talked, the more daylight sifted into nighttime. Jacob went to a motel. I brought food in. The girls and I slept in sleeping bags on the wooden floors that clumsily tipped over more stuff.

    Time to leave tomorrow morning, 8:00am. My next door neighbor Kate insisted on making Jacob, Kailee, Emily and I breakfast before we began our trek over fifteen hundred miles away. We all agreed. I was about to kiss everyone goodnight when my doorbell rang. All of my friend's were on my porch wanting to say a final goodbye. walked out to be voraciously greeted with hugs. Simultaneously, Deana's daughters, Ashley and Elly broke down, sobbing. The domino affect began. We all began to cry hysterically like it was the last time we would be together. On one hand, I was thoroughly overcome with emotion. On the other hand, I was ready for our new adventure. All our friends were unreservedly supportive of what we had to do. I was so torn, at least momentarily. My friends left, still crying. I tucked Kailee and Emily to sleep, wiping their tear-stained faces. I collapsed on the wooden floor, zipping open my sleeping bag with the hopes of partially receiving a decent night's sleep. I looked up at the ceiling and recollected again, what I so loved about this land. People came here to heal. People came to rejuvenate their souls. For some, it was but a short time. For me, it was years invested into some of the most memorable moments of my life and some of the most hurtful as well. I slowly closed my eyes.

I could not believe morning was peering through again. The time swept. I just remembered falling asleep at 11:00 p.m. I showered, dried myself with a towel that had been sitting out for days. I threw on clothes that I had packed in a night bag along with Kailee's and Emily's belongings. I awoke the children, helping them to wash. Quickly they were dressed. In less than a half an hour, my doorbell was ringing. Jacob was rearing to go. My dogs looked terribly morose, though I let them know we would be right back. We all walked two houses down to be greeted by an enormous breakfast Kate had set our for us. Conversation was light. My friend and I looked at each other one last time. We embraced for what seemed like endless moments. Thank yous were exchanged.

Inside my house, I looked around again, walked in every room, noting carefully if I had left anything. I took it all in, remembering the very good times. The fireplace lit with hot ambers glowing at midnight, with marshmallows browning on long skewers. Soft music playing in the distance. Incense burning to add an aromatic ambiance. Children giggling, running in and out of rooms. Dogs howling and wrestling, playing on wooden floors, sliding across them unexpectedly. The light from the sunsets streaming through the crease on the curtains. Then, the vicious anger. Doors slamming, loud voices. The arguments. The infringement of an unwelcome wrath in a warm and loving space had invaded the years that were once safe. I shuddered. It was time to go. I said goodbye to my abode, got in my car, with Kailee, Emily, Succi and Stella packed in it. Jacob ahead of me, was waiting for my signal with the enormous truck and my car attached to the hitch. "Make wide turns Jacob." That's what the rental place told me. "WIDE TURNS!" We were off.

Chapter 29

Twenty-nine and a half hours later, through torrential hurricanes in Virginia, an overnight pit stop at a 99 Motor Inn, cafeteria like food and a drive that seemed as flat and as long as one could imagine, we arrived in Sarasota, Florida on a Saturday evening, 9:00 p.m. to be exact. It was hotter than hot, approximately ninety-eight degrees with full blown humidity. Three quarters of the way down, while driving through Georgia, Jacob and I began to fling the layer of clothes we had on, off, over our shoulder to wherever they landed in our vehicles. I could actually see Jacob undressing. Drinking water, juices, sodas, anything we could find became habitual. Despite how foreign this new land was to us, despite our exhaustion, we were able to absorb the beauty of this magical place as we entered into Sarasota.

Prior to my leaving Cape Cod, my mother made a trip with her friend to Sarasota, where she would eventually lead me to a realtor and a house to live in. I met my landlords through phone calls. Eventually money was wired to them. Later, a set of keys with a list of exterminators was sent to me. They were animal lovers and animal owners, one less predicament to have to deal with. Thus, I was able to secure a small home that would accept dogs, regardless of the fact that I never even saw the house or the area. I did know however, that I was to be west of the Tamiama Trail, near a particular school district. This rental was located in walking distance to the elementary school Kailee and Emily would attend.

After asking for directions at a gas station, we found our way to a very, itsy bitsy cottage. Jacob and I did not even think the truck's contents could be emptied into its space. Without further a due, and within minutes of arriving there, five gentlemen appeared ready to help unload the truck. One of them I recognized. Miracles happen everyday.

I once had a client in Cape Cod who moved down to Florida with her husband and her daughter. She was only twenty minutes away from where I would be living. She knew of my pending arrival. She arranged to have her husband along with his friends at my new home to help Jacob and I. The irony was the fact that she did not know when we would pull in, nor did they know the exact address of this very small house. Somehow, by the grace of God, they were there, almost simultaneous to our arrival. Another sign for me to fully trust. I blessed each and every one of them silently. I set off to help unload an enormous twenty-five foot truck with the rest of them. It was 9:20 p.m. With what seemed like an eternity to eventually be able to leave the state of Massachusetts, the truck became completely emptied within a forty-five minute time span. Everything was filled, box on top of box in this very tiny space. Our lives were in these boxes. The more I looked at what I brought down, the more overwhelmed I became. Another timely humility check for me. Unclutter the clutter. Sweating profusely, Jacob and I thanked everyone. People shook hands. They all exited. Jacob headed to a motel. The girls and I looked at each other. We were deliriously exhausted and hungry all at the same time. We managed to pick at unwrapped food still lying in bags near the front door. I pulled the mattress down on the floor, found the pillows and a blanket where all of us slept, snuggled close to one another. I could not get over how hot it was. Each climate was so radically dissimilar. In my slumber-like state I found the thermostat, turning on the air. Something new to acclimate to.

I was too tired to do anything else. I collapsed back down with Kailee and Emily. Into a deep sleep I fell. One hour passed when I stirred. I jolted upright. I caught my eye on something moving quickly on the wall across from us. I noticed Succi's eyes following it but Succi simply sat there, barely moving. That was my cue. I got up, letting out a huge yelp. For approximately forty-five minutes, I attempted to slay a cockroach that was about the size of my car. The difficulty was the fact that this creature sped faster than lightening. It also flew, making me far more cautious to get too close to it. It finally dawned on me that I was actually in the tropics. There were enormous bugs that were indigenous to this native land. I endured a challenge that consumed me. This roach outsmarted me. My biggest concern was to protect the girls from anything grossly crawling on them. I was up. My watch read 3:00 a.m. With my adrenaline pumping, I decided to get up the girls' bedroom together, still with one eye scouring the walls.

At approximately 4:45 a.m., I managed to set up Kailee and Emily's room. I found the sheets, the comforters and I arranged their dressers. Picking up each child, I gently tucked them into their beds. They were out cold, most likely from the extremity of the heat and our long journey down here. I got into bed with Emily, only to be awoken by the brilliance of the warm sun's rays peering through the bedroom. I glanced at my watch. It was 8:30 a.m.

Our bell rang. Stumbling over boxes and furniture, I opened my front door. To my relief it was my brother Jacob. I was so elated to see him. He came to say goodbye. The girls jumped out of their beds, running to greet him as he gave each of them monstrous bear hugs. He was going to drive the truck back to a dealership in Sarasota, where he would then have a rental car awaiting him, for his drive back to Atlanta. I was instantly overcome. In that very moment, I was clearly cognizant of the fact that I knew no one down here. My brother was a familiar face for me. Thank God I had my children. Jacob helped me to ease my fear without ever knowing it. I had so much of my work cut out for me. Without warning I sobbed like a baby in front of him. He grabbed me so tenderly, not knowing how to comfort me. He looked so alarmed because I appeared to be in such a state of intense sorrow. He was completely taken off guard. He kept asking me if I was okay. The more Jacob asked, the more I cried. Kailee and Emily looked at me, unsure of how to handle their own emotions. Jacob held tightly on to me. I was so eternally grateful for his unconditional love. I told him to have a very safe trip home. I thanked him a thousand times over. He looked back over his shoulder, waved goodbye to me while tears of sadness poured from me as I stood on my front step.

My whole life flashed in front of me. What was I thinking? I was fifteen hundred miles from anything I knew. I left family members, many dedicated and loyal friends, a neighborhood I was comfortable in and a practice that was booming. I took an extraordinary leap of faith coming down with only three thousand dollars in my pocket. I had previously met up with innumerable introductions from bugs, wild tiny creatures that looked liked salamanders crawling outside in heaps all over my house with intense heat to boot. I was alone. I wiped my face, walked back into the house, found some dry cereal and bread, fed the girls, gave them fresh towels and told them to grab a shower. I fumbled through boxes to find some toiletries.

The rest of our day was spent unloading boxes, arranging furniture, re-arranging furniture, finding any nooks or crannies to put things away in. By the end of the day, it was ferociously pouring like we had never experienced. The thunder roared and bellowed continually. Stella was terrified. She was horribly discomforted by a storm of any kind. Storms were torrential here, resplendent, with huge cracks of lightening slamming against the sky. The sounds were so loud they reverberated in our bodies. Stella hid. Succi sat placidly, stretched out on the back, enclosed veranda, known as the Florida room or lanai. It was a tiny space, screened in, but the view outside was lovely. Huge, native plants with flowers in bloom encircling the trees, wrapped themselves around our house. For all the years I spent money on plants up north, I had most of them here in my backyard. The air was distinctive. It was a smell that was not describable. You knew you were in Florida, simply by the lingering odors.

Kailee and Emily came running into me with warm smiles expressing their need to eat. I filled the dogs' bowls with fresh water. As I proceeded to lock the door, Succi and Stella looked at me as though I was leaving them for good. This time however, furniture was in its place, belongings were put away, their dog bowls were set in a specific location near the kitchen table. Less disarray, less confusion. Regardless, they were just as new to this space as were we. I promised them that I would be back in a short amount of time. I locked the door. We were off.

I have always had a very good sense of direction. However, we arrived in Sarasota at nightfall, thus my remembrance of streets and location was limited. Unfortunately, the surging rain did not make it easy for me to see anything clearly. I ventured up the main highway known as Tamiama Trail, a road that divides the west side from the east side. It was covered with shopping stores and restaurants of all varieties, some splendid in statue and some not. We stopped at a fast food place, much to my chagrin, as we had spent years nourishing ourselves on whole foods. I was too tired to argue with myself on this. Flexibility was everything. I acquired much in the last few years. We would survive. The rain was terribly strong, making it very difficult for the girls and I to open our doors. We bee-lined to the entrance of the restaurant. A huge, crack of lightening reechoed. We all stopped short of the door. The intensity of the crack shook us up a bit. We all looked at one another. I thought of poor Stella, most likely terrified again by the thunder. As we entered the eatery, we opted for a table near the window, where we ordered our food, merely waiting for its arrival. Within seconds of us sitting down, a pleasant customer came over to us. She told us not to sit near any windows during storms. She continued to say that the leading cause of death in Florida was being struck by lightening while sitting near windows or on the beach. We thanked her. I looked at Kailee and Emily, they looked at me and we all moved to another table. Another humbling lesson to learn: Never sit near a window during a thunderstorm. We were not yet, true transported Floridians, nor did we know enough of these mini lessons to put them into practice yet. Kailee, Emily and I never sat near a window again when we went out to eat.

As we completed our meal, the rain completely stopped. The sun shone as if it never could shine as brightly. The girls and I decided we would walk Succi and Stella when we got home. We could also explore the neighborhood. We left. The heat was intense. Entering our new home, we gathered the dogs. I proceeded out the door with both dogs on a long leash. Stella tried frantically to catch the geckos scurrying on the sidewalk, making the walk troublesome. The girls were behind me, talking to each other. I came to a small, patch of grass near our home. Suddenly, I screeched like I never had before. People would have thought I was being terrorized. Kailee and Emily completely stopped in their tracks, looking at me with huge eyes. An extremely long, black snake, approximately two inches in width withered its way over my shoes. Stella went crazy, while Succi merely watched it. Another lesson. Never walk in grass up to your ankles. Before I moved down to Sarasota, my friends jokingly and very lovingly questioned me on why I would want to move to a state that occupied over twenty-three species of snakes. I had an enormous phobia of these creatures. I simply put it out of my mind. As I was told, only three were deadly. "Red on yella, kills a fella." That was my lesson on little red and yellow coil snakes. Black snakes were harmless.

Whether that black snake was harmless or not, it still found me. It also emotionally tortured me. I knew the snakes would find me because I had fear of them. In eastern philosophy when a snake passes your way it is noted to be good luck. It is vital to take heed of something positive coming your way. I could certainly use the luck. Besides almost passing out, I would most definitely take heed of not meeting up with any more snakes that evening. The girls and I walked fast, shortening our walk. Unfortunately, we did not appreciate that evening stroll as much as we could have. I was too preoccupied looking under my feet than observing the splendid fruits and coconuts lushly dangling from a variety of trees. Tomorrow was a big day for Kailee and Emily. They would begin their first day at Southside Elementary School. I wanted them to get a good night's sleep. Our walk was shortened, I suppose for a good reason.

We all washed up, reminiscing about our day. We decided we would watch one television program. It was 8:00 p.m. There were boxes still to be emptied in my room, which was the tiniest of rooms in our house. All I could get in was my bed and a dresser. I decided I had three more days before I began my job as a Women's Intervention Specialist at a drug rehab facility. I would have time to unpack. Spending time with the girls was far more important to me. As Kailee and Emily nestled on the couch, located inches away from the kitchen, we all heard a jar spill over. I did not think anything of it. I walked over to the kitchen counter. I noticed that all my glass, antique jars filled with grains were turned over on their side, half opened. As I turned my eye toward the window in the kitchen, a huge rat appeared before me. My scream was bigger than before. Kailee and Emily jumped up. "It's a huge rat!" I shrieked. "Run!" Then in my disoriented state, I thought run where? Not only did I terrorize the kids, I also became lost in my own fright. It was late. I decided to call one of the exterminators my landlord had given me. Forget about the time. Though my love for animals was enormous, somehow these beasts were not welcome in my home. As I dialed the telephone, a man named Harry answered. In my panicked voice I told him a rat was in our house. He could sense I was terrified. I explained to him we had just moved in. He asked me where the rat was. I screamed so loudly I probably made Harry deaf in one ear. "It's here," I yelled.

He, in heightened emotion asked again where, only responding to my anxiety-ridden voice. I apologized, still screaming and in my intermittent fear, I told Harry that the rat was staring at me. He was on the kitchen counter. Harry said he be over immediately.

Sure enough, Harry arrived at our house, placing traps everywhere. He said that fruit trees will produce so much fruit, the fruit will drop to the ground. The rats gather the goods. Eventually they stash their goods elsewhere. Rats are inherent to fruit trees. Regardless, these rats only appeared to be interested in my goods and our space. I did not comment further. Harry was as gracious as he could be. Within minutes Kailee comes running in, in a voice so high, exclaiming that there was a rat in her bathroom. Thank goodness she had the audacity to shut her shower door, a glass stall. I began to cry. Harry looked at us. He explained that this house had no one living in it for a good year. He put more traps in the bathroom. "This will do it. Call me when you hear the trap shut. I will remove them." He also said that he would put some poison under the house making sure they would never appear again. Meanwhile, I needed to listen to the traps catching the rats. I knew these rodents were utilizing our living accommodations, free of charge. I thanked Harry, walked him to the door and said goodnight. I begged Kailee and Emily to sleep in their beds as the bathroom was close to their room. We had shut the bathroom door. Folding a towel, I stuffed it under the door. I knew the rat would be left inside. As I tucked them in, I assured them they would be fine. I promised I would sleep with them until they fell asleep.

Quietly and peacefully as I watched my beautiful children innocently fall asleep, I stepped back from the previous events. I started to cry and laugh equally. I was so beyond exhaustion and sanity presently, I could not believe our prior's day events. Roaches, snakes, rats, what next? I walked out of their room and found the sofa. I flicked on the television, still looking over my shoulder at the kitchen counter. About a half and hour later, I heard a very distinct wailing. A slap could be heard from the back bathroom. The rat had just been caught. It had also died. In my craziness, I started to weep, feeling very sorry for a creature I really did not intend to make die. Its death overcame me. I really thought I was going nuts. I shut off the lights, collapsing on my bed, noting that I would call Harry first thing in the morning. I fell quickly asleep.

The glow from the clock revealed 3:08 a.m. I awoke in a panic, not being able to see. I could not place where I was. I was sweating. My heart was beating profusely. I was crying intensely. My exhaustion took over. Everything that could have happened to me did today. I was so confused beyond belief as to why I was here in Sarasota. I questioned everything I was doing. I sobbed beyond control. It was an understatement to say I was terrified. The aloneness I felt was extreme. Did I have courage or was I merely stupid? More crying and so much so, I began to choke in my sobs. Tears forced my eyes shut. My heart hurt so much. I could not stop weeping. In a very primitive way, my cries were coming from a place I did not understand. I looked at the clock. Two and a half hours had passed. It was 5:31 a.m. The girls would be up in an hour or so. I was totally fatigued from crying.

However, I could not stop myself from doing as such. Instantly, in my awakened, yet, painful state, I heard, "Cin,Cin?" My crying came to an immediate halt. I sat up in my bed, looked around, listening very quietly. Again, I heard "Cin, Cin?" I thought I was hallucinating, but I was not. "Michael, is that you?" He said, "Yes." "Are you okay?" Again, without uttering a spoken word, I replied, "I am." He said, "Cin, don't worry." Silence. I looked around. More silence. I just had a telepathic experience with my brother. I knew it was him. No words were stated out loud. I could hear everything in my mind's eye and respond accordingly. When Michael was alive, he always called me Cin. I knew I was not dreaming. I knew my brother was always concerned with his family. I felt privileged to have him come to me. I lay in my bed, peacefully. I shut my eyes one last time. "Shrrrrrrrl!" The alarm clock sounded as did the pounding in my heart. I lost that instant peace.

Chapter 30

First day of school. The jitters. The excitement. The knots in the stomach. I was so proud of Kailee and Emily. They had so much grace. They looked lovely. I gave them money for lunch as I had yet to do a food shopping. We decided to take the car given the fact it was their first day. We had to go into the principal's office to solidify their teacher assignments. The girl's gathered their belongings. As we approached the car sitting under a small carport, without warning, a huge crawly creature fell on top of my head. Kailee and Emily looked up at me, hesitating, trying not to laugh. I began to yell, "What is it, what is it, get it off!" Instantaneously, the girls let loose, laughter coming out of their sides. I was yelling even louder. I must have looked ridiculous. Whatever fell on top of my head felt like the texture of the Gumby dolls that were popular when I was a little girl. Kailee and Emily could not help themselves as they continued to laugh uncontrollably. Seconds later, this thing fell off my head, staring directly at me, landing on top of my car, ready to bolt inside my car window, already half open. It was a huge lizard, huger than huge, with bulging eyes and a bloated stomach. I shuddered, got in the car as fast as I could, rolling all the windows up, despite the heat and the humidity. I said nothing during the car ride to school. New Lesson: Shut all car windows when you leave your vehicle, evening and morning.

In my frenzied state, I managed to drive to the main entrance of Southside. The girls and I walked in to the office. We were then greeted by the secretary who eventually led us into the principal's office. All the paperwork had been previously processed. We exchanged hellos and intros. I was given instructions as to where each of the children's classrooms would be. I then walked Kailee and Emily prospectively to their new teachers, praying quietly that their day would go smoothly. Watching, Kailee and Emily nervously walked into their rooms, every student staring at them. I told the girls to hold their heads high, not to be afraid. How could they not be? They too, left all their close friends, the familiarity of their town and their home. I knew they had to have some apprehensions. I also knew they were wondrously courageous. My heart triggered tears from my eyes. The doors shut. I turned, heavy-hearted. I made my way outside to my car. More tears. Another hurdle for me to tackle, within a forty-eight hour period of our arrival to Sarasota.

The morning was going smoothly until I was drastically caught off guard. Arriving back to our little abode, within ten minutes of me entering my foyer, I responded to a knock on my front door. I was somewhat taken aback. I hardly had any time to meet anyone in the neighborhood. A huge, burly man in a uniform had asked if there was a Cindy Barg living here. I nodded. He then handed me a sealed envelop. He left just as quickly as he came. I opened up the letter reading its contents. I was horrified. My heart sunk. I was to be in Cape Cod tomorrow, in court to hear a plea about my ex- husband lowering child support again.

It was quite obvious that if I did not show up, child support, automatically, would be lowered. My ex knew full well that my appearance in court could not occur. It was physically impossible for me to be there. I just drove over fifteen hundred miles to a new area which was barely familiar to us. This was deliberately planned. Panic set in, my adrenalin was flying. All the old tapes in my mind played. I so wanted my ex not to act from a place of fear. I prayed he would just forgive and let go. Yet, as much as I attempted to dig deep, I was also broiling with anger. Too much of my energy was expended on tackling his fear which he turned into vindictiveness. That was much too painful for me. My child support was recently lowered before I left, though I attempted with integrity to keep it where it was, already at bare minimum allotments. This was such an abusive action, I was filled with rage of unmanageable proportions. I paced the house continually, seething with an anger that frightened me. Minutely small, within my soul, I also comprehended, however brief that I could do nothing. I had to let go. It was such a slap in my face and Kailee's and Emily's face. I struggled with both emotions.

Everything and anything that I could feel I did. All of the pain in my marriage came into view. Old emotions of our union reproduced in my mind. I wanted his pain to soften. I wanted Allen to know that my leaving was not about hurting him. It was about beginnings again, helping wounds to potentially repair themselves. It was about time. It was about healing, regardless of how temporary that may be. I knew Allen to be a highly sensitive individual, yet I also knew that such sensitivity could be a detriment. No matter how desperately I tried in vain to understand his actions, I simply could not justify them anymore.

All of us inevitably, have to be responsible for the actions we partake in and how such actions affect others. Unfortunately, when fear takes over, our humanness and our spirit is marred by resentments and hatred. Our thinking becomes representative rather than participatory. Disharmony in pain causes more chaos. Harmony in pain seeks to create a higher order that emphasizes understanding. Nonetheless, I called my attorney. She would be present for me in court. The next day child support was lowered. My inability to tangibly speak for myself was a determining factor.

From a earthly standpoint I felt defeated because he won. From a spiritual standpoint, I knew a lesson would eventually appear to me. Ideally speaking, that was an enlightening thought. Realistically, I was livid and I did I want to be a victim of his malevolent actions. Realistically, I wanted to fight like hell. I wanted to argue the injustice of it all. Yet, I had enough of defending myself. I spent years desperately trying to be heard by a man who never could hear my voice. The hurt inside of me never did completely dissipate. My heart was half broken for most of the years I was married. No matter how I attempted to defend my position, my honor was always forfeited. Letting go, despite my inner protests was of great significance. Fighting my ex was meaningless now. What was the use and for what? Feelings of unexplainable wrath still harbored inside me though. Part of me was emotionally bottomed out. Michael's murder further accentuated my need to want to detach myself from hurtful people, blessing their essences from a distance. I also needed to acknowledge my truth. Living my life in resolution to what I believed in was essential for me. Reacting to my ex's ill will of me, only subjected to me to more abuse. I allowed my buttons to be pushed, many of them old, raw wounds, not yet healed. I wanted our new life to exist. I wanted happiness. Allowing abuse to hinder me was detrimental to my spiritual growth. It was also a detriment to Kailee's and Emily's evolvement. Unmistakably, trusting what I knew was mandatory.

Love and fear can never coexist together on this earth plane. Painfully, I was especially reminded of this during my married years. Striving to live my life with love being the underlying principle for conscious living, was vital to my existence. Yet, losing myself in my ex's anger and his humility became my preoccupation. Fear inevitably superimposed itself into my soul. Harboring intense agony and anger was crushing my spirit. It was a very vicious cycle, one I was gravely aware of, but one I could not always dismiss myself from.

Despite the fact that my ex-husband sent letters via his attorney on a monthly basis, threatening custody and visitation rights, put me in a tizzy momentarily. I trusted and I prayed. That was all I had left. Eventually the letters stopped. My ex's attorney withdrew from my ex. My ex defeated his own purpose. Fighting an exhausted fight was his issue. It no longer became mine. Slowly, I could begin to acclimate to life here without fearing going to the mailbox.

Kailee, Emily and I did not leave garbage unattended or out; too many bugs, too many unusual critters roaming about. We walked in short-cropped grass. No snakes would be present. We stayed away from windows when it down poured. We shut everything off in the house when it stormed. No burned-out power surges to be concerned about. We stayed away from the ocean when it was lightening and thundering. We cropped down the fruit trees, pulling down grapefruits and oranges when they were in bloom, giving any determined rat zero incentives. Kailee and Emily had made wonderful friends. I belonged to a spiritual center known as The Center for Positive Living where I met some of my closest friends, through intimate dinner parties and healing circles. My work was hard, draining and low paying, but I was grateful to have it. The days were intensely hot, the nights lovely with some of the magnificent skies ever to be seen. I had real neighbors that exchanged conversation with me, Kailee and Emily. The children and I belonged to a wonderfully progressive synagogue. Siesta Key Beach was rated one of the top ten beaches in the world. We were but two miles from this wondrous ocean land, where we spent many an evening and a day, collecting shells, finding sand dollars and witnessing droves of dolphin families swarming the waters. Kailee was active in theatre, Emily in gymnastics. We were settled in, starting our lives anew. Compared to my first month, being broken in all too quickly to life in the tropics, snakes, roaches, rats, geckos, other unrecognizable creatures, summons from a sheriff, weekly letters from attorneys, I was able to surpass the worst of the worst. Yet, I had this lingering, unsettled feeling inside of me. I could not pinpoint where, or how or what it was. It just loitered in my soul.

One morning in Sarasota I was driving over the South Bridge where magnificent boats floated underneath. I was forced to stop allowing a rather small boat with a huge mast to open the drawbridge. As I was sitting peacefully, admiring the scenery with glorious egrets flying above, tears sprung from my eyes involuntarily. I was becoming more and more accustomed to such outbursts, I merely went with the flow. Yet, the sorrow I harbored was deep. My soul yearned for a reprieve from a pain I could sometimes recognize, but not dispel. For the moments I sat on the bridge, my mind once again reverted to Michael's death. I could not help myself from the imperishable grief welling inside. I broke, sobbing, revisiting in my mind's eyes my brother's tortuous ending to his life. This bottomless pit of exhausting pain lasted but seconds. It was done. The drawbridge closed. I looked out onto the water once more and drove. It was like a clip from a film that replayed over and over again at the most unexpected times.

In spite of all the intrusions of life's experiments I have been tested with and touched by, living my life with a peaceful pride used to be commonplace. Somewhere, along the way, my fire was slowly burning out. The serenity I once knew was hiding somewhere. My soul was disquieted. I was too distracted, however, to really want to fully notice.

Chapter 31

A full year had passed without any major glitches. Still, no word on Michael's trial. The children and I moved over to the east side, to a space that was larger and far more comfortable. Putting up a fence allowed the dogs to be in their glory as they could roam freely about. My neighbor, across the way, became my very best friend. We spent many evenings conversing about life, resting on the wooden swing attached to my outside porch. We were both adventurous. We loved change. We were passionate about living. Each of us had our share of tragedy. We were equally sensitive about the importance of living life. We had a mutual respect for our individual beliefs and our life-styles. Lil was a delight to have so close by.

Our street was long, connecting to a much bigger thoroughfare opening to more traffic. Neighborhoods were different here. Families came and gone. Sarasota was a tourist area, attracting people from all over the world. On one hand, the eclecticism from such diversity was appreciated. On the other hand, it was hard to establish roots because the area was transient. Our neighborhood also contained many elderly folks. It was a very common statement for Emily to say "That person must have died," when a For Sale sign would appear in front of the house. In most cases, that is exactly why that house was being sold.

Lila and I would comment on how especially quiet our neighborhood was. Meeting people was difficult. We barely knew any of our neighbors. I knew more of the dog's names in the area than I did the names of people who inhabited my street. The heat from the sun during the spring and summer months was so extreme, people tended to stay inside. It was very important to remain connected though. Otherwise, it was very easy to get lost in a crowded solitude.

I understood well what that felt like. I was a master at isolating myself during painful times in my life. The choice to do so was not always a conscious one however. I loved people. I was exceptional at accommodating others, making them feel good about themselves. Yet, I would retreat within my soul, not sharing much of my own personal struggles. I was an extraordinary survivor. In many respects, I had this remarkable ability to walk through life with a strength and a knowledge that usually guided me. I knew how to adjust. I attempted with a sincere modesty to value that whatever I needed to know, it was for a specific reason. Inevitably, such lessons would appear to me later on. The beauty of hindsight. Yet, I had this knack for going full circle, repeating specific lessons over and over again, utilizing different experiences. Many of these lessons were exhausting, painful and hard.

Ironically, many of my clients believed my life was devoid of personal problems. They saw me as an individual who was capable and strong, a rock for their obstacles, a person who could direct them gently, unreservedly and with honest intent. Yet, I was hard on myself during those times when I needed to love myself more. When I was vulnerable in my marriage, my ex was not available to me. Risking my pain was much too great. Unsuspecting, none of my clients would have known that for years, I cried myself to sleep, night after night, for hours on end. None of my clients would ever have known how difficult it was for me to ask for help, when I gave help so freely. What I did for others was purely out of compassion and genuine loving. Ascertaining tenderness for myself was difficult. Choosing experiences that brought me back to the silent suffering I had known only escalated feelings of failing myself. Surely, I should have known how illogical it was to plague myself with such thoughts. Intellectually, I understood. On a heart level, I agonized.

The pace was much slower in Sarasota. Cares were not visibly shown. Stress was minimal. Siesta Key Beach afforded me tremendous opportunities to merely let go. Sitting down on the white crystal, quartz sand, staring into the vast ocean took me to a place of deep tranquillity. If I was distressed, it was short-lived. The ocean was quietly therapeutic. The sun baked my soul, allowing me to acquire an inner peace that was full and comforting. Dismissing worry became easy. Simply, I could tuck away any cares, bundling them up into the water's crest. When critical thoughts of my choices stared out at me, the ocean became my refuge. Returning home, I was unrestrained, relaxed and free. My inner anguish could neatly be put away, at least temporarily.

Chapter 32

Time passed. One year drifted into one and a half years. I finally became cognizant of my discontentment with my work situation. Placing pregnant, addicted women into rehab centers drained me and consumed me. Despite my valiant attempts at persuading women to relinquish their drug habits for the sake of their unborn children, their drug of choice became more important than their lives and their children's lives.

Dignity and self-respect had no value for these women. Also, my frustration was mounting to huge elevations toward the agency I was affiliated with. My talents at bringing the numbers in, meeting quotas to fill beds appeared far more significant than actually helping these women get well. There was so much dysfunction within the organization I was becoming unclear as to who needed the help, the employees or the clients. Clearly, I had to make more changes. My talents were not being utilized well. My mind was no longer being sparked. My soul was thirsty for something more, but my body always felt fatigued, clouding my ability to move forward.

Craving a work situation that afforded me more creativity swelled within me. Yet, I had no idea what I wanted to do. Practically speaking, I needed to sustain an income that would bring me sufficient funds for my mortgage payment, my car loan, utilities and other expenses accrued within a family household. Despite the ability to indulge myself in endless activities in Sarasota, I was also gravely aware of how low paying the state of Florida was. Private practice was not presently the answer as I did not have enough money in the bank to support our existence, nor did I have the energy to build a clientele. My resourcefulness had always been a strong asset for me. Yet, I was shuffling around to find extra motivation to stay afloat. Again, my fire seemed to be waning.

My years of devotion to serve others brought me tremendous rewards however. Invaluable insights, deep reverence and extraordinary compassion opened up my heart to levels of loving that were gifts in my life. Nevertheless, the unremitting sadness present in my soul also manifested itself more visibly. Quiet wailing emerged from me at night while tucked in my bed, out of earshot form Kailee and Emily. This lament was deep, an emotion I could not control. My heart felt tortured. My soul was weeping. I wanted Kailee and Emily not to want for anything, I did not want them to be aware of my pain, a pain I could not even pinpoint. They saw enough in my marriage. They saw too much death at an early age. They were already well beyond their years. They were still children. I wanted them to remain that way, at least for a while, despite their innocence already lost.

I knew that tomorrow would come. I knew I would be grateful for waking up. I knew I would be grateful to see my loved ones. I knew I needed to simply be, to accept, regardless. I gave myself more than enough time to become accustomed to life here. It was time for more changes. Yet, I was completely baffled as to my direction.

During my first week living in Sarasota, I began acupuncture school. Five evenings a week and every weekend were the time requirements for classes. I was a month into my studies. I did not have enough support systems or financial stability to back me up and I could not focus in the evening to maintain the rigorous academic schedule. I had to withdraw, regardless of my dream. I would not have been able to fulfill my school commitment with due diligence and I did not have enough motivation to sustain me. Moving was a challenge in itself. Taking care of my children and tending to their needs was also a priority. I needed to forgive myself. Not an easy task for me.

Finally, I received a certified piece of mail from the State of Massachusetts from the District Court System. The time had come. Michael's trial was set for April of 1997. Memories swarmed my mind of my brother's death. Anguish was all too familiar to my soul. I knew this day would come. Rearranging our lives was becoming so familiar. Kayla and Emily would miss one week out of school. Sarasota school vacation was in March. Both girls were fully vested in their lives. They were doing exceptionally well in their classes. I had three months to come up with plane tickets, find friends to watch my dogs and prepare ourselves for our trip back up north. Kailee and Emily would not be present at the trial. They did not need to be privy to all the details of their uncle's massacre. Despite the circumstances that would bring us back to Massachusetts, Kailee and Emily would have the opportunity to see their cousins and their father.

It was hard to predict if the weather would be inviting. April could bring as much snow as it could bring the warm sun. Yet, all of us were out of touch with anything that sunk below seventy degrees. Locating boxes filled with old, winter clothing would be challenging. I already knew Kailee and Emily probably outgrew them.

My biggest conflict was coming to terms with the actual events of Michael's death. None of my family members really knew why Michael was murdered nor did we know the details surrounding his death. We did know that he was slashed to death with a samurai sword. What I did know is that we all silently asked innumerable questions with no answers present. Now, the answers would come. So would unbearable suffering. My heart was barely healed. Opening up these wounds offered me very little comfort. Nobody talked about the pending trial. Like anything seemingly normal, we did the best we could to prepare ourselves for the inevitable. Nothing could have prepared us for what we did hear.

Chapter 33

Two and a half more months slipped by. Arrangements were nearing completion for our trip north. A few friends would stay at my home on different days, tending to my dogs. Kailee and Emily would bring with them, a week's worth of homework to make up while they were away. Winter clothing was sparse. Their dad would supply them with extra heavy clothing when he picked them up at Logan Airport in Boston. I would see Kailee and Emily off, get my rental car and proceed to go to the police headquarters in Lynn. I would then locate my brother Jacob, who was flying in from New York City. My mother was being driven by her friend from upstate New York. It was done.

The state of Massachusetts supplied Kailee, Emily and I with airline tickets. It is customary for some states to give airfare to family members of the murdered victim who are living far away. I was totally unaware of such protocol, but very appreciative of the state's offering. This was a great help to us. I would have preferred to have secured tickets to something far more worthwhile though.

Once a murder takes place, the family of the victim is assigned a victim-witness advocate. Ours was a woman whom we were blessed to know. Connie was always there for us, without resignation, keeping us as informed as possible. For nineteen months, my mother had innumerable conversations with Connie, establishing a solid and trusting rapport. Despite questions that were continually asked, Connie provided an answer. If she did not know, she would call back soon after with a pending resolve. We also found out that our attorney would be a fairly young man in his forties, committed, dedicated and hard working. David Dunn was the prosecuting district attorney for Lynn. He had known the system. He had seen just about everything. He also wore a pacemaker in his heart. Not surprising, given the nature of his work. Our case was one that was most horrific and sorrowful he had ever worked on. Unfortunately, this agonized my mother.

As much as we needed some closure on Michael's murder, none of us were looking forward to unveiling the details of his death.

Chapter 34

My dogs looked at me with that familiar expression, knowing all too well that Kailee, Emily and I would be going away. This time though, the house was not in disarray. I had to believe that they would believe we would come home soon. I knew these beloved animals did not have a sense of time. They would just wait. They would wait and be there for all of us to return. I was already looking forward to my departure back to Sarasota. We had not even made it to the airport yet.

After hugging my dogs, shutting doors and whatever else I did, Kailee, Emily and I were in my car driving to the airport, but minutes away. After landing in Atlanta, Georgia, for a brief layover, we would resume our flight to Logan Airport in Boston, arriving at one in the afternoon.

It was an uneventful flight. Shortly before we came into view of Boston, the Captain on the plane offered a thank you for flying with his airline. He immediately said that the temperature was thirty-eight degrees. I shuddered. The girls and I looked at each other, not uttering one word. I pulled out some clothes from a tote bag I had with me, handing them to Kailee and Emily. Better to have more layers than none at all.

I looked to my left, being caught off guard observing huge amounts of water as the plane was nearing the runway. I forgot how close to the water you are when the plane makes it descent into Boston. A discomforting view. We landed. We were here, a very familiar place. This city use to make my heart sing. Instead, my heart felt a gut-wrenching ache. I recognized that same feeling when I would cry at night. I composed myself for a moment. We proceeded to walk out of the plane. Kailee, Emily and I saw their father anxiously awaiting their arrival. He looked at me sensitively. I looked back at him the same. All the past fights, our cruelty to each other dissolved for an instant. I now remember what attracted to me to Allen years ago. When I first

119

met him, even before I uttered one word to him I knew I was going to marry him. He hugged me. I began to cry like a baby. Kailee and Emily got enormous hugs from their Dad. I thanked him for picking up the girls. Without words being mentioned, Allen nodded lovingly, walking hand-in-hand with Kailee and Emily. He knew I had to face a week of horror and pain. I knew that he knew. I waved goodbye, telling him that I would call soon, keeping him posted. He looked back at me one more time. Within seconds of his stare, he disappeared with the girls to find their luggage. He was gone. My heart sank. I felt terribly alone.

I knew this airport well. I knew this city like the back of my hand. My heart felt like it was going to split in half. When Michael was murdered, I had no desire to live near Boston anymore. Anytime I used to venture into the city, I felt alive, excited, mingling with the buzz and the sophistication Boston generated. The loss of Michael left me so depleted, the positive energy I once felt for Boston was substituted with a hollowness. A dark void filled my stomach.

I swallowed my pain, realizing all too soon that I had to get my luggage and my car rental. In another half an hour I would be driving to Lynn, a town filled with dreadful recollections. The trial would be in Salem, a town adjacent to Lynn, at the main facility, the Salem District Court.

Salem is a renowned city known for its witches, witch trials, its spells, its magic, its voodoo, its history, its cobblestone streets, its metaphysical bookstores. How uncanny that now Michael's murder trial would take place here. Instead of burning at the stake, Michael's murderer would have to sit and wait for his sentence, shackled in chains. A witch would know however, of her impending death. Michael's murderer is innocent beyond a reasonable doubt, until proven guilty. No one would know the outcome.

Chapter 35

Driving, though I was extremely cognizant of where I was going, I was equally as distracted. Smelling the ocean was a sign that I was becoming closer to my destination. Seagulls were dancing above me, making huge sweeping motions with their wings, cawing as they flew. I recognized this wall. Occasionally, I wound up there after visiting my friend Laura, who had lived further out on the north shore, before she died of cancer. Sometimes I would merely sit on this stone fence, gazing into nothingness and everything. The ocean brought me to such a place of peace. Anywhere I could devour its essence, I would. Suddenly, I had this morbid curiosity to see the house my brother was murdered in. It was but a stone's throw to the block Michael had lived on. Getting back into my car, I took a left on Preston Street. I drove up to this huge white house. I stopped the car directly in front of the driveway. Uncourageously, while facing the front of the house, I rolled my window down. One would never, ever suspect that a brutal killing took place here almost two years ago. The sun was shining gloriously. Flowers were starting to make their way up from the ground. Green buds were appearing on the trees. Enormous windows reflected the warmth of the sun's rays, as streaks of golden hues rippled the glass. A stone walkway edged its way up to the main entrance. Victorian houses cradled next to this one, also beautiful in stature. This house could have been depicted in Good House Keeping, Town House or Architectural Digest Magazine. The loveliness and charm of this space was enough to mesmerize anyone. While quietly listening to the ocean's waves gently tumbling, I forgot that Michael was violently murdered on the second floor.

Blinking from the invasion of the sun onto my window shield, abhorrent memories reverted back to me. One week after Michel's murder, rummaging through his wallet, I found dry cleaning stubs yet to be picked up. The store was in close proximity to his house. For some reason, rather than divert myself onto a different street, I chose to drive by the murder scene. Yellow police ribbons lined every crevice of this dwelling stating: "Do not cross over. Police investigation." A chilling feeling crept up within me. I was overcome with emotion. Distraught beyond belief, my face became soaked with heavy tears. My body began to tremble. Those intense emotions I felt two years ago, were equally acute now. My stomach felt squeamish. The fear Michael experienced had to be of colossal proportions. Nothing I imagined could suffice for what Michael went through.

Amazingly quiet, I started the car, proceeding to the police station. Not looking back, I managed to choke my emotion. Otherwise, my eyes would have been blinded by my sobs. Within minutes, I arrived, only too quickly reminded of two years ago, when Jenna and I came upon this same street, this same neighborhood to be confronted with my brother's murder. Finding a parking spot, I walked in, my body feeling weak at the knees, my heart pounding until I was met by a familiar face. Jacob found me. What a tremendous relief. We hugged somberly, holding onto each other as though we were lost souls reunited again. My mother had yet to arrive. However, within moments, like an orchestrated plan, my mom and her friend walked in the front door. Seconds passed before we were greeted by a uniformed person. He handed all of us hand-written directions. We exchanged brief conversation, held each other, following one another out to our cars, caravanning one behind the other. The car ride was a mere fifteen minutes. We landed in front of this lovely stone hotel. It reminded me of a bed and breakfast inn. Quaint in structure, its foundation was set close to the cobblestone street. Finding parking was cumbersome. The spaces designated for hotel patrons were behind the building. They were terribly small. With some maneuvering, we all managed to find hidden, empty spots, with the intention of not moving the cars until our departure at the end of the week. Grabbing bags, simultaneously, we all entered the front door, checked in and walked to our prospective rooms. One half hour would pass before we would congregate in the main room of the hotel. We would then walk over to the District Court where Connie, David Dunn and others would brief us on the trial, set to start the next day.

It was so apparent that we were all so powerless. Yet, in respect to Michael, we would do anything for him to see this through, honoring him in whatever capacity we could. If the trial took more time we would see it to the finish. We would sustain and continue our vigil, unconditionally. We all knew if the situation was reversed, Michael would have been here for all of us, regardless. We were bound together with a genuine commitment to honor Michael.

Finally, we all met downstairs. No one spoke. Walking beside one another, we began our trek. Two more blocks would take us to the Salem District Court. I realized I was freezing. The clouds were heavy, little sun to speak of.

My shoulders were hunched up. My arms wrapped around my body to maintain some warmth while my legs felt stunned by the cold. Forty degrees was warm to many New Englanders. It was a promise of a potentially decent spring and a calm summer. Walking quickly, I yearned for Florida's sun. Forty degrees seemed like five below to me.

The streets were quiet. Despite the warmer than usual New England Spring weather, the neighborhood appeared isolated and distant. Perhaps, given my state of affairs, anything close to my view would seem detached from the world's reality. My truth was a far cry from normalcy. One block away, we would open the door to new, emotional injuries, exacerbating the old ones.

The District Court looked like any Bostonian office building. Red brick covered its frame, stately in nature. Attorneys, lay people, police officers, court reporters flowed in and out of the doors. Some dressed up, some casual with shirt tails hanging out of their suit pants, others with run in their stockings defying the race against time to meet docket times on the daily calendar. It seemed ludicrous for me to notice such petty details on people. Eclectic characters filled this place. Some looked dismayed at life, others appeared harried, while still, others seemed to be distinctly unruffled.

As we entered the building, we were met by metal detectors and armed officers. A heaviness set within me. The bottom of my stomach turned. Jacob emptied his pockets of change. A beep was sounded. Jacob then took off the watch Michael had worn. Very protectively, Jacob placed the watch on the wooden tray near the detector. He then walked through the detector without a glitch. I could sense that Jacob was somewhat agitated. Gathering his belongings, he walked to the main office where we stood waiting. David Dunn, a tall man with curly blonde hair came out to greet us, despite the somberness of the occasion. I managed to peek into his office. There were pictures of his children smiling on his desk and on the wall. It was an austere, bare office that seemed to suffice for David. He was a normal guy, with a normal family, friendly in nature but also serious. Connie, the victim witness advocate approached us, shook our hands, asking if we needed anything. She led us to an even barer room with one broken window and an old, beat up couch. This was the waiting room. A room designed for family members of murdered victims. It was more disquieting to know we were not the first people who passed through this room. As I later found out, Lynn had the highest murder rate in the state of Massachusetts. It is known as, "Lynn, Lynn, City of Sin." Such news added no relief. To no avail, as we sat and merely waited, we were able to see men walking slowly, bound by chains at their feet and their hands. Another uneasy sight.

I was terribly naïve when it came to crime as it related to my own personal experience. Equally, I desperately wanted to know how a person could go wrong. I could not comprehend why anyone would risk losing their lives over committing a crime. Yet, if a passion is that strong, touching the deepest springs within our soul, good, bad or indifferent, I suppose then, it is possible not to think of the consequences. As a soul entity I believe we all come in choosing a life plan that will hopefully help us learn lessons. Committing a vicious crime as part of the divine plan seems to be a heavy price to pay to learn lessons: A price that not only affects the person who did the killing, but one that also affects the victim and the survivors of the deceased person. I continued to watch these individuals in their chains, wondering what got them to where they were. No answers appeared.

After formal chit-chat, we were introduced to more staff. Still confined to this barren room, all we could do was sit and wait. We sat and we waited for a very long time. The day was almost over. It was obvious that David Dunn was overworked, tired and ready to go home to his family. We were briefed a bit more on some of the details of Michael's murder trial. Tomorrow, beginning at 8:00 a.m. we would discuss what would happen in the morning, what judge would be residing over the case and specific issues related to our case. Another half an hour passed when my mother's cousins walked in. They had flown in from Arizona. It was good to see them despite the circumstances that brought them here. We gave them the information we had, we walked out and discussed dinner plans. All of us would meet in a hour at the hotel restaurant.

Waiting on the elevator, my need for some privacy was urgent. Now would be a good opportunity to secure that seclusion. I felt estranged from the world, almost aloof from where I was. Yet, in a small way, I wanted someone to hold onto, someone I could lie here with without having to exchange words with. Once inside my room, I pulled back the covers on the bed attempting to rest my body for a few moments. I decided to run a bath. To my dismay, this room, though lovely, only had a shower. It was most narrow and terribly tiny. I was taken aback by how I was going to fully immerse myself in its space. With some finagling, I stood under the hot spray for a long period of time, dowsing my tired body. I redressed ready to meet the rest of my family downstairs.

There was nothing much to discuss as we ate our dinner. We were merely anticipating the trial to begin tomorrow. I was grateful for my cousin Kris. She was a wonderful buffer for this raw moment. She was quite an evolved soul with many similar beliefs to mine. Thus, our personal conversation took us to another level of an unspoken knowledge that soothed my soul. Her husband, Jay, my mother's cousin was equally as gracious in his giving. Contrary to what lie ahead, the evening went well. They were a tremendous support for all of us, especially my mother. We all exchanged goodnights.

As I made my way to my room, my body slowed to a snail's pace. The traveling, the whole day had caught up with me. Laying gently down, I placed a call to Kailee and Emily. The line was busy. Looking up at the ceiling, I drifted off. Seven hours later, I was awakened by the phone ringing. The hotel operator informed me that is was 6:30 a.m.

Chapter 36

Though my life was accustomed to early am hours, I would have been completely satisfied staying in bed for an extended period of time. Getting ready in very little time was easy for me. I was expecting a day of momentous emotional discomfort. There were no preplanned meetings with my family, thus, congregating at the courthouse at 8:00 a.m. was the consensus. Picking up my watch on the nightstand, it read 7:03 a.m. I rolled out of bed, meandering to the bathroom, where once again I adjusted the shower nozzle with the hopes that I would receive a decent wash. I had to stand awkwardly against tiled walls to be immersed. An indefinite amount of time passed before I shut off the water. Dried and dressed, I flickered on the television, curious to know the temperature outside. Forty-one degrees. Another over cast day prevailed. I pulled on my heavy, wool sweater, stood in front of the elevator and waited for the door to open. In minutes I was on the street, walking to the District Court.

Tuesday morning, in the height of rush hour, the roads were impeccably quiet. The air was brisk, picking up an east wind, making my walk become a quick stride. I clung to my sweater as if it were all I had on. I found a shortcut that curtailed my travel time in half. Although only blocks away, rambling through cobblestone parking lots behind buildings helped to diminish the wind. Looking forward, I could glimpse the courthouse through a narrow driveway. Almost there, a gust of wind blew so vigorously, my shawl blew off my shoulders. Scrambling to run after it, I snagged a run in my stockings. All I could do was live with it. They could be replaced. I reminded myself quickly of the importance of what was important in life. Catching my breath, I came out from the driveway, onto the street, facing the courthouse on the opposite side. My heart sped up. The beats became an incessant, pulverizing pounding in my chest cavity. My hand automatically went to my heart. Pressing harder, I was hoping to ease the pain. Momentarily, a car quickly sped by, forcing me to waver on the curb. Focusing on my heart was no longer significant. Getting across the street safely became the priority. Adjusting my shawl, I deliberately looked to my left, then my right and darted across the street into the courthouse. As I stepped inside, I was taken aback by the long line of people waiting to go through the metal detector. I was approximately tenth in line. Nothing to do but wait and watch. More people in chains appeared. Lawyers were impatient, fighting with the plains clothes man sitting at the metal detector. They were to be heard at the top of the hour. No movement. No special treatment. It seemed like forever before the line moved. I was up next. I was also praying I would not beep. Making it through, I quietly sighed, approaching the barren room I had yet to become fond of. Peering behind me, I noticed my brother coming inside the building, followed by Kris and Jay. There was no watch on Jacob's wrist. He breezed through. Jay had to empty his pockets. Kris whisked in. Finally, Jay was able to pass through without a sound. We all exchanged hellos. Chatting nonsensically, my mother walked in looking discomforted. Her friend was close at hand. We were not as clear as to what would take place, thus, we merely engaged ourselves in conversation. Connie walked out from another hall, leading us to the same room we were taken to yesterday. She offered coffee. Everyone declined. She explained to us that we would have to wait a bit more before the trial began. Trial protocol, so to speak. So we sat. One hour led to two. Two hours led to three. The anticipation was gruesome. Being forced to sit without any action precipitating, made the time dreadfully draw on and on. We talked, we stared at the holes in the wall, we readjusted our legs, we stood up, we sat down again and we waited. I noticed one of Jacob's legs was continuously stomping the floor. Nervous energy. Kris and Jay remained extremely patient. My mother insisted on pressing an issue that there were no answers for. Jacob was getting agitated with her. As she insisted, the more agitated Jacob became. Finally, in his desperation, raising his voice with tears welling in his eyes he shouted, "How can you persist about something inconsequential when your son was murdered?" All talking ceased. Discomfort was swallowing everyone. Everybody's emotions were at a heightened state. No one was in a reasonable frame of mind.

Connie suddenly appeared in the room. It was quite obvious she sensed the tension. Gently, she recommended we all break an hour for lunch. The judge had yet to appear for our case. All we could was comply. I was far from hungry and restless equally. My despair was heightening as was my need to lift myself. Refusing to dine with my family, I decided to walk the cobblestone streets near the hotel, venturing into some bookstores I passed earlier along the way. No one seemed to mind. Hugging my family, I breezed through the metal detectors again without a glitch and headed toward the door. The wind had picked up tremendously. Though I was anxious to solo a walk, I also knew I would be chilled to my bones. Nonetheless, this brisk respite was what I needed.

As terribly sorrowful as it was to be in Salem, I appreciated the many antiquated storefronts this town had to offer. Salem was filled with eclectic shops, some artistic, some avant-garde, some new age and some modern. Within minutes I opened the door to a most soothing vintage gallery brimming with old books, clothes of the past and herbal remedies. The smell was sweet, but pleasant. My soul tingled with a nostalgia that was comforting. This space brought to me a level of calm, away from the real world to a quieter dimension. Everything was so tranquil. I took it all in as if I had known this before.

Browsing, I tested herbal concoctions and lotions, I read spiritual texts and draped vintage clothing over my body. Forgetting what lie ahead, I relished the hour I had been there. Placing things back in their place, I thanked the clerk and left.

It was getting darker by the hour. Clouds hovered in huge clumps over me. No room for sun today. Picking up my pace again, I grappled to hold onto the peace I just secured. More traffic appeared. Honks could be heard from cars. People were in a hurry. The peace was jilted. The courthouse stood there as I had left it. However, there was a homeless drifter standing to one side, in layered, tattered garb, with his hand held out. Not such a good place to be begging was my thought. However the policeman at the door never bothered to notice.

Looking sadly back at this man, I entered the building, walked through the metal detector, approaching the only room I knew. Jacob was already there. Other family members were still out. One and a half days had passed and the trial had yet to begin. So little information was given to us. Sensing Jacob's frustration, I merely found a spot on this tired sofa and rested. Mom, Kris and Jay entered, asking if there were any word on when the trial would begin. No answers. Once again, all of us found our designated spots on the couch, old imprints still left on the cushions. We stared into nothingness, holding any conversation possible to hold. Another hour had passed. We continued our chit-chat. It was now three in the afternoon. Jay made a very gracious attempt to secure information on the trial. Leaving the room for a few moments, he came back in, dismayed to learn of nothing. Finally, and with the hour closing toward 4:00 p.m., Connie came in, greatly apologizing for the delay. She exclaimed that the judge who was going to sit for the trial no longer could. We were confused. The judge recanted his responsibility to be present for Michael's murder trial, opting to go to Europe instead. A conflict of interests, so to speak. My anger was brimming very slowly, yet it was building to a boiling level that was still unbeknown to me. Jacob paced harder, his knuckles clenching. My mother looked tortured. Connie explained that another judge may be able to sit. We had to reappear tomorrow morning at 8:00 a.m. to determine the fate of this trail. Despite our very frazzled states, we acknowledged her generosity, left and made dinner plans for later in the evening.

Nothing seemed to be accomplished. The mere fact that we were completely unworldly about court trials, let alone murder trials put us in a vulnerable place. We had no control over anything that concerned this murder trial. We too, were victims of a different nature. Our hands were tied, we hand no access to confront the court's manipulative way of putting people on hold, despite the circumstances. There was absolutely nothing we could do. We walked away feeling very emotionally and physically spent and enormously had.

Dinner was uneventful. The anger I experienced two hours ago was once again brewing. I felt taken advantage of, used and invalidated. Michael's justice had yet to prevail. The way things were progressing or not progressing, made me question if justice was even a reality. My passion soared at this issue. What kind of judge would even commit to sitting at a murder trial only to decide to set his vacation as a precedent? Overly fatigued, I dismissed my presence from the table. Walking back to my room, I collapsed on the bed, still fully clothed, crying hysterically. My sobbing was a mixture of pain and anger. My family and I waited so long to see this through and with heart wrenching anticipation. It was very obvious once again, how abusive the court system can be, without any due regard to people, their feelings and their lives. However, as I struggled unmercifully to open myself to the knowledge that everything happens for a reason, somewhere deep within me, I accepted. Though distraught with grief, I believed this was a blessing of some sorts. The universe has a miraculous way of presenting other opportunities in order that the highest good prevails. I desperately needed to trust that despite how insensitive this judge had been, another judge would be there to see this trial through and to see it through with a compassionate conscious. The hardest challenge was waiting. Time was always passive, especially when results were anticipated.

Throwing my clothes over the chair, I dialed the phone, hoping to connect with Kailee and Emily. Allen picked up. Relaying the information I had, he then passed the phone to Kailee and Emily. What a relief to hear their tiny voices. Tomorrow I would most likely see them. Presumably, we would head back to Sarasota, resume our lives and wait patiently until the next trail date. As I was hanging up, my body caved onto the bed. The haunting visions of my brother's murder subsided over the months each time I attempted to sleep. Though in my mind's eye, I still managed to see images of this enormous samurai sword reducing Michael to nothingness, no matter what the time of day or night. I decided to think of Kailee and Emily. With that, I gently closed my eyes, praying for a peaceful sleep. Seven hours later, I awoke to a brilliantly sunny morning.

Chapter 37

Hurrying to get ready, I made my way upstairs to see Kris. She was packing her luggage, somehow knowing we would all be leaving today. We walked downstairs, into the dining area and grabbed some melon. The rest of my family was already present, guessing the events of the day. Soon enough, we were once again making our way to the courthouse. Today the sun shone as bright as it could possibly shine. A very slight nip was in the air, but tolerable it was.

As we all scurried inside, Connie met us right at the door, urgent with pending news. Walking fast, the barren room we sat in for endless amounts of time, became home to us again. All of us sat down. Connie began to explain that there simply was no judge who could reside over our case at such short notice. We would have to return home, until another judge could sit for Michael's murder trial. Momentarily, nothing was spoken. The silence was so strong, I finally said something to break the agony of a mere explosion soon to happen. "You mean to tell us that after almost two years of anticipating this trial, we would now have to wait for another date?" Nothing short of a slow-witted statement, Connie merely looked back at me, nodding yes. Again silence predominated the room. Jacob began to pace, keeping silent at the same time. My mother refused to believe that the trial was not going to take place. Questions began to fire at Connie from everyone and from every direction. Politely, she answered them. The courts would rearrange our plane schedules, accommodating our flights home today, regardless of availability. That was it. Two and a half days of waiting patiently and no trial. None of us truly would feel the impact of such neglect until a later time. The anger was not directed at Connie or David. It simply was an anger that had nowhere to go.

As a last ditch effort I found Mr. Dunn's office, asking if I could please talk with him. He nodded, telling me to sit down. Not even a moment to spare,

I could feel my blood rising. With sincere intent I professed my disappointment, discrediting the court system's inability to treat the human race with dignity. Furthermore, I wanted David to fight for us, to reprimand the judge for his wrongdoings. He listened patiently. My final words to him were forthright. They grazed humility and anger simultaneously. He nodded. He knew his hands were tied, as were mine. Embracing his resignation, I gently gestured goodbye, thanking him all the same.

Unfortunately, I have come to know the injustices of the court system, despite the circumstances that put us there. David's ability to push harder for a judge to accommodate this trial was virtually impossible. It was no fault of his. He was a prisoner to the insolence of his surroundings. Months of preparation to prosecute the murderer meant nothing to the courts. For David, it was mere frustration and waiting. I came to know later that David and Connie were profoundly moved by our family's devout commitment to Michael and to this murder trial. Unknown to us, rarely did family members ever show up when someone was murdered in Lynn. David prosecuted many cases for a John Doe or a Jane Doe. No close to kin even came to claim the body. David was left to fight alone. We loved Michael. We would never forsake him. This made David that much more frustrated. He felt our devotion. He even shared our pain. He too was a parent who adored his children. Delays troubled everyone, including David.

Walking away like a dog with a tail in between our legs, my family and I felt persecuted, lost, bewildered and very, very tired. As we found our way back to the hotel, there simply were no words to convey what we wanted to express to one another. Kailee and Emily would be coming soon. Our flight was to leave in three hours. Checking out, Jacob, Mom, her friend, Kris, Jay and I sat around a round table in the dining room, quietly attempting to review the past days' events. Our luggage was securely set in our vehicles. More waiting. A very humbling lesson. Often what we want control over, there is none.

Two beaming girls came running into the dining hall, embraced with warm and tender hugs. Kailee and Emily were here full of inquiries, with little information to give to them. A bright moment in our day.

Chapter 38

I had a lot of time to think on the plane ride back to Florida. My mind wandered every which way it could. The girls were amusing themselves pleasantly. Though anxious to resume our lives again, I was taken aback by my inability to look forward to another day. One of my greatest strengths was my passion for living. Though such passion was somewhat muddled in the last few years, now, I was stunned, too emotionally tired to even care. These last few days brought me to another earthly reality that timing is everything and staying in the moment is a very good place to be. Whatever my passion, I could no longer locate an ounce of it. Building myself up for what I thought would be a tremendously painful trip, turned out to be even more draining and more distressing. There was still no resolve to Michael's death. Perhaps there would never be. Convicting his alleged killer would not bring Michael back, nor would it end the torment I experienced over his death. This gut-wrenching, searing emptiness welling in my soul, only escalated to heights of emotion that literally and physically ripped me apart inside. If my passion was there it was surely superimposed by this wretched ache. Finally, my eyes shut.

We landed in Sarasota. Kailee and Emily were anxious to get home. The distinct odor of Florida became acutely visible to us. April 18th brought sweltering temperatures and tremendous humidity. The second we walked outdoors, every pore of our bodies experienced the intense heat. Despite the fact that it was 8:30 p.m., there was no respite or comfort for our tired bodies. However, the warmth somehow soothed my pained soul. Collecting our bags, we headed to our car, quietly left in its place in long-term parking. Making our way inside, I immediately turned on the air conditioner. Traffic was sparse. Home was but ten minutes away. Rounding the corner to our street we could glimpse the side of our house. Kailee and Emily would go back to school tomorrow. I was off for another three days. Though I could opt to resume my work tomorrow, I decided I would not return until the following Monday.

As usual, my loyal canines were ecstatic for our arrival. Nothing could have sufficed as their loyal love for us was supremely generous. The house was cool, the way I had left it. None of us had any desire to unpack our suitcases. Kailee and Emily took out what they needed, showered, ready to relax before their evening sleep. Their homework had been finished back in Boston, thus, they were free to enjoy the rest of the evening, at least the next hour. It was obvious that Succi and Stella were anxious for an evening walk. Given the fact that much of my last days were either spent sitting in a desolate courtroom waiting, or sitting and waiting in a restaurant with my family or sitting, waiting on a plane, I was more than happy to oblige them. Slipping on shorts and a tee shirt, I gathered the dogs, their leashes and we headed out the door.

The night was impeccably still. Hoards of stars shimmered throughout the night sky. Nothing moved. The intensity from the heat was overwhelming. Yet, I managed to allow myself to slip into the unconsciousness of the night, obliterating from my mind the previous day's events. Rounding the bend to our block, Succi and Stella seemed most content. It was getting late. The exhaustion from my trip had finally took hold of me.

My home was peaceful. Candles, plants and gentle music filled my space with a loving warmth. As I kissed Kailee and Emily goodnight, without warning, I could feel my frustration mounting. Regardless of the serenity I experienced inside my home, I was struck by the discord inside myself. No sense could be made out of the last three days. Perhaps none was suppose to be made. Yet the unsettledness pushed me to a motivation I would not have suspected.

Well into the wee hours of the morning I began to compose a letter to Judge Bonner, the judge who was suppose to sit at Michael's murder trial. Rewriting and erasing I attempted my final draft. I was hardly comfortable with being told that my family and I would have to wait for yet another trial date. I was also well aware this letter may never get to him, nor would I ever receive an answer. There was not much to lose and without expectation, my thoughts flowed from my deepest feelings. My intent was not to blame, rather if remotely possible, my intent if anything was to inform Judge Bonner. I wanted him to know what it may have been like to be a family member of a loved one who barbarically died in his city as opposed to being a perpetrator in his courtroom. I wanted him to know how painfully difficult it would be to rehash the horror of how my brother was desecrated unmercifully. I wanted him to be aware that none of our lives would ever be the same, nor would our feelings of humility and frustration ever be acknowledged by his unilateral decision to opt to go to Paris than to sit for this trail.

My expressions spoke of genuine pain and genuine anger. The cold, barren, icy walls of a linear courtroom setting seemed to be reflective of his decision to dismiss this trail for another date. I signed the letter, stamped it and set it out on the mailbox for the mailman to retrieve later in the day. Falling onto my bed, I attempted a few hours of sleep before the sun would soon awaken me.

Chapter 39

A week later, as I was returning from picking up Kailee and Emily from their prospective activities, I noticed a yellow envelop sticking out of my mailbox. Running, the girls opened the latch, handing me the mail. Glancing down, I distinctly read the return address: Massachusetts District Court. With my heart racing in trepidation and in anticipation I opened the letter. Michael's murder trial was set for June 1ˢᵗ of this year. Less than one and a half months away, this would be the final date. A woman judge was assigned to the case. Without a shadow of a doubt, this trail was going to take place. Overcome with emotion, I turned away from the girls, allowing tears to saturate my face. It was done. Though I never formally received a response from Judge Bonner, it was quite apparent that whoever got this letter in hand, solidified results quickly. I was very grateful and sorrowful equally. There was nothing I could have done to make my pain over Michael's death go away. Some days were better than others. Some days were horrifically haunting. Once again, gathering the tenacity of spirit and courage to face this ordeal was momentous. The girls would pack for six weeks in the summer as their school year would be finished. They would stay with their Dad, while the rest of my family would sit through the trial.

Arrangements were being made well in advance to ensure a comfort level in my home for my dogs and my children. Kailee and Emily would be allowed to finish out the school year, not missing the last week of school with friends and collective parties. That was very important to me and for the girls. Kailee and Emily needed a semblance of continuity and balance in their lives. However, the day after school ended, they would be boarding two flights, rush into Boston, exchange parents and hug goodbye until I saw them in August. As for me, I would race to Salem again, tuck myself inside a very lonely hotel room and wait patiently for the trial to begin.

Chapter 40

Nearing the end of the flight path, the skyline of Boston once again became visible. Meeting the children's father at the airport was done smoothly and without any impediments. After a few words were exchanged, I quickly secured my rental car with the hopes of being in Salem by 8:00 p.m. I would then meet the rest of my family, go over some details for the following day and attend the first murder trial in my life and hopefully my last. Vehemently kissing my children goodbye, I told them I would call at the end of the week. Zooming past people, luggage, porters and security personnel, I obtained a compact car, darting out of Logan Airport only to be deadlocked, bumper to bumper in traffic. So much for meeting with my family on time. There was not much I could do but sit and wait. Apparently this was becoming a common thread in my life, waiting, being forced to stop, merely attending to the very moment I was in. Nonetheless, I waited.

What appeared to be a long, arduous time, traffic finally moved. A long sigh came out of me. The confinement of being stationary in an immovable vehicle for over a forty-five minute period was enough to make me want to scream. Yet, despite the circumstance, somehow my patience became a huge factor in helping me to get beyond this trivial stuff. Amazingly, I found my way into Salem, in front of a lovely hotel with plenty of parking. Getting out, I gathered my belongings, checked in at the front desk inquiring if any of my family members had yet to arrive. To my surprise, no one else was here. In many respects, I took this as an opportunity to unpack, shower and unwind. Quietly, I entered my room, quite stately in nature. This room was bigger than my last one, not nearly as warmly furnished though. Sensing a bath might be good, I walked into the bathroom only to be dismayed with finding a shower available to me. However, this space was much bigger and more accommodating. Throwing my clothes onto the freshly made bed, I scurried into a very hot shower, temporarily cleansing myself of the pain and the dread of the unknown days to come. Feeling somewhat refreshed, I dried my hair. I then pulled out a book I had brought with me. Already halfway through it from previous weeks, my mind wandered away from the pages in front of me. My concentration was gone as my eyes shut periodically while I lay on the bed. A gentle knock appeared on my door. As I asked who was there a familiar voice responded back, "It's Jacob." Extremely grateful to hear his voice, I wrapped a rope around me and opened the door. We hugged and talked for a few moments. Jacob's room was below my floor, around the corner. He wanted to clean up before mom arrived with her friend. We agreed to meet downstairs in a half an hour.

Fatigue was somehow winning me over. More than relaxed, I could barely move. All I needed to do was to dress and wait downstairs. My body collapsed down onto the bed again, where I fell into a deep sleep for approximately ten minutes. Awakening, I bolted upright realizing I needed to be downstairs shortly. Flinging on a pair of jeans, I ran a brush through my ear, put some lipstick on and ran to meet Jacob. My state of mind was disoriented. Awakening abruptly, I was yet to be fully present. Jacob and I decided we would head to the dining room where we sat at the bar. Though alcohol never appealed to me, I ordered a glass of wine, sipping slowly as conversation was exchanged generously about Michael. Quiet pauses ensued, along with reflections of time spent with him. We even managed to emit laughter about those moments when laughter was shared with Michael. It was again, terribly bittersweet. Jacob exclaimed that it was very difficult for him to enjoy a Yankees Game. The last time Jacob saw Michael was the time they participated as spectators in Yankee Stadium in the fall of 1995, one week before he was savagely killed. It was most apparent how vulnerable we were and how susceptible to our emotions we would always be when discussing Michael. Stares and silences were sufficient. Finishing, we both walked to the front desk to find out that our mother had arrived and had attended to her room on the third floor.

Climbing in the elevator, I had a flashback to when Michael was ten and I was nine. We had gotten stuck in the elevator in our grandparent's apartment building in the Bronx. I became terrified and began to cry. Michael was so distressed over me being upset, he pushed all the buttons at once. Miraculously, the elevator gently slowed to the ground floor, opening the door for us. Michael waited for me to get off. He then jumped out, his face too, as white as a ghost, though he never let on that he may be afraid. As usual, he was concerned about me.

Jacob and I found my mother's room. We knocked on the door. Mitch, her friend and companion for years answered, directing us to our mother. We all hugged. It was terribly difficult to comprehend the illogical state of why we were all here in the first place. Yet, such absurdity was a reality. It was a reality that exuded excruciating emotions of the most profound variety. Discussing dinner plans, we directed ourselves to the hotel dining room. Appetites were sparse, the time was getting later and later, but such a gathering gave us some strength in the sense that we were together and we would get through this.

After a brief and casual meal, we all excused ourselves and dispersed to our prospective rooms. Preparing early, I ironed what I was going to wear for tomorrow. Too late to call the kids. It was 11:18 p.m. Climbing into bed, though physically pooped, I simply could not fall asleep. My body was immobilized from exhaustion. My head was spinning with unknowns. Staring up at the ceiling, restless in thought, did nothing for my comfort level. Momentarily, I had this picture of an enormous sword in my mind, soaked in blood, oozing with a jealousy and a hatred of a faceless killer, holding the weapon. That is all I could think of. It was deplorable, this vision that came and went whenever it chose. Angry at myself for even allowing these pictures to supersede my will, made me feel that much more defeated. Slowly and with genuine deliberation, I struggled to shut my eyes. I needed to sleep. I was desperate. My stares won out. 6:30 a.m. came. I could barely move.

Chapter 41

My body ached. Perhaps it was preparation for what was to come. Lacking inspiration, I crawled out from under the covers, walked to the bathroom, locating the nozzle in the shower. Vaporizing the bathroom, I gladly stepped inside the stall, smothering myself with warmth. June 1st, 1997. The thermometer outside my window read only forty-nine degrees, a far cry from the blue skies and ninety-one degrees in Florida. Standing under the nozzle for what appeared a sufficient amount of time to coat myself with an incandescent glow, I was ready to get out. Rapidly, I dressed, blew my hair dry, put on some make-up, grabbed a light sweater and made my way downstairs to the main foyer of the hotel. A quiet anxiety festered in my solar plexus. Nothing would have stopped me from being here, yet, to be here in a place that spoke of only tragedy and an unspeakable atrocity brought me to a suffering that bore through me. I simply did not know how to manage such discomfort. Furthermore, not being able to handle such emotion only served to heighten my pain.

Jacob appeared out of the corner of my eye. Dressed in a suit and tie, he was coming down the stairs looking quite somber. Noticing me, he made his way closer to where I was standing. Exchanging hugs and a silence, we waited for our mom and her friend. Not withstanding the silence, my mother finally appeared looking horribly distressed. No one was particularly hungry. However, a good cup of coffee was agreed upon before we trekked over to the courtroom. Little conversation being said, all of us in tow, walked sadly to a destination none of us wanted to be privy to. Entering the courtroom we were immediately met by Connie and David. The plan was to direct us to a room out of earshot and eyesight of the killer's family. In that instant however, my glance caught a woman's stare way on the other side of the hallway, where eyes meeting eyes was a powerful as it could be. I said nothing. She said nothing. I later found out that woman was the killer's wife. In my heart of hearts, I never wanted to feel any animosity for her family. In many respects I felt terribly sorry for them, knowing all too well they would carry with them a horrendous burden for the rest of their lives. Yet, I also felt a dislike for them. It was such an imposing emotion. One, I know, was unreasonable as well.

Walking briskly into Mr. Dunn's office, David sat us down and very compassionately explained to us who would be sitting on the bench and approximately how long the trial would last. We knew we would be here no longer than a week, possibly shorter. David was very confident with the prosecution and he was eager to see Jerry Cooper put away. He was sure he could prove beyond a reasonable doubt that Mr. Cooper premeditated this vicious murder. It was all so foreign to us. Our hearts were tattered and broken, our minds were confused, our souls tortured. The best we could do was to be here, for Michael's sake and for his honor, despite the fact he had none when he was being hacked to death.

Quietly, Connie walked us through empty, cold corridors to another hall, down a stairway leading to the courtroom. Entering to the back of this lofty and very unfeeling room, we all noticed Mr. Cooper's family congregating on the left side, waiting for the trial to begin. We were escorted to the right side of the room, a stone's throw from their view of us. A big, rather strong looking bailiff was placed in front of our row, right next to Jacob, where he stood throughout the ensuing days of this trail. It was apparent that this was done deliberately. Somehow, placing an armed officer near Jacob suggested Jacob may have enough rage to jump over the rail and lunge at the murderer. Directly in front of our view, his back to us, was Michael's murderer, Mr. Cooper, shackled in hand and leg restraints. He looked enormous and rather menacing. He frightened me.

"Good morning Counsel. Ladies and gentlemen, my name is Eliza Dooley and I am an Associate Justice of the Superior Court. There are two indictments against Mr. Cooper. The first alleges that on October 14th, 1995, Mr. Cooper did assault and beat Michael Barg with the intent to murder him, in a most cruel and atrocious manner. Such assault and beating resulted in the murder of Michael Barg.

The second indictment alleges that a home invasion did occur at the home on 8 Preston Road in Lynn, Massachusetts. The home invasion was against Michael Barg and another occupant in the home, Diedre Fort. The defendant, Jerry Cooper denounces that he is guilty of any of the crimes charged in those indictments. It is imperative for you to understand that when you sit as a witness in this case, if you know anything about this case or anyone on this case, your ability to be fair and impartial may be affected. Once you are sworn in, you will have taken an oath that says you will render a true and just verdict.

I will begin with Counsel for the Commonwealth. Please introduce yourself." "Thank you your Honor. Ladies and gentlemen, my name is David

Dunn. I am an Assistant District Attorney. It will be my responsibility to present the evidence for the Commonwealth."

"And the counsel for Mr. Cooper?" " Good morning ladies and gentlemen. My name is Jake Botere. I am a lawyer in the Commonwealth of Massachusetts. I have offices in Boston. It is my privilege to defend Mr. Cooper."

The moment Mr. Botere said that it was his privilege to defend Mr. Cooper, I literally got sick. I understand that a defense attorney's responsibility is to defend his client despite whether he may be guilty or not. My insides ached. I could not defend someone who I honestly believed was lying. Although, such evidence had yet to be established beyond a reasonable doubt, I knew that Mr. Botere knew that his client was guilty. My gut spoke of it and from the moment the trial began, I had lost all respect for Mr. Botere.

Judge Dooley continued, addressing the jury: "We anticipate approximately seven days to try this case. The court is empathetic to the time that is being taken out of your lives. However, the constitution in Massachusetts states that all of us must perform our civic duty and sit as a juror. We will do everything to expedite the trial. But you are required to perform your civic duty. I have a number of questions to ask you before the trial begins. If any of you answers yes to these questions, please hold up the yellow card that we have given you.

Are any of you related to the attorneys, to Mr. Cooper or any of the potential witnesses in this case? Have any of you have any interest or stake in this case of any kind? Have any of you expressed or formed any opinions about this case? Are any of you aware of any prejudices that you have for either the prosecution or the defense? Is there anyone here who does not comprehend that in any criminal case the defendant is presumed innocent until proven guilty? Is there anyone here that does not comprehend that the Commonwealth has the burden of proving guilt beyond a reasonable doubt and that the defense does not have to present any evidence in its own behalf? Do you all understand that if there is an issue of lack of criminal responsibility, the Commonwealth must prove that the defendant was legally sane at the time of the alleged crimes? If there is an issue of lack of criminal responsibility, is there anyone here that does not understand that the Commonwealth has the burden of proving legal sanity at the time of the alleged crime? Is there any evidence of the defendant's consumption of alcohol and/or drugs that would impair your ability to listen objectively to all of the evidence, rendering a true and just verdict? Do any of you have any reason why you would not be fair and impartial and be able to render a true and just verdict based solely on the evidence and the law? Finally, is there any reason you would not be able to perform your civic duty?" No yellow cards were raised.

Furthermore, the judge said, "The indictments presented here are simply accusations. They are not evidence of guilt and you will not consider them evidence of guilt. In a criminal case, the burden of proof is on the Commonwealth. The Commonwealth has brought the accusation. Thus, the Commonwealth has the burden of proof. The Commonwealth must prove beyond a reasonable doubt each and every elements of the crimes which are charged in those indictments. It is a rule of law that compels each and every one of you, the jury, to find the defendant not guilty unless and until the Commonwealth convinces you from evidence that they introduce beyond a reasonable doubt that the defendant is guilty as charged. The presumption of innocence stay with the defendant all during the course of this trial. If at the end of the trial the Commonwealth has failed to sustain its burden of proving the defendant guilty beyond a reasonable doubt, you shall find the defendant not guilty."

I was feeling terribly overwhelmed by the wordiness in the presentation to the jury. I was only hoping the jury took everything in as sensibly as possible. However, the closing remarks to the jurors by the judge was exceptionally clear to me. The jury needed to determine the facts of the case. Once they determined the truth, they needed to speak the truth and render a verdict. In a nutshell, that was their responsibility. Also, it was made doubly clear-cut that no juror could discuss the case among themselves or with anyone else until deliberations were discussed to find a verdict. Any premature conversation could affect the outcome of the verdict, supporting or contradicting evidence. Objectivity was essential.

Opening statements began with the prosecuting attorney, David Dunn: "Ladies and gentlemen, at 12:30 a.m. on October 14th, a Saturday morning, 1995, this man sat in his home in Medford. He had a few drinks. He took a couple of pills of anti-anxiety medication. He also wrote a note to his wife saying, Cally, I'm sorry, and I do love you, Jerry." David continued by saying that Mr. Cooper went to his house to specifically get a samurai sword where he then proceeded to take the sword and get into his car. Mr. Cooper drove his car to a friend's house, leaving a note stating that he was sorry for what he was about to do, disposing a large amount of money at that house. He did not communicate with anyone there. He then went to 8 Preston Road, got out of his car and approached the home. Walking up the stairs, with the samurai sword in a sheath and a billy club in the other hand, Mr. Cooper opened the front door of the house. The key he had in his possession no one knew about. The locks had been changed on that house to specifically prevent Mr. Cooper from entering that home. Mr. Cooper walked inside the dwelling. There were three people living there. Sleeping on the third floor was Derrick Simpson, a retired state trooper and a friend of Mr. Cooper's. Diedra Forte, a woman whom Mr. Cooper had had an affair with, was sleeping in her bedroom on the second floor. Directly opposite Ms. Forte's bedroom was

Michael Barg's bedroom. He was also asleep. Mr. Cooper took the sword out of the sheath and proceeded to walk up the stairs. He went into the bedroom where Michael Barg was sleeping. He flipped on the light and began to swing the samurai sword at Michael. Mr. Barg awoke, attempting to get up, pleading in muffled cries to please stop. Mr. Cooper hit Michael Barg with such ferocity, the handle on the samurai sword broke, and he still, repeatedly hit Mr. Barg. Mr. Barg, out of reflex put up his hands to defend himself. Michael Barg was found face up on his bed, his legs over the bottom of his bed, where moans were audible out of Mr. Barg's mouth minutes after his brutal attack. All in all, twenty-three separate sword wounds were found on Michael Barg, where he was left to die and suffocate in his own blood. Of those twenty-three wounds, the majority of them would be fatal, leaving slices in his body and his head. Mr. Barg did die on his bed, with no chance of protecting himself. Mr. Cooper also waited until Mr. Barg died. He then left the room.

Mr. Cooper with the sword still in his hand, went across to the opposite room to where Diedra Forte was sleeping. Diedra Forte, six months earlier, had broken off the affair she and Mr. Cooper were engaged in. Mr. Cooper grabbed Diedra, dragged her across the hallway to Michael Barg's bedroom, holding her against her will in the doorway, making her look at the scene in the bedroom. "See what you made me do, see what you made me do," Mr. Cooper forcefully said.

It was Mr. Cooper's intention to kill both Michael Barg and Diedra Forte. Yet, in the moment as Mr. Cooper vehemently was holding Diedra, the love he had for her resurfaced. Mr. Cooper went back into Mr. Barg's bedroom and stood at the foot of the bed with the sword still in his hand. He walked out. He dropped the billy club in the hallway, threw the sword down in the floor of Ms. Forte's bedroom, where it remained there, stuck in the grooves of the floor. He then went outside, got into his car where he supposedly attempted to slash his writs, swallow a bottle of pills, all in the same time that he drove once around the block, again parking his car in front of the Preston home.

Pause. I was more than just aghast. My mother's face was streaming with tears, her pain so distinctly visible, so fragile she was, gasping each time she heard that Michael pleaded for his life. Jacob was terribly agitated, yet he remained composed, with tears visible in his eyes. My body slumped down out of sheer terror of what I just heard. These were mere opening remarks. I could not imagine what I would continue to hear. My heart ached so much, I began to have trouble breathing. Placing one hand on my heart and the other on my mouth, I closed my eyes with the hopes I could sustain myself from not passing out. My brother, my poor brother was savagely hacked to death in such a cruel and atrocious manner, he had to suffer. That in itself was enough. To die is one thing, but to die such a horrific and untimely, inhumane death was beyond description. My mother could never be the same. How could she? Michael was her firstborn child. She loved him unconditionally. How could she ever go on and expect to live a normal life? How could any of us?

Jake Botere introduced his opening remarks: "Good morning ladies and gentlemen. The issue in this case isn't going to be just whether or not Mr. Cooper was responsible for the death of Mr. Barg. The issue is going to be, ladies and gentlemen, whether or not Mr. Cooper was criminally responsible for the death of Mr. Barg, that is to say, whether or not at the time that conduct took place, which is as horrifying as you could possibly imagine. I have no qualms about saying that what bothers me the most about this case is whether or not you're going to be able to conform to the oath that you took. I am concerned whether you are going to be able to truthfully abide by the answers that you gave Judge Dooley with respect to whether or not you find the facts to indicate that Mr. Cooper is not criminally responsible. Hopefully you will return the verdict that I am going to be asking you again in closing arguments, the only verdict I suggest that the evidence in this case will dictate, a verdict of not guilty by reason of insanity."

At the precise moment, right after Mr. Botere's initial statements, all I could think of was how criminally irresponsible Mr. Botere was to even represent Mr. Cooper. Pleading insanity seemed a ludicrous plea, especially when Mr. Cooper knowingly took the time to stop, leave a note and proceed to do what he was going to do. Pleading insanity would allow Mr. Cooper to get away with murder, literally.

Mr. Botere summed up his opening statements by sharing that everything Mr. Cooper did was out of character for him as the evidence would state. Furthermore he exclaimed that Mr. Cooper was always a model citizen. Cooper went right into the armed forces soon after high school, he was discharged with an honorable discharge and his work ethic was impeccable. He continued by mentioning that Mr. Cooper was a very active man, involved with running and outdoor activities. He also had a good sense of humor. Apparently though, on the night of Michael's murder, such humor would never surface. Only the dark side would be visible, a dark side that no one ever wanted to acknowledge in Mr. Cooper, most likely in my opinion because they feared it.

Finally, Mr. Botere said that Mr. Cooper had been married for some twenty years. Some years prior he had also met Diedra Forte. She had been a waitress at the Mariott Hotel Mr. Cooper had bartended at. He was very helpful to Ms. Forte, giving her additional money whenever she needed it, buying her gifts and sending her on trips. Eventually Mr. Cooper became unfaithful to his wife. He began to have an affair with Ms. Forte. Ms. Forte also became quite friendly with Mr. Cooper's wife. Diedra and Mrs. Cooper exchanged numbers and went on outings together.

Enough was said about Mr. Cooper. Nothing in my mind allowed me to believe that Mr. Cooper was indeed a model citizen. Rendering judgment would not justify my feelings. Yet, because I was only human, I decided that Mr. Botere was digging a hole for himself and for Mr. Cooper. Mr. Botere was justifying the murder of Michael. Finally, Mr. Botere concluded that Mr. Cooper was cognizant of the fact that he could never hold onto Diedra Forte, regardless of how obsessed he was with her.

Michael, Diedra and Mr. Cooper had met in a sales transaction months prior, only briefly. All three of them exchanged conversation. Michael had stated to Mr. Cooper how attractive his girlfriend, Diedra was. Fatal mistake number one. Months thereafter, Diedra broke off her affair with Mr. Cooper. Diedra knew that Mr. Cooper was very controlling and had a threatening temper, despite the many moments Mr. Cooper was genuinely giving to her. A few months after their break-up, Michael called Diedre to get together. Diedra accepted.

Mr. Cooper was a married man and he knew that. He realized Diedra never really loved him. He did however, always love her. Diedra and Michael saw each other twice intimately. They were never boyfriend and girlfriend. They became friends and maintained a very casual and unassuming friendship. Mr. Cooper kept calling Diedra after their break up, insisting on talking to her for. He was becoming raged that he was unable to locate her. Again, he phoned Diedra. This time Diedra was home. She picked up. Mr. Cooper was screaming at her inquiring about her previous whereabouts. Diedra was so incensed, she told Mr. Cooper that she had in the past, been out with Mr. Barg. Fatal mistake number two.

Michael was looking for a new place to live. Diedra had an open room in the Preston house. The third floor was being occupied by retired State Trooper, Derrick Simpson, also a friend of Mr. Cooper. Months before, Mr. Cooper had gone to meet with Derrick at his apartment. He noticed the new key on Derrick's wall. Mr. Cooper stole that key, made a copy out of it and eventually put it back, supposedly without Derrick knowing as such.

Eventually Mr. Barg moved in. It was very clear that Michael had his own room and Diedra had hers. That unknowing decision was the final and most fatal mistake for Michael. Mr. Cooper became insanely jealous of Michael believing in his very abusive and controlling mind that Michael and Diedra were having a fullblown relationship. The only relationship that was truly visible was a mere friendship.

Cooper felt replaced. He assumed Diedra dismissed him for someone else. Diedra wanted out. Yet, she was terrified of Cooper. Michael, unknowingly presents an opportunity to Diedra, a glimmer of hope. Michael comes into the picture, so to speak, unsuspected of Cooper's rage. Though Michael sensed that Mr. Cooper was strange, Michael never fully understood the impact of Mr. Cooper's rage. For months on end, Mr. Cooper was furious at the fact that Michael had seen Diedra. Twice to be exact. He was beyond besieged with hatred for Michael. Thus, the hunt began. Plotting in his mind how he could kill Michael and Diedra, somewhere in Cooper's psyche, Cooper was going to win. There was absolutely no way Diedra would ever have Michael. Nor would Michael ever have Diedra. For all concerned, Mr. Cooper's vendetta meant murder. A murder that was the worst atrocity ever in the history of Lynn, Massachusetts.

Opening remarks were said. The court recessed for ten minutes. I simply sat with my family, saying nothing. All of us were immobilized from sheer pain. An eeriness permeated the courtroom. The bailiff remained still, statue-like, in front of Jacob, his hands clasped behind his back. The jurors came back silent in their pose, never looking any way but toward their seats. David Dunn and Jake Botere followed. Jude Dooley entered.

"All rise." Everyone stood up. "You may be seated." Everyone sat down. The prosecution called their first witness, John Whitaker, a commercial photographer. David Dunn began his examination: "Where do you presently live?" Whitaker said, "8 Preston Road. I reside on the right side of the home. At the time it was a two-family house." Dunn continued: "Who lived on the left side?" Whitaker proceeded: "The left side of the home was occupied by Diedra Forte, Michael Barg and on the third floor was another resident, Derrick. I believe his last name was Simpson." Dunn asked, "Who owned the house at that time?" Whitaker answered, "My father-in-law, Austin Cornell." Dunn continued, "At that time were you married and has there been any change in the house from then to now?" Whitaker said, "At that time I was not married. I am now. The house has been converted back to its original single family dwelling."

Dunn went on to ask a myriad of other questions ranging from Whitaker's whereabouts on the night of October 14th to what he was doing and his actions thereafter. Whitaker responded by saying that earlier on Friday the 13th, he was in the Bay Tower Room in Boston, proposing to his girlfriend. He went on to say that many of his employees, neighbors and friends had known of his pending proposal. Whitaker had left the Tower Room approximately at 10:00 p.m., returning home to announce their engagement to his in-laws, who resided directly behind the house on 8 Preston Road. When Whitaker and his fiancée had arrived home it was around 10:45. At that time Whitaker announced the news. A bottle of champagne was opened. Employees, other friends and neighbors began coming in to celebrate the news. The celebration was still going on at 1:00 a.m. in the morning, October 14th. At around 1:20 a.m., Whitaker was opening another bottle of champagne when he had heard a distinct commotion at his back door. Whitaker's fiancée began screaming. She yelled for Whitaker. She shrieked, "Joe, Joe." Whitaker immediately ran over to his fiancée where he saw Diedra Forte. Whitaker had only known Diedra casually. Whitaker had just moved into the right side of the house late in August.

Diedra was only wearing a long tee shirt. She was hysterical. She had been screaming and crying uncontrollably. Whitaker's mother-in-law and fiancée grabbed Diedra attempting to soothe her. Diedra continued to scream saying that there was a huge fight, a terrible argument at her house. Diedra yelled wildly. Whitaker realized, in between Diedra's intermittent sobbing, that something terrible had happened at the house. Whitaker ran to the back of 8 Preston Road, about one hundred feet from his in-law's home. He approached the kitchen. Many lights were on. There was also an uncanny silence in the home. Whitaker passed through a hallway and saw another roommate, Derrick standing at the base of the staircase. Derrick appeared very shocked, possessing a glassy look on his face. Derrick said nothing to Whitaker. Whitaker happened to notice a gray Volvo sedan parked in front of the Preston house with its lights still on. Whitaker then turned his head and looked over to the stairwell noticing blood all over the front foyer. Whitaker rushed throughout the rooms, looking in the downstairs rooms, only to find nothing. He then noticed a long trail of blood leading up the stairs. He followed the blood up the staircase also detecting bloodstains on the walls. Focusing on the Oriental rug in the middle of the floor near the balcony, Whitaker recollected seeing an object sitting there. He thought it was a broken chair leg. Whitaker never touched the object but proceeded to walk straight into Diedra's room. Nothing was in there. Whitaker then went into the opposite room. Every light was on. Peeking into the room, he saw a body on the bed, covered in blood. Whitaker became dazed. Immediately he looked away. He then went back inside realizing what he had seen. Whitaker was grossly taken aback. He realized that he had seen a naked body on the bed with hideously, severe wounds all over the body. Assuming that there was nothing Whitaker could do, he ran to find a blanket to cover the body. He also realized how terribly severe the situation was. Whitaker then heard people downstairs and in a moment of cognizance, his response was not to let anybody see what he had just seen. Whitaker ran downstairs. He told his father-in-law not to go upstairs. He said he believed that Michael Barg was dead. A call to 911 was made. Whitaker had only known Michael for a very short amount of time as Michael had just moved in two weeks prior. Whitaker said that Michael was horrifically unrecognizable.

At that distinct moment, I noticed my mother trembling. It was terribly obvious the excruciating agony she was in. Paralyzed in my own anguish, I could not comfort her. No one could. Jacob put his head down, tears streaming down his eyes. The dignity Michael never had ripped us to pieces, let alone that fact that he was not recognizable to the human eye. Michael had piercing blue eyes with a gleaming smile. He had thick, gray hair cropping his face. He was considered exceptionally handsome. What was left of him on that bed was unimaginable to me.

Whitaker went on to say that two police officers arrived at the home within minutes. Whitaker directed them to the stairwell. Both officers ran up the staircase without question. Whitaker stood downstairs and waited. Silence. Seconds passed when all of a sudden Whitaker heard one of the offers yell out loud, "Jesus Christ! Call the Sergeant, call someone." They were screaming. One of the officers ran downstairs. The other remained upstairs. Whitaker cleared out of the house to check on his fiancée. Diedra was being taken care of by his mother-in-law. She was offered some clothes and a pair of shoes to put on. Diedra was terrified to go back into her house. Whitaker's mother-in-law offered Diedra a place to stay for as long as she needed.

Mr. Dunn had no further questions for Mr. Whitaker. Attorney Jake Botere did not want to cross-examine. Mr. Whitaker stepped down. The second witness to be called to the stand by David Dunn was Officer Haverill. Again David began to ask questions that would clarify answers of details of what this Officer had witnessed and what actions were taken. Haverill merely described what had taken place when he arrived at the scene of the crime.

Haverill had only been an officer for three years. When he arrived at the house he noticed a gray vehicle with a body slumped over the wheel. The vehicle was parked on the side of the street. The body in the car was a white male covered in blood. Immediately, Derrick Simpson approached Haverill and began to exclaim excitedly that there was a person upstairs not breathing. Haverill went to his cruiser, took out a medical bag and darted toward the house. Concurrently, many police had begun to arrive. Haverill, along with another fellow officer went inside the house to the second floor. As Haverill was going up the stairs he noticed a considerable amount of blood all over the walls, the carpet and the floors. He also observed a billy club on the floor outside one of the bedrooms. In the entrance to one of the bedrooms, a sword was stuck in the floor. Haverill then saw a white male, lying face up, on his back, with legs dangling off the bed. Haverill began to evaluate if there would be any need for medical assistance. He then drew his service revolver, securing the second floor believing there was still a suspect inside the house. He found no one. His Sergeant, Sergeant Denno came inside, up the stairs, telling Haverill to go downstairs.

Cross-examination began. Jake Botere questioned Haverill about his whereabouts after he left the bedroom of Michael Barg. Haverhill said that he went to retrieve some crime tape to block off the crime scene. Once Haverill began to secure the area he observed EMT'S administering aid to a white man slumped over the wheel in the gray Volvo.

Redirect Examination by Mr. Dunn, "To your knowledge, did anyone attempt to administer aid to the person upstairs?" "Objection," said Botere. The

Court: "Sustained." Mr. Dunn: "Did you see anyone do that?" Mr. Botere, "Objection." The Court, "He may have that." Haverill answered, "No, we I didn't." Mr. Dunn, "Thank you. I have nothing further." Mr. Botere redirected cross-examination by asking Haverill if the condition of the body was that severe, could it be concluded that Mr. Barg was not alive? Haverill then answered, "Correct." He was then asked to step down.

Sergeant Denno approached the stand. David Dunn once again asked him to verify what Haverill had witnessed. It was concluded that the condition of Mr. Barg was horrendous. Denno stated that Mr. Barg was severely cut up. He had innumerable wounds and cutting injuries to his entire body. Denno could not help Mr. Barg. Denno's focus was on finding a suspect. He was not convinced one had yet to be apprehended. He then ordered his police officers to make another search in the house and outside the surroundings of Preston Road. Eventually Sergeant Denno walked downstairs out to the yard where he approached the back of an ambulance. Placing his right foot onto the step of the ambulance, he looked inside. The gentleman on the stretcher was identified as Mr. Cooper. Denno, looking up at a fellow officer in the ambulance had asked if a bad guy had been caught yet. Mr. Cooper turned his head slightly upward and said that he had killed the fucking bad guy. Immediately Sergeant Denno told his officer to read Mr. Cooper his Miranda rights. Denno then did a thorough search of the surroundings and met with other detectives arriving on the crime scene. Denno finally left at day break.

Why there was a trial in the first place threw me off guard, especially after hearing Denno's testimony. Mr. Cooper bluntly and outright admitted to killing Michael. It was almost as though Cooper took pride in committing such an act. Why in the world would a trial be necessary? The admission was made. What other evidence could there possibly be? Apparently, the Miranda rights also state that a person may have an attorney present. Mr. Cooper heard all of that when he was being read his rights. According to the testimony from the witnesses, no one remembers Mr. Cooper asking for one. Thus, when Cooper is brought in for questioning and is brought into lock-up, he now requests an attorney. Massachusetts law states the alleged suspect can have one. Botere now comes in the picture and recommends Cooper plead not guilty due to reason of insanity. Cooper agrees. Now a trail is in place, despite Cooper's disclosure of guilt.

In many respects this trial seemed like a mockery. Michael was brutally and savagely murdered. It was clearly obvious Cooper's intent to kill Michael. Jealousy is the oldest and most deadly of all emotions. People kill for love, though I hardly suspect Cooper even understood the meaning of love. Instead, Cooper's notion of relationship was rooted in possessiveness, self-centeredness and a need to control. Without that control, he felt helpless, useless, no longer the big man, no longer the man Diedra looked up to. Cooper's desire to placate his ego was far greater than setting Diedra free. Letting go meant defeat and Cooper could never live with that. What an insidious defense. Diedra knew of Cooper's ill will, his uncontrollable temper. Why would she jeopardize someone she thought was warm, kind and showed her compassion? Why did she not warn Michael? How senseless this all was. Michael died for nothing. He died because he was everything Cooper was not. Michael paid a very heavy price. A price that cost him, his life and a tortuous end to his being. Feeling distraught was an understatement to my actual state of mind. A five-minute recess was called.

Chapter 42

Again, we were all told to rise. Again, we were all told to sit. More witnesses were called to the bench. Justin Mackey appeared in front of the judge as he was being sworn in. He told the court he was a paramedic. Questions began with the prosecution. Mackey summarized. Mackey clarified again that he was a paramedic, not an EMT. There was a big difference. Paramedics can provide advance life support techniques, administer medications and they can execute a myriad of other life-threatening duties. EMT's cannot do as much medical work. Mackey disclosed that he had been a paramedic for over ten years. He also supervised and trained new paramedics.

Mackey received a call in the early am hours on October 14th about an incident two miles from his station. His response time to get there was three to four minutes. Once he arrived on site, he had noticed a host of police cars on the scene. He was instructed to an individual sitting in a Volvo in front of the dwelling. Mackey noticed that one of the officers was sick to his stomach, throwing up on the lawn because of what the officer had previously witnessed upstairs in the bedroom. Mackey turned his attention to the man in the Volvo and began to administer treatment to him. He observed a large amount of blood on the man's wrist. Mackey grabbed a towel, wrapping it around the wound on the wrist. Mackey also concluded that this wound was not arterial. It was not life threatening. The bleeding did not come directly from the heart. The bleeding was a lot slower. Mackey was assisted by another paramedic. Both men looked over the man, now known as Jerry Cooper. They cleaned up his arms and wrists, applied dressings and sent him off to another ambulance that would drive him to the emergency room. None of Cooper's wounds were devastating. Mackey accompanied Cooper into the ambulance, hearing Cooper repeatedly say, "I killed the fucking bad guy. I killed the fucking bad guy." The whole transaction between Mackey tending to Cooper's wounds and escorting Cooper into the ambulance was fifteen minutes. Mackey further concluded that Cooper was extremely coherent, alert, not in the least disoriented. His mental status was exceptionally clear. Finally, Mackey stated that during Cooper's time on the stretcher Cooper described in detail how he killed Michael Barg. Cooper smugly said, "I wanted to cut off his arms so he couldn't fight. I wanted to cut off his legs, so he couldn't run. I wanted to cut out his heart so he couldn't feel." David Dunn asked Mackey to reiterate if Cooper basically put it that way. Mackey answered, "Yes." Prosecution rested. My mother, my brother and I were sick to our stomachs.

Cross-examination began by Botere. Botere asked Mackey that if a person has no blood pressure then what happens? Mackey answered that I.V.'s would be administered. Mackey went on to say that Cooper's situation was not life threatening. Botere barraged Mackey with cross-examination that implied Mackey stated in the ambulance to other officers and paramedics that Cooper had no blood pressure and his pulse was very weak. Mackey denied he had said that. Botere forcefully interrupted Mackey, stating that he had said otherwise as written on the report made out on the morning on the 14th. He went onto to badger Mackey and exclaim that Mackey had indeed told others that Cooper was bleeding excessively, his blood pressure was not audible and therefore fluids had to be pumped into the veins. Mackey answered again, "It was not a life-threatening situation." Botere continued, "No sir. Assume that the conditions were life-threatening." Mackey replies, "You want me to assume?" Botere answers, "Yes. I want to assume what is in this report as…" "OBJECTION!" yells Dunn. Botere asks again, but in a different manner, "Is that a life-threatening situation when there is no blood pressure?" Mackey answers, "Yes."

Redirect examination by Mr. Dunn: "The report you were just shown. Did you write these statements?" "No," says Mackey. Dunn continues, "I'll show you these pages and ask you if those are a copy from the report you made at the scene?" Mackey replies, "Yes sir." "What do they state?" questions Dunn. Mackey says, " Cooper's blood pressure was 110/80. His pulse rate was 114. Mackey steps down.

What a disgrace to the legal system and to Botere. Botere portrayed everything but the truth. His adulterated impropriety at misrepresenting evidence, picking at straws to save his client was a low blow to humanity in general and especially to Michael. I almost felt humiliated for Botere. Observing him bulldoze answers and witnesses did nothing for his credibility. Instead, he left a blanket of minimization, undermining the system we apparently have in place to determine guilt or innocence. He was an actor. The courtroom was his stage. Money would be his reward, despite the outcome. Fortunately, Botere would not have won any Oscars.

It was approximately 2:00 p.m. I was just as anxiety ridden when I first sat early in the morning to hear opening remarks as I was now, sitting in the afternoon. Desire to eat was nonexistent. More witnesses were to testify today. Exhausted emotionally, heart broken and nettled with frustration, hearing more of Botere's counter examination was agonizing. I thoroughly disliked him because he knew he did not have a case. I disliked the fact that he manipulated, tugged on the truth and made witnesses out to be stupid. I especially disliked him because he was to collect a large sum of money despite the outcome for his client. I could only pray the jurors felt the same way.

A final witness stepped up to the podium for the day. He was Officer Jeremy Dell. Officer Dell described what he encountered when he arrived at 8 Preston Road. Originally he went to the vehicle where he saw a white male, behind the steering wheel with cuts on his wrist. The ambulance had yet to arrive. Within a three-minute period however, the ambulance came and immediately three paramedics got out and began to administer aid. As Dell got closer to the car, he heard Cooper say that he wanted to die. Dell left the car and watched two fellow police officers look terribly dejected and emotionally distraught, sitting on the lawn. Both officers had just come from inside the house. Dell went over to another Sergeant and the Sergeant said to Dell that the guy in the car was making incriminating remarks. Dell proceeded to watch the paramedics put Cooper on a stretcher. Dell identified himself to Cooper and read him his Miranda Rights. Dell asked Cooper if he had understood what was being read to him. Cooper said that he understood. Finally, Cooper asked Dell, "Is he dead. Is he dead?" Dell responded by asking him what he meant by that. Cooper said, "The guy upstairs, is he dead. I cut him real bad. Excuse me. I take that back. I cut him real good." Following Cooper to the hospital, Dell had asked Cooper, once they were in a room if Cooper wanted to talk. Cooper had said yes and began to unfold the details of how he planned to murder Michael and exactly what he did. Cooper's speech was calm, collected and very coherent. Cooper went onto to explain that he had awoken Michael up. After one massive blow to the head, Michael somehow was able to get out of bed. Michael attempted to defend himself, but Cooper, wildly and frenetically swung harder and harder at Michael. Michael desperately begging Cooper to stop, fell back onto the bed, lifeless. Cooper continued his brutal attack on Michael, striking Michael with such force, slashing his body continuously, blood splattered everywhere. Cooper finally left the room. He then grabbed Diedra across the hall, bringing her into Michael's room. Realizing he could not kill her, Cooper said to Diedra, "Look what you did." Conversation stopped. Officer Dell's Captain arrived, Captain Rhett. Dell and Rhett went to the station to file a report.

Sobbing, my mother was distraught beyond belief. Jacob was seething with pain and anger. I was a mess. None of us could comfort one another. Our pain was so immense, we were paralyzed by our emotions. This was the second time I had heard gruesome details about how Michael lost his life. Each time Michael's death was disclosed, more piercing facts would be revealed. It was a horrific nightmare. The day had yet to be over. Botere would be up next, attempting to discredit Dell. My stomach felt like it was going to throw up.

Botere wasted no time. In less than five minutes Botere continually questioned Dell's accuracy about what he had written on the report. They ranged from Cooper's alcohol level to his intoxication level if any, to his eyes being glazy, to his mind and speech being incoherent and to his laceration on his wrist. It was a nonstop bombardment of attempts to get the jury to see that Cooper could not be accountable for his actions. Dell answered with a coolness and a calm and with a forthrightness that left everyone believing Dell. Eventually he was asked to step down.

Much was happening at Godspeed. I was sure the court would be recessed until the next day. Dell would be the last witness. I was wrong. One more was added with the hopes to expedite the trial and the eventual verdict. Terry Earnhardt was sworn in. David Dunn asked what she did, where she worked and her relationship to Jerry Cooper. Terry replied by stating that she had met Mr. Cooper at one of the lounges at Logan Airport. She had been employed there for almost eight years as a bartender. She and Mr. Cooper worked the same shifts with the same hours. She had known Cooper since 1987. David Dunn had asked if she had known Diedra Forte. Terry said that she did. She knew Diedra since 1987.

Dunn had questioned Terry about Cooper's temper at work. Terry disclosed that Cooper would get very angry with employees at various times throughout the work shift. He would literally snap at people, yelling at them with an intensity that often left others feeling as though they were walking on eggshells. Afterward, he would not talk to them at all. Some employees even broke down in tears. Days later, Cooper would justify his behavior by bringing in gifts to the people he intentionally had hurt. Or, he would merely ignore the fact that his actions even occurred.

Dunn went on to ask Terry if she knew that something more had manifested between Diedra and Cooper. Terry concluded that Cooper had approached her and told her that he was having an affair with Diedra. At this time, Terry had already left her job at the airport due to pregnancy. She and Cooper kept in touch via the phone, functions with mutual friends and family gatherings. Terry knew Cooper was married. Over the years, Terry had come to know Cooper's wife Cally. Terry pleaded with Cooper to tell his wife or to end the affair. Terry was terribly uncomfortable with the deception and she felt it was wrong. Eventually Terry revealed that Cooper and Diedra were having problems and much of their relationship was spent arguing. Both parties would break up and then get back together again. However, by the summer of 1995, the relationship finally terminated. Cooper was highly agitated. He lost control over Diedra. Terry concluded that he was very angry. He assumed Michael and Diedra were having a relationship. He felt exceptionally betrayed.

October 13th was the last time Terry had a conversation with Cooper over the phone. Terry was considering going back to work. She made a call to the bar and Cooper answered. Cooper was extremely upset. He began to tell Terry that Michael had come into the bar to be with Diedra. When in fact, Michael was merely coming in simply to say hello. They were roommates. Cooper went on to say that he and Michael had a loud confrontation. When in fact again, Cooper saw Michael enter into the bar, Cooper left his post at the bar and went over to where Michael was sitting, grabbed his arm and pulled Michael toward the door, for no apparent reason. Cooper was furious to see Michael at the establishment Diedra was working at. He had told Michael never to come in again. Cooper was asked to see management immediately.

The following morning, October 14th, Terry got up as usual, made breakfast for her children and later on, before noon she went to the mailbox. In it, an envelop from Cooper was there. Terry opened the envelope. To her dismay, thousands of dollars were located in a note. Terry handed the money to her husband who counted it. Five- thousand, seven hundred dollars to be exact. The note was as follows: "Terry, you are a good friend. I am sorry I did what I did, but I could not live like this. Love you, Jerry. This is a few dollars I have saved not going with Diedra. It's for you. I love my wife, but I cannot go on."

Terry's initial thought was that Cooper had committed suicide. She immediately called Cooper's home, but there was no answer. She proceeded to call friends and other family members. No answer. Finally, she called 8 Preston Road and Derrick Simpson picked up the phone. Terry was then told the details of what happened earlier in the morning.

Botere cross-examines. Botere suggested to Terry that Cooper and his wife Cally had a good marriage. Terry said that Cooper relayed to Terry that he loved his wife. Again Botere persisted that Cooper had a good marriage. Terry firmly answered that was not what she said. Cooper told Terry that he loved his wife. Botere went on to cross examine Terry about Cooper's devastation of his break-up, his anger with Michael Barg and his feelings of betrayal from Diedra. Terry replied that she suggested to Cooper in the spring of 1995, that Cooper get some help.

Early in September of 1995, Terry went to visit her husband one evening at Long Wharf in Boston where he worked. Incidentally, Cooper and his wife walked in simultaneously. Cooper sat down next to Terry disclosing his frustration with Michael and Diedra. Cooper could not let go of his anger. His entire conversation was centered on the resentment he still had toward Michael and Diedra.

It was very apparent that Cooper had a temper and anything could set him off. He was like a walking time bomb. Despite the fact that customers may have liked him as well as fellow employees, he was a bully and he used intimidation to hurt people. He would go to lengths to minimize anyone that posed a threat to him. Michael stood up to him one time. That in itself was humiliating for Cooper. Every portion of the testimony was evident of how angry, jealous and controlling Cooper was. Botere always attempted to paint the better side of Cooper. However, I knew differently. Cooper's dark side was ugly. The anger he possessed was of an intangible nature, such that no one really sees the visible wounds when they are inflicted onto another individual. There are no viable black and blues on people's bodies that speak of such anger and abuse. Cooper knew when he was angry and he knew how to use people to make himself look better. Remorse? Rarely for Cooper. The only genuine feeling he experienced was flat out inferiority. The irony was that Cooper's own inadequacy only served to minimize himself. However, Cooper would not want others to know that. It was all so obvious and all such a terrible tragedy for Michael.

I resorted back to my beliefs that there is a divine plan in the making for everyone. Was it divinely planned for Michael to meet Diedra? Was it divinely planned for Cooper to meet with Michael? Was it divinely planned for Michael to become a roommate at the Preston Home? Everything that happened to Michael, was it orchestrated for these events to take place? I was completely baffled. I understood that we all have the free will to change our lives. When opportunities present themselves, we have the ability to either take the opportunity or say no to it. If only Michael could have seen inside of Cooper. He did in a sense, but not with much seriousness. Perhaps we are not meant to see all the time. Perhaps we are merely meant to be without censorship. Michael was much too young to die. His death was terribly malevolent, without any justifiable reason. Yet, is there ever a way to reason with death, especially when it involves someone you are close to and you love? Maybe in time. Maybe in years, I would find peace with these questions. Maybe in time, my heart would mend. It was horribly heavy. It hurt. I hurt. I was terribly sad for Michael. I was terribly, terribly sad.

4:38 p.m. We would hear one final witness for the day. My eyes began to tear. I did not think I could get through one more testimony. All of it was so overwhelming. Then I thought of Michael. Reminding myself what he went through, I felt ashamed for my lack of strength presently. Recomposing myself, I listened and waited patiently, though my insides were most fragile and quite withered.

Derrick Simpson stepped up to the seat. Dunn proceeded by asking background questions and his knowledge of what he knew between Cooper and Diedra. Simpson had been a State Trooper for a good amount of years. He came to know of Cooper by being introduced to him through a friend. He and Cooper established a very solid friendship, sharing scuba diving, jogging and various other outings. Eventually Simpson knew that Cooper and Diedra were dating. Cooper told Simpson that Diedra was moving into a house and she needed roommates. That was in 1993. Simpson took the third floor bedroom, the only bedroom on that floor. On the second floor, Diedra inhabited one bedroom, while another woman lived in the bedroom opposite Diedra's. Cooper would come over often visiting Diedra and sometimes Simpson. Simpson was unaware that Cooper ever had a key to the house. In 1995, Simpson noticed there were problems arising between Diedra and Cooper. One day thereafter, Simpson was leaving to go outside to do errands when Diedra introduced Michael to Simpson. Simpson said that it was a pleasant exchange as each man shook hands. It was brief.

Toward the end of August or after Labor Day, Simpson saw Michael again. Michael had just moved into the bedroom opposite Diedra's. It had been vacant for quite some time. Prior to Michael moving in, Simpson overheard a conversation Diedra had had with Cooper on the phone. Every roommate had separate phone lines. It was late in the evening and Diedra was becoming highly agitated. In fact she was screaming on the phone. Diedra yelled for Simpson. He came down to calm her but she looked very frightened and distraught. She wanted to change all the locks on the doors and the windows. Two days later, all new locks were put into place. Simpson acquired a new key. He kept a spare key on the last kitchen cupboard door on a plastic hook.

Simpson received some phone calls from Cooper after the locks were changed. Cooper wanted to know who was now living there and when did they move in and for how long they had been there. Simpson described Michael physically to Cooper. He continued to answer Cooper's calls every time Cooper dialed Simpson. Simpson diligently relayed information to Cooper, as if he were implicating Michael to Cooper's inquiries. Cooper had asked if they ever had sex. Simpson willingly replied that only once did he hear them together before Michael actually moved in. That was it. Michael had separate living quarters from Diedra thereafter. Also, Cooper had no access to getting inside the house after Diedra changed the locks. Cooper suggested that he come over one day and both he and Simpson go scuba diving together. Cooper would pick Simpson up. While Simpson was rummaging through his closet to collect his belongings, Cooper found the spare key and confiscated it. He would later return the original key. That was what was surmised. Cooper had no other access to getting the new key. More calls eventually came from Cooper to Simpson. Simpson maintained his replies to Cooper.

I was outraged with this information. I could not understand why Simpson simply did not cut Cooper off from the get go. Simpson was being used as a pawn, a go-between and Simpson allowed it. Cooper appeared to have had this deadly hold onto people. Decidedly, I lost my respect for Simpson. I later found out that Simpson hid under his bed when Cooper was murdering Michael. He was frightened when he heard the sounds of the attack. Simpson knew Michael was viciously being hurt. A former State Trooper Simpson was and he hid. I was once again beside myself. To even hint to myself that maybe Michael could have been saved would be too much to bear. Stuffed down anger appeared to be my only outlet.

Finally, David Dunn asked Simpson the dreaded question, what he had heard on the morning of the 14th. Simpson said that he was watching the American Baseball League playoff games in his bedroom upstairs. He had heard footsteps coming into the house. Simpson assumed it was Michael. Diedra had come in earlier in the evening and was already asleep. That was approximately 11:00 p.m. He then heard Michael turn on the baseball game as well. Simpson shut off his television around 11:30. Michael shut off his at relatively the same time. Simpson fell asleep for a few hours. Simpson was awakened by sounds coming from the second floor. He heard the sound of pounding. It was as though it were a baseball bat or a fist. Simpson first thought he may have been dreaming, that it was a nightmare. The more awake Simpson became, the more voices became audible to him. There was a person screaming, "*Stop, don't, stop, don't.*" Simpson went on to say that the person he heard sounded as though he were in a lot of pain, in a lot of fear, in a lot of anguish and in a lot of terror. According to Simpson, the screeching lasted about three to four minutes. Simpson then heard broken screams coming from Diedra's bedroom. She was sobbing frantically telling Cooper to stop. Simpson put on a pair of shorts and a tee shirt and went downstairs. Before he got to the second floor, he observed a profuse amount of blood everywhere. He then saw Diedra hysterical in her bedroom. He told her to call 911. Afterward, he went into Michael's bedroom where he observed Michael lying naked on the bed, his legs prone toward Simpson, with an enormous amount of gaping wounds to his body. Out of instinct, Simpson went upstairs to gather a sweatshirt to help Michael. Simpson believed he could help stop the bleeding. After he returned from his bedroom, he heard a loud thud coming from the front door. Someone just left the house. Simpson went downstairs, but he could find no one. He went onto the porch and he still could not find anyone. He then noticed a light coming from a car that simply parked itself outside of 8 Preston Road. It was a gray Volvo. Simpson recognized this car to be that of Jerry Cooper's. Simpson never returned to help Michael.

Court was recessed. The judge concluded the day by saying that every member of the jury must fold their pens and their notebooks onto the chairs they were sitting on. They were not to discuss the case with anyone, nor could they discuss the case among themselves. They were also not allowed to read anything about the case or listen to any form of media. They were to be back in their seats by 8:50 a.m. tomorrow. Each member of the jury would find their pens and their notebooks on the chairs where they left them. They were dismissed.

We all rose. Not one person in my family said anything. Dinner was forthcoming. No one wanted it. Prospectively, we all headed in quiet directions. Intolerable sorrow transcended our beings. Crushing anguish penetrated too deep. Goodnights were not even exchanged. After Michael shut his television off that evening on the 13th, he had called our mother to tell her that he loved her. That would be the last time she would ever hear from Michael again.

Chapter 43

"All rise. Please be seated." Day two. Jacob, my mother, her friend and I sat in the same seats we sat in yesterday. The Honorable Judge had asked if any jurors violated what she had discussed with them the previous evening. Nobody raised their hands. Captain Rowan stepped onto the podium to be sworn in. He was Chief of Detectives for the police force in Lynn. Once again David Dunn began his inquiries. Once again, they were answered.

Captain Rowan explained that he received a phone call around 1:30 a.m. on the morning of the 14th of October. Conjecturing from information Rowan had at hand, he placed more phone calls to various detectives. By 2:00 a.m., Rowan was at the crime scene. Along with fellow officers Rowan scoured the house and the bedroom where the murder took place. He observed Michael still lying on the bed naked, again with massive wounds and blood splattered everywhere. He also concluded that no life was coming out of Michael. It was assumed that Michael was dead. Rowan talked with other police, detectives and EMT's on the scene. He left the dwelling approximately at 8:15 a.m., driving to Jerry Cooper's home. Callie Cooper answered the front door. Rowan identified himself asking if he could please come in. Mrs. Cooper let Rowan in. He then explained why he was there. He was led to a television room in the house where he confiscated an empty Sambuca bottle, a glass and a note that was written from Cooper to his wife saying, "Callie, I'm sorry, and I do love you, Jerry." These items were eventually brought down to the police station where they were processed for fingerprints and for further testing. Rowan escorted Mrs. Cooper down to Union Hospital in Lynn to see her husband. Once there, Mrs. Cooper went inside to see Cooper who was in the intensive care unit. Rowan approached the room stating that he needed to speak to Mr. Cooper. Mrs. Cooper had the option of leaving. She wanted to remain. Rowan advised Cooper of his rights under Miranda, asking if Cooper understood them. He had replied that he did.

Rowan went on to ask Cooper if he wanted to change any statement he had given to police earlier that morning concerning what had taken place on Preston Road. Cooper said that he did not. Rowan also asked Cooper if he was willing to talk to him now. Cooper acknowledged that he did. Cooper without emotion said that he had left his home in Medford, went to Lynn to kill Michael and Diedra and how he acquired the key to the Prescott home. Furthermore, Cooper described how he murdered Michael: "I went upstairs with a billy club and a sword. I dropped the club on the floor. I went over to where Michael lay asleep and I struck him very hard in the head. I continued to hit him all over. I walked across to Diedra's bedroom. I dragged Diedra across the hall to Michael's room. She pleaded with me not to hurt her. I wanted to kill her, but I still loved her. I couldn't." Dunn's final question to Rowan was if Cooper had mentioned to him that morning if Cooper had said anything about a psychiatrist. Rowan concluded that Cooper had told his psychiatrist whom Cooper was seeing prior to the murder that Cooper wanted to shoot Michael. Rowan had asked why he did not shoot Michael. Cooper said that he did not have a gun.

It was later found out that Cooper began to see a psychiatrist because he could not handle Diedra's association to Michael. Cooper was a married man. Diedra had relationships prior to dating Cooper. Michael had one official date with Diedra. No cross examination took place. Rowan stepped down.

Witness number two on day two of the trial took the stand. Dan Jenkins after being sworn in, alleged who he was. A bartender at the airport Cooper had worked at, Jenkins described his relationship to Cooper. Jenkins went onto conclude that Cooper was a friendly guy everyone looked up to. Jenkins added however that Cooper did have a temper and when his temper flared, Cooper was extremely verbally abusive. The next day Cooper would bring flowers or a card in to make up for what he did the previous day. Jenkins went on to describe how he saw a relationship unfold between Diedra and Cooper. Jenkins also went on to state that during the mid part of the summer of 1995, Michael Barg called on the phone to speak to Diedra. Jenkins answered the phone at the bar. It was at this point Cooper forcefully pushed Jenkins into the back room, screaming at him for allowing Diedra to speak to Michael. Jenkins said that this was a public place. Anyone had the right to do what they wanted. Eventually Jenkins concluded that he also observed the dissolve of Cooper's and Diedra's relationship over time. There was much tension at the bar between Diedra and Cooper. One night, Michael had come to the bar to say hello to Diedra. Continuing, Jenkins said that Cooper became so enraged that Michael was there, Cooper went over to where Michael was sitting and screamed at Michael. Michael walked away, out of the bar. Cooper was so furious he could not work anymore that evening.

Botere cross-examines the witness. Botere suggested that Jenkins and Cooper had a friendly relationship. Jenkins replies, "Sometimes." Botere asked if there were times they did not work well together. Jenkins replied: "We would not work well together because Cooper always wanted things his way. Cooper would always bring the tension to the bar." Botere inquired if receiving a personal call at the bar was against the rules. Jenkins again replied and said that no one abided by it. People had received personal calls all of the time, including Cooper. Botere further pushed Jenkins to explain what happens when an employee was not doing his or her own fair share of working harder. Jenkins explained that everyone kept their own tips. Waitresses tipped out money to the bartenders on their own accord. Botere again questioned that if a waitress was not quick enough, wasn't that enough reason for anger to be expressed? Jenkins said that it did not matter. Even though everyone may have wanted to work as a team, each waitress had their own customers and what they did and how they performed their job duties would only reflect on them.

Botere was trying very hard to justify Cooper's volcanic explosions. Somehow, justification did not come across. Dunn recrosses: "Was it out of character for Cooper to get angry?" Jenkins said, "No. He pushed me around." Botere recrosses: "You say he pushed you around. What do you mean?" Jenkins said, " One time, he got so mad, he punched me in the arm. It left a welt on me for a week and a half." Jenkins stepped down.

Botere screwed up royally. I understood thoroughly what David Dunn was attempting to do. It was already obvious how Cooper's character was. It seemed so apparent that if nobody else in this courtroom could detect how explosive Cooper was, they were equally in as much denial as Cooper. Botere truly had nothing to defend. Moreover, Botere probably did not give an iota about Cooper. He was merely doing his job, or attempting to do it. I felt as though he was excavating a bigger hole for himself and for Cooper and for what? At this point, Cooper certainly did not look good. Botere had no means by which to make Cooper appear better. The nausea I experienced in the pit of my stomach intensified that much more. More witnesses appearing on the stand would only confirm Cooper's belligerent posture. As quickly as the pace was going, enough was said to implicate Cooper. After all, Cooper did implicate himself in the murder of Michael. Was that not more than enough? Jacob looked more angry than I ever knew him to be. My mother was far away, trembling and deeply hurt. I was full. I was ready to hear a verdict.

More bartenders and employees were sworn in. Details were revealed, verifying Cooper's behavior and attitude concerning his anger and his ferocity toward Michael. It was concluded that Cooper was so beyond angry he was yelling inside the human resource's office that he was going to kill Michael. Other conversations employees had with Cooper confirmed that Cooper indeed made statements that Cooper wanted to kill Michael. Cooper blamed others for not helping Cooper find a solution to his anger and to his pain.

The night of October 13th, Cooper looked fairly calm. When his shift was over, Cooper gathered his belongings and left his place of work. Normal was the consensus the employees described Cooper as looking when he left for the night.

Finally, in a last ditch attempt to discredit Michael and Diedra, Botere asked the last witness who took the stand why the rules were never enforced about personal phone calls. Botere suggested that if they had been abided by and employees were fired as a result of receiving them all of the time, then there would not have been any provocation for Cooper to be so angry. David Dunn countered by asking the same witness that if all the phone calls were terminated, how many employees would be left working? The witness replied, "Very few." Recess was called.

My family and I had the option of eating lunch. We had approximately one hour before the courts would intervene. All of us desperately needed air. We decided on settling together at an open air café, but our appetites were insufficient to makes us want to eat any proportions of food. Finally, we talked. We were appalled by this whole trial. Botere was clearly out of his league when it came to Dunn. Money was the obvious motivation. Disgust prevailed. So much was out of our hands. We knew we were highly biased when it came to Botere and especially to Cooper. Nothing indicated in the trial thus far, that Cooper was innocent. It was as plain as the noses on our faces, even to Botere. Despite the fact that we had almost two years to come to terms with Michael being dead, this trial continually brought up pain that had yet to be touched upon. It was an ongoing process of trying to go on with life and being slammed in the face simultaneously. I understood that Michael was gone. However, I could not reckon with the searing wounds that made themselves so clear to me. Yet again, surviving was what I did best. I had to go on. I had to go on for myself, for my mother, Jacob, my children and for Michael. Normalcy. I now question that. Squelching my pain kept me in a comfort zone. Stepping out of it, brought too much suffering. Balance was unreasonable.

1:50 p.m. read my watch. We paid for what we did not eat and walked quickly to the Superior Court. Adjusting back into the hard wooden pews, I closed my eyes for a moment, imagining myself with my children. I would have given anything to smell them, to touch them and to merely be with them. Soon, was my desire.

"All rise." We rose. "All be seated." We sat. There was a side bar conference in progress between the attorneys and the judge. Connie, the victim witness advocate who was sitting patiently with us during the trail, explained what was happening. Pictures and a video-tape of the crime scene, including Michael and his bedroom would now be introduced to the jurors. Doctor Fitch the State Medical Examiner, would be called to the stand to define and to explain the photographs in precise detail. It was apparent by the agitation at the judge's seat, this display would be very graphic and very, very difficult for any human being to consume. It was advised that we all leave the courtroom while this testimony was being heard. Jacob and I opted to stay, though we were exceptionally uneasy about doing as such. This was hardly a courageous act. Perhaps in my mind and Jacob's mind it fueled itself as a catalyst toward some closure. When in fact, it would only act as a catalyst toward unleashing pain we had yet to know could possibly exist. My mother was strongly advised not to stay. Connie escorted my mother out. That decision was wisely made. I believe if she had heard how her son was desecrated, the broken heart she already had, would have stopped functioning.

Connie came back, sitting between Jacob and I. Doctor Fitch was introduced. He was known as the Associate Chief Medical Examiner for the Commonwealth of Massachusetts. He attended the medical school at Wake Forest University in North Carolina. He eventually completed his training in anatomic and clinical pathology at Mt. Sinai Hospital in New York City. After passing his medical boards, he became an Assistant State Medical Examiner in New Jersey. Since 1987, he had been employed as Associate County Medical Examiner where he eventually was promoted to the Chief Medical Examiner by the state of Massachusetts.

Doctor Fitch performed an autopsy on Michael on October 14th at 11:00 a.m. Michael's body was shipped to Tewksbury Hospital, about one hour from Lynn. That is where Fitch's office was located. David Dunn had then asked Dr. Fitch some standard questions concerning autopsy procedures.

It was apparent that David wanted the jury to know how qualified Fitch was in his field. Dr. Fitch had performed over 4,000 autopsies, he had published six papers in forensic pathology and he had already testified over three hundred times in various courtrooms throughout the Commonwealth of Massachusetts. Dr. Fitch went on to explain how the autopsy on Michael was performed. I coiled in fear. Jacob did not move nor did he sense my discomfort. My insides wanted to yell out in pain, but nothing came out.

Before any doctor attempts an autopsy, he wants to know some history of the person he will be examining. In Michael's case, Fitch would look at Michael's unclothed body to see the presence or absence of injuries or normal findings. He would perform a thorough examination where he would make a Y-shaped incision on Michael's thorax, his chest and his abdomen, and inspect all of his organs from the neck down to the pelvis. He would then observe the brain. In addition, Fitch would look for obvious injuries that would be the cause of death. He would attempt to find if there was any diseases in the body that would have attributed to the cause of death.

According to Dr. Fitch's discoveries, Michael was five feet, nine inches tall. He estimated Michael's weight to be one hundred and sixty pounds. He found multiple slashing wounds from Michael's head down to his feet. Other than those wounds, there were no other findings that would conclude that Michael had died from another cause. It was in no uncertain terms that Michael died from multiple sword wounds. Twenty-three definitive wounds were located on his body and any of the wounds could have been potentially fatal. Even a small cut could have been deadly because of the quickness in which it can become infected and affect the entire body.

Dr. Fitch had before him innumerable photographs of Michael's injuries. Each was labeled arbitrarily with letters. At this point, Dr. Fitch was going to introduce each injury in precise detail, explaining to the jury how horrific this killing was. I would never be prepared for what I was about to hear. Nor do I think any preparation would have sufficed.

Picture A: Injury on Michael's left forehead. It was measured to be two inches in length and was approximately forty-five degrees in a horizontal position. In layman's terms, this wound went through the entire thickness of the scalp and struck right into the skull. Picture B: Measured six inches in length, extending down from the corner of the left eyebrow down over the cheek and to the jaw line. The left side of Michael's face was peeled off. Picture C: Measuring three and a half inches in length. It went from the corner of Michael's mouth, cutting the upper lip. Picture D: A half-inch superficial wound, extending on the tip of the nose on the left side, not ripping through the entire thickness of the skin. Picture E: Approximately three inches on the left side of the head, extending down to the temporalis muscle. This is the muscle that aids in chewing. The nature of that wound would never allow Michael to chew again. Picture F: Thirty degrees down the back of the head, passing through the entire thickness of the skin. Picture G: Three and a quarter inches stretching through the entire thickness of the scalp, striking the skull. Picture H: On the left side of the neck, below the ear. It was six and a half inches in length, hitting a large muscle that goes from a big bone to the neck, through the neck down to the sternum. This injury would never allow Michael's nerves to function again. That wound also hit the spine. Picture I: Ranging one half to three quarters inches below wound H, on the left side of the neck. Though superficial in nature, this wound went through the entire thickness of the skin. Picture J: Located over the middle of the neck in the front, measuring three inches in length. This injury would never allow Michael to have the use of his Adam's Apple or his tongue. Picture K: Found on the left shoulder, known as the clavicle, measuring one and a half inches. Michael never would have had the ability of his collarbone after that blow.

At this time, Dr. Fitch was asked to show the photographs he previously described to the jury. Summarizing briefly, Dr. Fitch, beginning with Picture A and ending with Picture K reiterated Michael's injuries. Gasps were audible. I could barely detect these pictures, only catching mere glimpses of the color red located on all of them.

Dr. Fitch continued. Picture L: Twenty-four inches in length extending down to the left side of the abdomen. This wound began at the top of Michael's head and literally stretched as far down to his middle belly, cutting through muscles of the abdominal wall. David Dunn stopped Dr. Fitch momentarily, asking Dr. Fitch to tell the court which wound was fatal. It was surmised that any one of them could have caused almost immediate death. The blood vessels located in the head, causing extensive bleeding if injured, go to the back of the heart. This injury can cause air to be sucked and caught producing an air embolism, killing an individual very rapidly. Given the nature of the neck injuries, large blood vessels that are cut can also cause excessive bleeding to take place, producing air embolisms as well. Both of those strikes may have caused Michael's death within minutes. Michael could have suffocated to death, both from the embolisms and from choking on his blood.

Picture M: Situated on the right arm and down the chest region, measuring twelve inches in length. It cut through every one of Michael's bicep muscles, tricep muscles and chest muscles. The only thing that was not affected was Michael's humerus bone. Again, Dr. Fitch was asked to show these pictures to the jury. More aghast looks became visible. Picture N: Anatomically, it measured nine inches in length, extending from the end of the forearm to the thumb, to the tip of the thumb. Michael would never have the use of being able to flex his arm or hand again. Picture O: Found on the left foreman, amounting to one half inch in diameter, injuring the front of Michael's wrist and the base of it. Picture P: On the left forearm measuring eleven and a half inches in length. This wound cut Michael's arm off from the elbow down. Picture Q: Found on the left forearm, cutting into the flexor muscles. Picture R: One inch in length and found on the back of the left hand, affecting some tendons that move the bones in that hand. Picture S: Situated on the left arm, five and three quarters inches in length. This wound struck right through the deltoid muscle. Picture T: Discovered to the right thigh near the top, in the front and in the middle. Measuring eleven inches in length and five inches deep, it cut the muscles of the thigh. Also, this injury cut a large artery and a vein, which could cause almost immediate death, due to loss of blood.

David Dunn interrupted asking if he could enter two exhibits to the court. Botere objected. The court overruled the objection. As per request of David Dunn, two exhibits were entered. They were photographs of Michael's foot. Dr. Fitch explained that he had yet to describe these wounds, labeled as Picture

U and Picture V. Dr. Fitch continued his findings. It was found that on Picture U and V, also known as exhibit 10, huge lacerations extended themselves from the tip of the big toe all the way down to the base of the toe on the sole of the foot. The other laceration could be described as a half inch cut on the arch of the foot.

Finally the last wound was depicted. Picture W: Located in the middle of the chest, measuring thirteen inches in length going all the way through the muscles of the chest wall. This injury was so severe because it not only cut into Michael's breast bone, but it also it also severed the dome of the liver. The liver is protected by the rib cage. Yet, the cartilage of the rib bone was completely cut off. The force upon which the blow was handed onto Michael's body had to be of enormous magnitude.

I was completely debilitated. Nausea filled my stomach. I was beginning to think what a sick bastard Cooper really was. I was also doubting my ability to think rationally and clearly. How could anyone resort to such evil and desecration of another human being? How could anyone actually act upon doing such harm to another individual, especially to the degree of complete butchery that Cooper did to Michael? Every human being knows what it is like to have buttons pushed. We all are capable of reacting in the heat of the moment, but to this degree? Cooper's hatred was so intense, Cooper committed a ferociously barbaric murder.

I was baffled as to the fine line Cooper crossed, or if there was a fine line. Cooper premeditated killing Michael. It was his intent to do as much harm to Michael as possible. He wanted Michael dead, out of the picture, away from Diedra. Cooper had to be sane to plot this vengeance out. Yet, while Cooper was butchering Michael, he did so with such a maliciousness, that each strike led to another impassioned strike and so on and so forth. Struggling with the notion of sanity and insanity, being on the edge or over it, why did Cooper not stop after one blow? Surely, one wound was enough to render Michael lifeless. Could such jealousy precipitate an abominable atrocity? Cooper's jealousy extended well beyond normal hurt and rage. Cooper enjoyed slicing my brother to death. I struggled with understanding if a fine actually existed.

My brother. My mother's son. Jacob's brother and best friend. Michael was inhumanely slaughtered like a cow in a slaughter house, literally. There was nothing left of him. My only rationalization I could make was knowing that Michael would have never been the same if he survived. The physical and emotional trauma would have been of such immensity to Michael, he would have been permanently, psychologically scarred for the rest of his life, not to speak of the physical disfigurement of his body. It was a blessing that he died. However, it was no blessing though that he suffered and died the way that he did.

Tears flooded Jacob's face. My body was shaking. Connie merely sat with us, embracing our pain. I was not ready to face my mother. Dr. Fitch was not yet done. David Dunn asked the most agonizing question, "Is there any way for you to know once these wounds were inflicted, how long Michael Barg lived?" Dr Fitch replied, "A very short period of time."

Jacob and I knew Michael had to experience horrific agony, even during that short period of time, which never could be determined. Merely having that knowledge left me with an excruciating emptiness that would sit with me for the rest of my life. Given the atrocious and horrifically cruel way Michael died, I was hoping the jury would be moved enough, based on the visual evidence they witnessed, to convict Cooper. Those pictures would most likely haunt them for the rest of their lives.

David Dunn's final question: "The sword used to kill Michael Barg, how much force would it take to inflict these wounds?" Dr. Fitch's final answer, "Given the fact that this particular sword was rusty and not very sharp, an extreme amount of force would have had to been used to impose these injuries." Botere did not cross-examine.

My mother was escorted back into the courtroom. Jacob and I never moved from our seats. By our postures, it was obvious to our mother, how deeply affected we were by what we previously heard. Too stunned, she never inquired about Dr. Fitch's testimony. Once the courtroom was settled, it was decided by the judge that the court would intervene until tomorrow morning. Again the jurors were given identical instructions they were given yesterday concerning confidentiality in this case. "All rise. The court is dismissed."

The very sorrowful irony of all, according to the autopsy report by Dr. Fitch, Michael had not one diseased organ in his body. He was an exceptionally healthy man.

Chapter 44

Day three of the trial. Diedra Forte was sworn in. I had so many emotions swirling in my head about Diedra, I was hoping to remain as calm and equitable in my assessment of her. David Dunn began by asking Diedra where she was employed, for how long and how she met Jerry Cooper. Diedra was asked to speak up. She was very nervous.

Diedra was a waitress at the Cheers Bar in Logan Airport. She had been working there for the last ten years where she met Mr. Cooper. Eventually they had become friends. Their friendship was established for close to two years before it turned into a romantic liaison. Diedra knew that Cooper was married. Diedra met his wife at company get-togethers and weddings. Cooper and Diedra had a close, but very volatile relationship. Both Cooper and Diedra's schedules were very similar, placing them at work together. Though Cooper never went to Diedra's house, he did make personal phone calls to her. Diedra explained how fun-loving Cooper could be, but how equally hot-tempered he was as well. Throwing objects at employees or screaming at them, was typical for Cooper. Once again confirmation of Cooper's erractic temper was validated.

Approximately three years into their relationship, Cooper had told Diedra that he loved her and he would have liked to have married her. Diedra told Cooper that would never happen because their temperaments were so different. Diedra described Cooper as being very controlling. He would call her every night at eleven in the evening to check on her, see with whom she had gone out with and what she did. It was also discovered that Cooper's domineering behavior started well before Michael ever came into the picture, beginning when Diedra and Cooper became romantically involved.

In June of 1995, Diedra had ended her sexual relationship with Cooper. There was an excessive amount of fighting. Despite their sexual relationship terminating, Cooper called Diedra frequently. One evening in July Michael had called Diedra, asking if she would like to go out to dinner. Diedra accepted. Diedra knew that Cooper would call her at a specific time during that evening. Diedra also knew that Cooper would call her at the time she was out with Michael. Diedra understood if Cooper was not able to get her, he would continue to call her the following evening. Sure enough, on a Monday evening, Diedra had picked up the phone knowing all too well that Cooper would be on the other end. Cooper had inquired of Diedra's whereabouts. Diedra replied that she had been out with Michael Barg. Cooper went into an uncontrollable rage. He was screaming at Diedra. He told Diedra that she was a fucking bitch, a whore, a tramp and that she used him. He continued to scream that she would never get away with what she did. Diedra hung up, emotionally a wreck and terribly frightened.

Soon after, Cooper called back, but Diedra would not pick up the phone, until later that evening. Diedra pleaded with Cooper to calm down. It would be three times Diedra would talk to Cooper on the phone that evening. Cooper continued to call incessantly. Diedra's answering machine picked up the rest of Cooper's calls. Diedra was so immobilized with fear she made a decision to have all the locks in the house changed. Once the locks were changed, Diedra only saw Michael a few more times during that week. When Diedra went into the work the following week, Cooper insisted that Diedra stop seeing Michael. Diedra refused Cooper's request. Cooper in front of employees and patrons yelled "bitch" to Diedra. Cooper emotionally abused Diedra for a few more months.

Diedra and Michael only dated for about a month, agreeing that they merely wanted to be friends. Diedra described Michael as a very gentle, kind man. She said that he was very soft spoken and laughed easily. She also stated that she remembered one of his hands shook from a car accident he was in when he was fifteen years old. She went onto to say that Michael, a passenger in the car, lost his father in that accident. Years later, as a result of that car accident, Michael suffered from epilepsy forcing Michael to use his opposite hand to write with. She concluded that Michael despite what he had endured, was an exceptionally loving person.

By the end of August of 1995, Diedra had placed an ad in the local paper looking for a third roommate. The bedroom across from hers had become vacant. Michael called asking Diedra if he could rent out that room. He wanted to attend law school nearby. The place Michael was living was no longer accommodating for him. Michael moved in, where he shared a portion of the rent. Neither Diedra or Michael were lovers, nor did they continue any relationship outside of merely being friends. They were strictly roommates. Cooper was informed by Diedra that she and Michael were roommates and nothing more. Cooper did not believe Diedra.

One month after Michael had moved into the Preston house, Michael drove to the bar where Diedra worked. His intention was merely to say hello. Cooper saw Michael enter and yelled at him to leave. Michael completely ignored him. Enraged, Cooper walked away from his post, went over to where Michael was sitting, grabbed Michael's arm and hurriedly pushed Michael out into the hallway near the entrance of the establishment. Diedra saw what had occurred. She was terribly upset. Diedra immediately confronted Cooper exclaiming that Cooper had no right to do what he just did. Cooper simply walked away, laughing. Diedra made a formal complaint to the manager. Diedra also found out that Cooper had too made a complaint about Michael showing up at the bar. It was decided by management that Cooper would be work at a different terminal away from Diedra. However, only for a short while that Cooper was transferred he began to complain that he could not make enough money at the new terminal. He wanted to come back to his old post. He was granted that request.

When Cooper returned, life became miserable for Diedra. Cooper was belligerent toward Diedra. It was Diedra who was asked by management to go home early so nothing would escalate. Diedra was so upset at this point, because she never provoked the disagreements. Also, Diedra was losing wages from being sent home before her shift was over.

Eventually, tension between Cooper and Diedra subsided. Diedra noticed that Cooper was more calm, joking with customers and interacting with staff. Time passed. The summer was over. Fall time was in full bloom. The night of October 13th, Michael had once again come into the bar to merely have a drink and to say hello to Diedra. Diedra could not go over to where Michael was sitting because she was still working. However, Cooper caught a glimpse of Michael sitting at a table. Without notice, Cooper went over to Michael and whispered something to Michael. Michael remained sitting. Raged with anger, Cooper ran over to Diedra screaming at her to ask Michael to leave. Fearfully, Diedra approached Michael telling Michael that Cooper was furious. Michael replied that Cooper would get over it. Michael stayed for an additional fifteen minutes and left the bar. The manager of the bar came out asking that Diedra go home. Her shift was almost over. Diedra complained the she should not be the one to leave. The manager explained to Diedra that Cooper was in the back room, angry and hysterically crying simultaneously, saying that he wanted to kill Diedra and Michael. Diedra cashed out and proceeded home to Preston Street. She and Michael got home at the same time. Diedra told Michael how ridiculous she thought it was that Cooper was so angry. Diedra went upstairs to her room. Michael stayed downstairs, flicked on the television to watch the baseball playoffs. Around eleven in the evening, Diedra shut off her light and went to bed. She could still hear the baseball game being played on the television downstairs.

A few hours later, Diedra had awoken from her sleep. She could hear moaning noises. Diedra became confused. She thought the noises were coming from outside her window. Immediately, Diedra turned on her lamp on her night table. Diedra then arose from her bed and stood to the right side of her bed. Her door had been closed. Standing only in a nightshirt, before Diedra could move, her bedroom door was abruptly opened. Jerry Cooper was standing perfectly still looking at her in a manner Diedra could not describe. There was blood on Cooper's face and arms. Crying out, Diedra said, "Jerry, what have you done? Why are you here?" Jerry yelled, "Go look at him. See if you like him now." Diedra was so frightened she could not move. Cooper then grabbed Diedra, dragging her into Michael's bedroom. Diedra saw Michael lying on his bed covered in blood. She immediately ran back into her bedroom terrified that Cooper was going to kill her. Screaming, Diedra begged Cooper not to kill her. Cooper stood in front of Diedra saying nothing. Within moments, Cooper threw something on the ground. Diedra noticed it was a sword. Cooper was in a rage. He had a horrible look of hatred on his face. Diedra became more and more in shock, stating that she could not believe what she had just seen. She believed that Michael was still alive. Cooper looked at Diedra one more time. He then walked out of Diedra's bedroom, walking down the stairs. Shrieking uncontrollably to her other roommate, Derrick Simpson, Derrick ran downstairs to Diedra's bedroom. Diedra said that she thought Cooper killed Michael. Simpson told Diedra to call 911. Yelling into the phone, Diedra said that a man was dead or maybe alive at her house. Hanging up, Diedra ran out the front porch with the cordless phone still in her hand. At that moment, Diedra noticed Cooper's car rounding the corner making its way back to her house. Diedra again screamed to Simpson, "He's back, he is going to kill me." Hastening back into the house, Diedra ran through the kitchen, out the back door, yelling for help.

Police arrived, bolting around to the back of the house. Diedra was convulsing in fear. Not realizing it, Diedra had blood on her shoulder and her shirt. Her feet were splattered with the blood she had trampled on in the house. She became more hysterical. The police asked her what had happened. As Diedra was sobbing and yelling she attempted to tell them what Cooper had done. Still, Diedra was screaming that Michael needed help, Michael needed help. After police assessed Michael, they told Diedra that they were afraid that Michael was gone. More hysterical, Diedra was told to wait until further questions could be asked of her. An hour later, Diedra was taken to the police station in Lynn where she was interviewed about the murder that had just taken place.

Botere began counter examination. Botere was so tough on Diedra I thought she was going to break. He insisted that because she was in such a state of shock at the time of the murder, her incriminating remarks concerning Cooper were unjust. Botere also wanted to introduce pictures concerning the first time Diedra and Cooper had socialized together.

Cooper's wife Callie was also at this particular function. Diedra and her former boyfriend attended as well, all mutual friends of the wedding party. Botere wanted to show the jury pictures of Diedra wearing a very provocative dress. The judge ruled no. There was no significance for it. Botere protested. The judge was getting annoyed and reiterated no. It was Botere's intent to show the jury and the court that Diedra brought attention to herself by wearing the clothes that she wore. That would have been Cooper's incentive for asking her out initially. At least that is what Botere implied.

That was it. Botere took the lowest step he could take. He was a master at making it appear that Cooper had a reason to be incensed. Botere was placing blame on Diedra for Michael's murder. In fact, Botere consistently attempted to place blame on everyone else's behavior to justify Cooper's actions. The scenario was becoming so common to my ears, the repugnance I felt for Botere had not changed. I had heard that Botere was one of the top criminal attorneys in the state. If this was top notch for the state of Massachusetts, I was ill with worry concerning our judicial system. I was more than dismayed to think that Botere could be allowed to practice law. As each minute passed into hours and hours passed into a day and days passed into a week, the logical and most evident conclusion to be made was the fact that Botere literally had nothing to draw upon. Thus, given his ill equip defense, everything could validate his supposition. Where else could Botere turn? Certainly not to Cooper. Everyone else became Botere's pigeon stool.

My heart was barely at ease, knowing that such display of debauchery made my brother's death seem so meaningless. Everyone knew the motive behind Michael's death, including Botere. Yet, to utilize our time and the court's time in such a useless and demeaning way was perverse to me. I was also dumbfounded by Diedra's admission that she directly told Cooper that she was seeing Michael. Somehow, I felt that Michael was set up by Diedra. If not consciously, at least out of Diedra's sheer, frustrated ignorance. What in the world would Diedra have to gain by telling Cooper such information? She knew his temperament. She knew such information would incense Cooper. In moments of rage, our human frailties are quick to display themselves. Despite Diedra's fury at Cooper calling her every night at eleven, I am still haunted and disturbed by her disclosure.

Botere continued. He had deliberately asked Diedra what gifts Cooper had given to her. Her reply included gold jewelry, rings, bracelets, a stereo system and stuffed animals. Botere then asked Diedra if she still had any of those gifts. Diedra exclaimed that she merely put them away, that she did not look at them anymore. She also went onto say that Cooper was quite lavish. Botere asked that Diedre explain what she meant by lavish. Diedra expounded that he was merely generous to everyone, especially if she and Cooper were with others, Cooper would pick up the tab. Another in for Botere. Another way for Botere to embellish Cooper's character. Another way for Botere to demoralize my brother's death. Botere gloated when he said that was typical for Cooper's nature. Cooper was incredibly generous. So what if he was? He still murdered Michael. He never allowed Michael a chance to defend himself. How generous is that?

Botere pressed the final issue with Diedra. "Cooper expected you to be faithful with him, did he not?" Diedra answered yes. "He expected you to be faithful to him, even though he was married?' asked Botere. "Yes," said Diedra. "And you expected him to be faithful to you?" taunted Botere. Diedra replied, "I didn't expect him to be faithful. He was married." Botere reiterated, ""So on the day that he was hysterically attempting to reach you and he couldn't, you knew you were being unfaithful to him?" "Yes," responded Diedra, "but I was going to tell him." "And that is when you told Cooper that you had been out with Michael Barg, isn't that correct?" asked Botere. Diedra said, "Yes." "Was Cooper furious?" asked Botere. Diedra said, "Yes. I knew that he would be upset. I knew that he would be very mad." "Didn't you feel that Cooper would go nuts when he found out that you had gone out with Mr. Barg?" inquired Botere. Diedra responded, "I didn't know if he was—how angry. I just knew he was going to be very mad." Botere persisted, "Cooper eventually came to you and pleaded with you not to go out with Michael Barg, although he said that you could go out, but not with Michael?" Diedra said, "Yes." "Did Cooper not cry over the fact that you had established this relationship with Mr. Barg?" continued Botere. Diedra said, "Yes." "You knew that Cooper hated Michael?" Again Diedra said, "Yes." "So what did you do to rectify the situation?" asked Botere. "I simply let Michael know how upset Cooper was," replied Diedra. "At one point, Michael confided in you and said that Cooper was crazy," retorted Botere. Diedra responded, "Michael thought he was jealous and he said that Cooper would get over it."

Little did Michael know how Cooper would not get over it. At one point in an encounter between Michael and Cooper, Cooper threatened Michael if Michael did not stop seeing Diedra. Michael looked at Cooper and told him that he was a married man and what difference did it make to Cooper. Tragically, though it was a seemingly sensible reply to Cooper, it was also a statement that defied Cooper at all odds. Cooper went into a rage. It was a rage that would be prolonged at least until Michael's last breath.

Cooper and Diedra worked together on the evening of October 13th.
Cooper was still furious with Diedra for going out with Michael, in spite of the
fact that both Michael and Diedra were simply friends. Cooper's last words
to Diedra were, "I hate you. I'd like to kill you. I wish you were dead." At
that moment, Diedra was asked to step down. The jury was adjourned until the
following day.

Chapter 45

Many witnesses from Cooper's place of work had came and gone, all verifying Cooper's personality. Day four sped by. Day five opened with that of a psychiatrist. It was a testimony that will always stay with me.

Cooper had seen Dr. Cohen just twice, a few weeks before Cooper killed Michael. Dr. Cohen was called by a social worker Cooper had been briefly seeing for depression and alcohol consumption. The social worker thought it best that Dr. Cohen evaluate Cooper for further diagnosis. Dr. Cohen was affiliated with Harvard Community Health, the same organization Cooper attended when seeing his social worker.

Dr. Conner had been a practicing psychiatrist for only six and a half years. She is a general psychiatrist which means that she basically sees adults for some psychotherapy, while she treats other individuals for medical evaluations. Dr. Conner first saw Cooper on August 21, 1995. She did not however, recall if she had even discussed Cooper's case with the social worker who had also seen Cooper. In fact, it would be quite customary for Dr. Conner to have been briefed by the social worker via written notes, via verbal contact prior to Dr. Conner making contact with Cooper. No recollection was detected by Dr. Conner. Within seconds of Dr. Conner saying she did not have any recollection, she amended her statement. She went on to say that she would have had access to the social worker's notes prior to seeing Cooper. However, did she read them?

Dr. Conner's observations of Cooper were as follows as requested by Botere: Cooper was depressed and remained depressed over a couple of weeks before Dr. Conner saw him. At the level of what his depression warranted, Dr. Cooper thought it best to medically evaluate Cooper. She went onto to conclude that depression could have interfered with Cooper's functioning, the far end of the spectrum being suicide. Botere interjected, asking Dr. Conner if such depressive thoughts could warrant homicidal ideation. Dr. Conner reluctantly answered that perhaps they could. Dr. Conner continued. She knew that Cooper was on other medication for heart disease and high cholesterol levels. She also said that Cooper had explained to her that his present situation was contributing to his depression. However, Dr. Conner stressed that in order to diagnosis anyone, such diagnosis is made generally on symptoms displayed. Although it is helpful to have the psychosocial situations that put depression in prospective, most diagnosis is treated symptomatically. Cooper's symptoms included inability to sleep, diminished appetite, some weight loss, fatigue and suicidal thoughts as well as harm to others. At that particular visit, Dr. Conner prescribed more medication to alleviate some of Cooper's symptoms. Two weeks after that, Cooper had another appointment with Dr. Conner as follow up to his medical evaluation. During the second visit, it was Dr. Conner's impression that Cooper was doing much better. Each session lasted no longer than thirty minutes.

David Dunn was anxious to cross-examine Dr. Conner though he had never had a chance to speak to her prior to her testifying. Dunn went right to the punch: "During the course of your speaking with Cooper at any time did he tell you that he wished to kill either Michael Barg or Diedra Forte?" Dr. Conner replied, "He said he was having thoughts of killing himself, another woman and another man. He did deny his intent to actually act on the thoughts though."

It was at this time Botere cross examined, asking Dr. Conner if she thought that Cooper was a threat to others she would have informed the parties of his intent. Dr. Conner responded accordingly that she would have and she would have hospitalized Cooper. Dr. Conner thought none of these steps were necessary. It was also argued by David Dunn the medication that was prescribed to Cooper by Dr. Conner along with the medication he had been using would have a sedentary affect on Cooper when taken together. Finally after minutes of pressing the issue, Dr. Conner concluded for the most part, such side affects would be primarily a sedentary affect and sleepiness, not emotional liability, abnormal thinking or a paranoid reaction.

Dunn did a brilliant job in maintaining liability for Cooper's actions. Botere did the opposite. He claimed that the medication that Cooper was on and had been prescribed for him in part, aggravated precipitations of his heinous acts. Dr. Conner stepped down.

As a practicing psychotherapist, despite my good intentions in empowering others to get well, there are moments that is difficult to render whether the truth is being spoken. Trust takes time to establish as does rapport. It takes more than a half an hour to dive into the life and psyche of a person who may be a master at manipulation. Dr. Conner's profession speaks primarily of symptoms, treating that, not the whole person, not the underlying cause of what is really going on inside the person. Cooper's disclosure of wanting to kill others would raise suspicions and it is a disclosure that should not be taken lightly.

Yet, two half hour sessions are hardly enough time to render a conclusion that Cooper did not have any intent to act upon his actions. Pills and medicine are not going to stop a person from committing a crime. It was always Cooper's intent to kill Michael. His premeditated thoughts were already in place, months prior. How much preparation went into Dr. Conner's evaluation with Cooper? How much emphasis was placed on Cooper's admission that he wanted to kill others? How many sessions were devoted to getting inside of Cooper, deciphering his intent? Like many medical evaluations, it becomes a quick fix to treat the symptom, not to treat the root cause of what may make a person tick. On some level, prescribing a magic pill does not give responsibility to that person to take responsibility for who they are and what they do. It can certainly act as a catalyst toward feeling better at some point. Yet, the emotional work must be done. Dr. Conner did what she knew best. However, she did not press Cooper further offering indefinite sessions. She did not as a mandated professional insist that she was going to inform Michael and Diedra of Cooper's potential intent. Perhaps, such devastation could have been avoided. Perhaps such a rationalization on my part could ease my pain and my futility over the court system.

One of the last witnesses to appear was Dr. Galoway, a forensic psychologist who interviewed Cooper the day after he killed Michael. Her particular testimony would be essential in determining whether Cooper would be competent to stand trial. Dr. Galoway had spoken to Cooper in lock up. Cooper fully understood the murder charges against him. He also described in excessive detail to Galoway various interactions around Diedra Forte and Michael. His concentration and attention were very adequate and in Dr. Galoways's opinion, Cooper did not suffer from any thought disorder. In essence, Cooper was clearly cognizant of the fact of why he was in lock up and of the actions he perpetrated.

Finally, the last witness approached the bench: Callie Cooper, Cooper's wife. Mrs. Cooper stated that she had been married to Cooper since 1969. She relayed to the jury that both she and her husband had a good marriage. They had many years of vacationing and living a good life together. They had no children. They lived in a three family house they had bought in 1971 that was also occupied by family members. Cooper's father died quite early in life. He also had two older sisters and two younger sisters. He was in Mrs. Cooper's words, "spoiled by them all." Mrs. Cooper went on to say that she had many opportunities to meet Cooper and his co workers, emphasizing with a smile on her face that everyone appeared to have a good relationship with one another. Mrs. Cooper added that Cooper was always friendly with the waitresses at work. Oftentimes, the waitresses would call him at their house, asking his advice on baby showers and a myriad of other events taking place in their lives. Mrs. Cooper did not flinch or seem ruffled about her husband's involvement with these

185

co workers. She openly said that she always understood Cooper's actions toward them as being nonsexual. Mrs. Cooper accepted her husband's friendships. She did not have a need to question his behavior. At one point she met Diedra Forte at a mutual friends' wedding. During that time, Diedra had been with a boyfriend. A while after that event, Diedra was no longer involved with that particular man. Mrs. Cooper's husband remained friends with Diedra. He attempted to help her out of bankruptcy. Other times, he tried to find boyfriends for Diedra, fixing Diedra up with blind dates that Mr. and Mrs. Cooper knew. Mrs. Cooper claimed that Cooper felt it necessary for Diedra to have a boyfriend. As a result of Cooper's grandiose attempts to match Diedra with someone, Mrs. Cooper had the opportunity to become friends with Diedra. They went to the particular outings together, Mrs. Cooper usually being the one to purchase tickets for Diedra and herself. Mrs. Cooper was unequivocally unaware of her husband's relationship to Diedra. As far as Mrs. Cooper was concerned, her husband had many women friends. Also, she and her husband worked different shifts. Mrs. Cooper was asleep when her husband came home from work and he was asleep when she left to go to work. She said that her husband would always be talking to a woman on the phone. He enjoyed phone gossiping, talking shop of that nature. At the end of her testimony, it was asked of Mrs. Cooper if she still loved her husband, after she had found out about his three-year affair with Diedra? Mrs. Cooper replied, "Yes." She stepped down.

I was not shocked by Mrs. Cooper's posture. She was so passive and without emotion, I often wondered if she really did exist inside her body and where she was. She did not seem like an individual who would ever rock the boat. I also suspected that Cooper was the domineering partner in their marriage. My hunch was that Cooper was a master at deception. He knew how to placate his wife. Mrs. Cooper would always be loyal to her husband, despite the circumstances. Having a conscious was not even part of Cooper's constitution. What not a better scenario for Cooper? What a tragedy for Mrs. Cooper. It was as though Mrs. Cooper was on rote. She was devoid of emotion. She defended Cooper, despite his betrayal of her. The truth sometimes is much too much to ascertain. Mrs. Cooper did hear her husband's brutal massacre of Michael. Yet, she smiled. Conceivably, Mrs. Cooper was a pitiful character in all of this. Cooper's downright disloyalty to her, to their union and to their commitment together all spell emotional abuse of the most horrendous kind. Living with such an insidious ache can often dismiss that it actually exists, simply because it becomes so familiar. Perhaps for Mrs. Cooper, she could live with it.

I will never really know what went on behind Mr. and Mrs. Cooper's closed doors. I will never really know what they were together. In the big picture, such knowledge is trivial. Yet, what I do know is that her unconditional support of her husband, also validates Cooper's atrocious acts on Michael. Jacob and I looked at each other after Mrs. Cooper's testimony. We were significantly ill. I was too distressed to glance my mother's way. I knew her soul was tortured beyond description.

All the evidence had been concluded. Final arguments were to be heard the next business day. The jury would be instructed on the law and sent out to deliberate the case. "Hear ye, hear ye, hear ye. All persons having anything further to do before the Honorable Eliza Dooley, Justice of the Superior Court, now sitting in Salem, within and for the county of Essex, at present depart, give you attendance at this place Monday morning at nine o'clock to which time and place the sitting of this Court is now adjourned. God save the Commonwealth of Massachusetts and this Honorable Court." God, please get me through another day.

Chapter 46

Time passed all too quickly. I was anxious about the verdict. I was equally anxious about how long the jury would ponder the facts of the case. Walking together with my family into the courtroom once more, we all resumed our seats in the same sequence in the row we had been sitting for a week. Though my sleep was uninterrupted, a million and one thoughts were flying through my mind. That dull ache festered in my stomach again.

This is what I understood. There were charges on three theories of murder in the first degree. Firstly, there was an unlawful killing. Secondly, the killing was done with deliberate premeditation, that it was committed with malice afterthought. The jury would be told that there are three theories concerning malice afterthought, specific intent to kill or specific intent to do grievous bodily harm and unlawful killing by home invasion, punishable by life. Thirdly, murder by extreme atrocity and cruelty. The jury must come to an unanimous verdict in order to convict Cooper on any of the accounts. In other words, the jury would have to prove that Cooper inflicted injury on Michael, from which he died; that Cooper injured Michael as a result of sudden combat or in the heat of passion; that Cooper unlawfully committed the murder without legal excuse or justification. However, before any verdict could be rendered, closing arguments ensued. In any criminal case in the state of Massachusetts, the defense counsel is the first to address the jury in his closing remarks. Botere had the floor.

"I am sure it doesn't make me the first to say to you how much we all appreciate the fact that you people have had your privacy, your everyday life interrupted by having to sit on such a serious case as this case. I know that I speak for the government as well as the Court when I say that to you." Cut to the chase is what I wanted to voice to Botere. Yet, he went on. "We understand how much an invasion that is into your lives, particularly in a case when we have to be exposed to as graphic evidence as has obviously been such in this case. I realize with respect to time to argue, I will lose some of you if I argue every little bit of detail in this case. I will focus on the high points, summarizing the evidence."

Botere went on to say that the Court is going to instruct you that in this case and all criminal cases, it is the prosecution that has the burden of proof. The prosecution must prove each and every essential element of the case beyond a reasonable doubt. Also, when using your common sense and sorting through all of the facts in this case, they have the burden of convincing you that you are going to be sitting and making a verdict on every essential element in this case beyond a reasonable doubt.

Botere went on to state that his defense was insanity and such a plea would apply to all of the charges against his client. Furthermore, Botere stressed to the jury that David Dunn would have to prove beyond a reasonable doubt that Cooper was not insane on the early morning of October 14th when the crimes against Michael Barg were committed. The issue in controversy is whether or not based on the evidence in the case the jury had heard all the facts and is satisfied with those facts to believe that Cooper was indeed sane when he committed those acts. Botere also suggested that the prosecution miserably failed to convince the jury that there was any thread of evidence from which a reasonable inference could be made that Cooper was sane on the morning of October 14th.

Botere went onto to reiterate the evidence to the jury: Diedra Forte said that Cooper was easy going, that he had a good sense of humor. Fellow employees also validated what Forte testified to. At that point Botere piped in that he did not have to put his witnesses up to testifying that way. The fact the Botere even suggested such a statement made me wonder if Botere ever did that to his clients. Such disclosure made me that much more suspicious of Botere's integrity. He did say that even though Cooper did get angry at times and he had a temper, David Dunn was going to exploit Cooper as an extremely violent man. In my opinion, Cooper was a very violent man with an extremely volatile temper. Botere continued to justify Cooper's temper by stressing that Cooper's place of employment was a pressure cooker waiting to boil over. Botere emphasized the fact that where the bar was located added to any stress already existing inside the establishment. In other words, the people that came into the bar were coming in to be waited on. They were already under a lot of pressure simply because they were waiting for their flights. Such a place would warrant swearing, arguing and tension of the utmost kind.

I was wondering if what I was hearing was real. I knew where my bias lay. I also knew how my brother died. Botere went on to minimize the fact that despite Cooper's incensed temper, he would compensate by buying his employees flowers or a gift the following day. After all, Mrs. Cooper still loved Cooper. In spite of all the unspeakable acts that happened on the early morning of October 14th, Mrs. Cooper's love for her husband never waivered. Mrs. Cooper did testify to that in a sense. My hunch is that if Mrs. Cooper was to truly get in touch with what she could feel, there would be significant consequences for her. Consequences that would generate pain of the most unspeakable variety. And yet, she already sustained the consequences. Cooper took a bite of the forbidden fruit. He was married. He was having an affair for years.

In spite of Cooper's weakness, Botere summarized that there would be no reason to convict a man of first degree murder along with the two other two charges against him. The jury should not convict Cooper because they would all have moral feelings that went against that. Just because Cooper cheated did not make him a murderer. However, in Botere's summation, he concluded that once Cooper met Diedra and began an affair with her, Cooper's personality drastically changed. Both parties argued a lot. Diedra liked a manly guy and Cooper represented that, according to Botere. Cooper became like a father figure to Diedra. Diedra liked being controlled. Diedra liked the fact that Cooper bought her gifts. Diedre allured herself into Cooper's circle of friends. Then there came a time when Diedra could not be located one evening in July of 1995 because she had been out with Michael Barg. Botere continued and declared that by Diedra being out that night would cause Cooper to be outraged. Diedra simply sprung this news on Cooper, giving Cooper reason to flip out.

As I was taking everything in, it felt as though Diedra was now on trial. She was being persecuted for my brother's murder. Botere was literally blaming Diedra for Cooper's behavior and his actions. Also, Botere strongly hinted that as a result of what Diedra did, it led Cooper to commit vicious acts that he absolutely could not be criminally responsible for. Basically, according to Botere, Diedra rubbed everything in Cooper's face. After all, Diedra still had all the gifts Cooper had given her. How could Cooper ever be legally sane when he killed my brother? That was what Botere implied. Furthermore, the fact that Cooper was led to increased drinking while taking more antidepressants would validate Cooper's inability to be responsible on October 14th. Yet, in my opinion, Cooper was conscious enough and sane enough to make the decision to voluntarily increase his substance use. Botere's last words to the jury: "So I'm going to ask you based on the evidence that you return a verdict in this case of not guilty by reason of insanity on all three indictments in this case. Thank you." I was ill beyond repute.

David Dunn approached the jurors and in a resounding voice, Dunn reflected, *"I HEARD A MAN'S VOICE YELLING STOP, CUT IT OUT* and the man's voice started to scream in terror." "Derrick Simpson, friend of the defendant heard that over and over for what appeared to be minutes. At first, Simpson thought it was a nightmare, but as soon as Simpson became more awake, he heard the sounds of somebody pounding on someone and the person was screaming, *STOP, DON'T, STOP, DON'T.* It was terrible. It was a person in a lot of pain, in a lot of fear, in a lot of anguish and a lot of terror."

Dunn's words, the way in which he voiced them left me sobbing hysterically once again. Though I reiterated those statements in my mind over and over after hearing them from one of the witnesses days ago, I could literally feel my heart breaking. Dunn's opening arguments had already paralyzed me. The jury looked anguished. Dunn continued: "Ladies and Gentlemen, every night at 11 p.m., Cooper called Diedre Forte to check up on her. Jerry Cooper, though married, wanted control over Diedra. But a night came when she wasn't home. Cooper calls the next night. He was more upset. Finally on the third night, he got a hold of Diedra Forte. She told Cooper she had had a date, a date with Michael Barg. Cooper was wild, screaming at Diedra on the phone, calling her a bitch and other names. Ladies and gentlemen, jealousy and obsession are not insanity. They are perhaps the oldest motives known to man. However, we do not legally kill people in Massachusetts. As a result, this man is on trial before you. He now claims he is not responsible for what he did. And his excuse breaks down simply to one thing, motive, obsession, jealousy, most importantly, control. Cooper wanted to control Diedra. He wanted her to be part of his life even though he was married. When he lost control, he killed the man he thought was his rival. It was an evil act but not an insane act.

You will hear about premeditated murder. Did the defendant pre-mediate this murder? Did he plan it? Did he tell others that he was thinking of killing him? Did he even tell his psychiatrist that he wanted to kill Michael Barg? Did he go home, get the sword, write a note to his wife, stop off, leave some money for a friend, drive to Lynn and steal a key well before this murder was committed? No one knew that he had taken a key. Cooper learned that Diedra was dating someone else. He was so scary on the phone that she changed the locks on her house. Cooper snuck into the house stealing the key and said, "I did that because I wanted to take back a ring I had bought her." Why didn't he just take the ring that day he was in the house? He could have done that just as easily as to take the key. But, instead, he took the key so that he would have access so he could maintain his control.

Extreme atrocity and cruelty. That's what happened to Michael Barg. The medical examiner testified to at least twenty-three separate wounds with a sword. Some of the wounds are so large that they could have been made by more than one sword wound. He wasn't able to tell. There is, in fact, a piece of his left arm that is lying over on the right side of the body totally cut out of the arm. Eleven wounds are to the head and numerous wounds are potentially fatal. This was a violent attack. Yet the defense wants you to believe that the defendant is insane. After all, how else could he do this violent attack?

If you accept that argument then you're saying that anyone who kills with extreme atrocity and cruelty should be let go because the extreme atrocity and cruelty in itself proves that they are out of their head. What a great defense. It gives you absolute right to chop up people with a sword because you must be insane.

Felony murder. The felony here is home invasion. When you get a verdict slip, you have to be unanimous on these. You could find him guilty of any one. I suggest that when you think about the evidence, you'll find him guilty of all three.

The home invasion. There is a separate charge for that, coming into that house armed with a sword, this sword, the sword with the handle broken off during the fight and a billy club too, as a matter of fact, that he left on the floor, going up the stairs, flipping on the light and attacking Michael Barg, who was sound asleep in his bed in his own home. The indictment for home invasion does not require the actual use of a weapon. It requires some use of force. Was there force used on Deidra Forte when he grabbed her, that force, and dragged her into the other room? Look at him. See how you like him now. Those were the first things that Cooper said to Deidra.

Were these acts out of character, a man who had been having an affair for years with Diedra Forte, who was in love with Diedra Forte, who had a hot temper? He would yell at employees at work. He would scream at them so badly he would bring them to tears. Well, you cannot buy a bouquet of flowers to bring Michael Barg back. He is dead.

The defense says it is not trying to shift the blame to other people. You heard counsel very nicely, I think, say, I am not trying to shift the blame to Diedra Forte or anyone else. And then he goes on and on about what Diedra Forte did. Diedra Forte didn't kill anybody. Michael Barg didn't kill anyone.

You don't know much about Michael Barg other than he was a quiet, nice, friendly guy. He had a weak arm, a right hand that shook because he had been in a car accident when he was fifteen years old. He did what he could to avoid Cooper. He had seen Diedra Forte for only a month or two in a romantic relationship. He and Diedra only wanted to be friends and they remained friends, nothing more.

Are we talking about someone insane here? The defense has said there is no evidence of sanity, as you know from your common experience in dealing with people all around you, seeing how they operate, this is a man who the psychiatrist testified had no hallucinations, anything of that nature, heard no voices."

Botere objected loudly. Dunn continued: "You heard that psychiatric testimony." The court replies, "Sustained." Again Dunn states: "You heard that Cooper was able to do his job. Every witness who was here told you, every witness from the bar. Other than a few incidents Cooper had with Diedra Forte, Cooper was himself, he interacted with the customers normally.

There are so many other things. This little piece of paper, Callie, I'm sorry, and I do love you, sorry for what he is doing to his wife, not to Michael Barg. But he is sorry here. You have to look at this. You have your own judgment and your own common sense. Cooper knew what he was doing and what he was setting out to do. He knows it was wrong, but he is going to do it. There is not one witness who testified, including the social and the psychiatrist who said he ever had a mental defect. The defense says there is no evidence that he was still functioning. Not only was he going to work everyday, that during the period of time from July through October, when he committed this crime, when he is learning that Diedra Forte has broken up, that he went on at least two vacation trips. Does that sound to you like a person who is insane? We would like to think that the commission of evil is only done by insane people, but that is just not true. There is actually nothing strange as murderers who go about killing because they're jealous and they perceive someone as your rival for a woman.

The defendant remembers getting out of that car, going up those steps, carrying the sword, the sword in one hand, the billy club in another, unlocking the door, putting on the lights, going up the stairs, going to the bedroom where Michael Barg was sleeping, flipping on the lights. He remembered that Michael Barg got up and out of that bed and tried to defend himself, standing naked in front of a man carrying this sword, saying stop, don't. He remembers all of that. He remembers Michael Barg putting his hand up to try and protect himself. He remembers going across the hall to the room of Diedra Forte. He tells in his statements why he went there. He went there to kill her too. But when he looked at Diedra and she standing in front of him, pleading for her life, he remembered what this was really all about, that he loved her. He made a conscious and rational decision not to kill Diedra Forte. But he was not going to let her off the hook. So he grabbed her and dragged her across that hall. He said to her, look what you made me do. Diedra Forte did not do anything. From that moment on Cooper has never accepted responsibility for this crime.

Ladies and gentlemen, when this trial started, you were told of the presumption of innocence. You do not know anything about the def   endant. You know that he is presumed to be innocent. You have no reason to think that any stranger who walks through that door committed a crime. But now you have heard the evidence in this case. Now you know beyond a reasonable doubt that sitting in that chair is a murderer. There is a murderer in front of you. It is now your job, not a pleasant job, but it is your job to render the verdict. The verdict means to tell the truth." With explosive expression, Dunn reiterated, "Mr. Cooper is a *murderer* and it is now your time to tell the truth."

With more tears streaking down my cheeks, the judge summarized, "Your function as the jury is to determine the facts of the case. You alone, are the sole and exclusive judges of the facts. You alone, determine what evidence to accept, how important any evidence is that you accept and what conclusions to draw from all of the evidence. You are to be completely fair and impartial, you are not to be swayed by prejudice or by sympathy, by personal dislike or personal like toward either side. You are the sole judges of the credibility of the witnesses. If there is a conflict in the testimony, it is your function to resolve the conflict and to determine where the truth lies.

The verdict in this case must be unanimous. There will be twelve deliberating jurors. There are sixteen of you. There will be four alternates in this case. We will choose the alternates at the end of the instructions. The way we do it is we take the foreman's card, put that aside and put the remaining fifteen cards in the box and pull out four. Those people will be alternates. You will all have to decide each one of the three theories in the first degree, deliberate premeditation, number one, number two, extreme atrocity or cruelty; and, number three, felony murder. Your vote must be twelve to zero or zero to twelve. Mr. Foreman, when you have a verdict, it will either be guilty, not guilty, or not guilty by reason of insanity. Those are the three options."

I looked at my watch. It was 2:43 p.m. A painfully long day and it was not over yet. The judge continued, "Mr. Foreman and members of the jury, at approximately four o'clock, I am going to be sending in a little slip of paper to ask you whether you wish to continue with your deliberations today or whether you wish to suspend and come back tomorrow morning at nine o'clock. We do not want to rush your deliberations. If at four o'clock you feel you want to stay longer, we will do whatever you wish. I just want you to be aware that we are also aware of the time that you are putting in. So, in light of that, I will be sending that in about four o'clock; and you should tell us what you wish to do. The jury may go upstairs now." A recess prevailed.

None of us were clear as to how long the jury would be out. As we have seen in the movies, or have viewed on the television, or have read in the newspapers, a guilty verdict is often rendered quickly when deliberations have been short. It was viable to me given the testimony and the graphic brutal killing, that the jury would render Cooper guilty. Though the court may appear linear in nature, there is a very fine, shady area within such confines that makes the difference between real truth and exaggerated truth difficult to discern. I also knew that many of my biases were impartial. I have never been a proponent of killing another person, despite what that person has done. Perhaps, if I were my mother and if I too had lost a child the manner in which she lost Michael, such a statement may seem preposterous. However, if someone was going after my children I would defend my children to the hilt without due consciousness to the consequences. As righteous as this may sound, I know in my deepest place when Cooper leaves this planet, he will have so much work to do before he reaches that level of peace that is often spoken about on the other side of life. I know that Cooper will be faced with rigorous lessons, regardless. Though this will never bring Michael back, that was my only solace to any justice that could possibly predominate. In the meanwhile, if Cooper is convicted and sent to prison, the control he exercised to sustain his ego, would no longer exist. He would finally lose that battle. He would have to accept being told what to do. He would not have that freedom anymore. Perhaps for Cooper, that would be his final curtain call, shackled and all.

My family and I decided to stay within the parameters of the court. We all, in dreaded and consumed silence, made our way back to our little barren room, where all previous family members have sat and where all future families will sit to wait, while others decide the destiny of someone else's unspeakable act.

One and a half hours passed when Connie walked in to tell us that the jury needed a bit more time to discuss the trial. All of our stomachs sunk deeper. They were already sunk deep enough, but this news sounded menacing, making us sick inside. We waited. Another fifteen minutes. Connie came running in. "The jury is ready. They reached a verdict." A swarm of momentous emotions swelled inside me so fast I could barely stand. My heart was beating with tremendous intensity, I felt as though it were going to burst through my chest walls. Jacob and my mother were equally as overwhelmed. Walking fast, we found our way back to the seats we had come to know. Cooper's family, looking equally as agitated, were on the opposite side, awaiting the verdict.

"All rise. All be seated." "Has the jury reached a verdict Mr. Foreman?" asked the judge. The Foreman replied, "Yes, we have your honor." To justifiably describe the vibrations throughout my body and my families would be an under statement. Jacob looked at me with enormous anxiety. His ability to sit still was becoming a huge gut wrenching hindrance for him. My mother kept her hand over her mouth, tears pouring down her face, worry magnified a thousand fold. I was so highly agitated, the anticipation of what was to come was almost unbearable to me. Our bodies were suppose to be our insulation, our protection. Yet, to Jacob, my mother and I, our bodies were so out of control with fearful expectedness of the worst magnitude, our breathing became audible through the impenetrable silence. I could barely contain my tortured state, nor could Jacob. It was as though the weight of my emotions became heavier than my actual frame.

Our anxiety heightening, Judge Cooley asked the foreman to please pass on the papers he hand in hand. The inevitable question, "Mr. Foreman, what say you on Indictment No. 9577 CR 3259, charging the defendant, Jerry Cooper with murder? Is the defendant guilty or not guilty?" Mr. Foreman replied, *"GUILTY."* The judge asked, "Guilty of what?" The Foreman responded, "Deliberate premeditated murder." The judge continued, "The charges under Indictment 3259?" The Foreman replied, *"GUILTY* of murder by extreme atrocity and cruelty, guilty of felony murder." The judge continued," What say you Mr. Foreman, on Indictment No. 9577 CR 3260, with armed home invasion, Count 1?" Mr. Foreman repeated, *"GUILTY."* Again the judge asked, "What you say on Indictment No. 9577 CR 3260, with armed invasion, Count 2?" Mr. Foreman said, *"GUILTY."* My whole family broke concurrently. We were hysterically crying. The pain we held in released, making it cumbersome for us to hear the rest of what the judge was saying. The judge stopped momentarily, respecting our states of mind. The courtroom was impeccably hushed. The judge proceeded, "Ladies and gentlemen of the jury, harken to the verdict as the court has recorded it. You upon your oaths, do say that the defendant, Jerry Cooper, is guilty on Indictment No. 9577-3257, charging him with murder. So you say, Mr. Foreman?" "Guilty," responded Mr. Foreman. The Clerk then asked, "And ladies and gentlemen of the jury, so say you all?" All the jurors affirmed. The Clerk asked another question, "Ladies and Gentlemen of the jury, harken to your verdict...Botere interrupts, "Your Honor, I would move that the jurors be polled." Hastily, the judge responded, "We haven't finished yet, Mr. Botere." The Clerk carried on, "Mr. Foreman and Ladies and gentlemen of the jury, on Indictment No. 9577 CR 3259, charging him with murder, do you find him guilty of murder as to all three forms?" The Foreman responded, "Yes, we do." "So you say Mr. Foreman, and ladies and gentlemen of the jury, so say you all?" asked the Clerk. Again, all the jurors affirmed. "Ladies and Gentlemen of the jury, harken to your verdict as the Court has recorded it, You, upon your oaths, do say that the defendant, Jerry Cooper, is guilty on Indictment No. 9577 CR 3260, charging with armed home invasion, Count 1 and Count 2. So say you, Mr. Foreman?" questioned the Clerk. Again the Foreman responded, "Guilty." The Clerk continued, "Ladies and Gentlemen of the jury, so say you all?" All the jurors affirmed. The judge spoke, "Mr. Foreman, members of the deliberating jury and alternates, I want to thank you very much for coming in and performing the civic duty that the constitution requires all of us who sit as jurors to listen to the evidence and to render a verdict as the conscience of the community. On behalf of all of the members of the court staff and the judiciary, I thank you for performing your civic duty. You are now released from jury duty."

My mother, Jacob and I stood up, holding onto to each other weeping and gasping for what seemed to be an undetermined amount of time. It was a catharsis of some sorts. Connie and David merely watched us, sorrowfully. Cooper's family was crying and glanced over once. I too, knew they were in pain. Yet, I could not offer any generosity of my heart. Pain is pain and there is no way to simplify and minimize another's grief, no matter what the circumstance. Choked in emotion, my afflicted indulgence to my family was all I had. There simply was nothing left. The judge finished," I am going to revoke Mr. Cooper's bail. I am going to remand him to the custody of the sheriff. Tomorrow morning at nine o'clock, we will have sentencing." David Dunn expressed, "I would just formally move for sentencing at this time." Botere piped in, "I am going to request more time than to tomorrow morning, your Honor. It would be impossible for me to effectively represent him in sentencing disposition with just this evening to prepare for it." The judge responded, "Based upon the jury's verdict, there is only one sentence to be imposed upon the case in chief and that the other sentence with respect to the armed home invasion I can understand. But, I'm not sure you need that much more time to establish a presentation on that." Botere loudly protested, "Of course your Honor has discretion. I think it's important that I present as good an opportunity as is possible to give your Honor the benefit. There is an awful lot of background of Mr. Cooper that I think may act favorably in his behalf. So I would ask your Honor for at least a week or two to make a proper presentation for sentencing." Objecting fiercely, David Dunn said, "Your Honor, the Commonwealth would strongly be against that. Mr. Barg's family members live in New York State and Florida. They have all flown in. They have been here for this entire week. It would be extremely difficult for them to come back. They all want to be present at the sentencing." Judge Cooley remarks, "Tomorrow afternoon at two o'clock." Whereupon, the court was adjourned.

Chapter 47

Friday came. We all slept in, insulating ourselves from the pain swelling inside us. No one wanted to talk today. No one wanted to meet for breakfast or for lunch. No one wanted to do anything. Getting up was burdensome. Hearing testimony after testimony and rebuttal after rebuttal was depleting. Today I could feel no hatred or dislike for Cooper. Today, I could only be numb, for it was the only way in which I could tackle the rest of the day.

Hatred was never a part of my constitution. I knew compassion well. Sensitivity ran through my veins freely. As much as I wanted to hate Cooper for what he did to my brother, somehow I could not feel any for him. His tragic and pitiful demeanor was all I saw. Cooper was an individual who hated himself, though I doubted Cooper was ever cognizant to recognize as such. Cooper opted to act upon his wrath and his extreme insecurities. Regardless of the fact that Cooper may be convicted, it appeared his victory was acknowledged. He killed Michael. That was enough for Cooper. That was his liberation. If convicted, Cooper would spend ions of years behind prison walls. In my eyes, that was hell. My family and I would have to live our own hell each day reliving and envisioning how Michael inhumanly died. There was no getting around that. It simply was. We had to accept that, regardless of any justice prevailing.

It was getting nearer to two o'clock. Finding my family members, we congregated near the courtroom doors, waiting for Connie and David. Entering the courtroom, we again made our way to our designated seats. Cooper looked enormous to me, eerie in a sense. He was heavily shackled. He had very thick, black hair and his body was big, far bigger than Michael's. I could never imagine being at the mercy of Cooper's vengeance. Something about his face made me wince. There was a weirdness about his expression, one I would never be able to get out of my mind. Turning toward the front of the courtroom, I heard the judge acknowledge Botere and Dunn. I regained my focus.

At this time, before sentencing, an impact statement from my mother would be heard. The impact statement is a personal expression to the killer about what he did, affected our family. My mother was asked to come up to the stand. Composed, my mother offered these words: "It took me months to put what I wanted to say on paper. Every tear that I had, fell on each letter and each sentence I wrote. I got a call the morning after I spoke to my son the previous evening, informing me that my beloved son, my first-born child, had been brutally stabbed and murdered. I think I looked up to God and screamed, *WHY*? We have been through other tragedies, but this is the worst, this is the ultimate loss, for a mother to bury her child. This is a devastation that doesn't go away. You don't wake up in the morning and say, I feel great. Your child isn't there anymore. Michael became our everything. He was our protector, our friend, our Arch Angel, our hero. And all that was taken away. How dare you take my child's life? How dare you do that? You never knew my son. If you needed him for any reason, he would have reached out to you. He was the good guy. You have it all mixed up. You killed him to get even with a woman. This is such a senseless killing. You have put us into such a life of sadness. Getting up in the morning, going to work, putting one foot in front of the other, taking a shower, getting dressed, it has to be thought out. This is complete devastation. Actually I think this a death penalty case, to be honest. Unfortunately, they do not have the death penalty here in this state. Ironically, I've never been an advocate for pro death. I am now. However, if you get life without parole, knowing that this can never happen to another human being because of your rage and jealousy gives me some satisfaction. You have changed our lives completely. You have turned our happy family upside down. We try to get along the best we can. I feel very sorry for your family."

David Dunn stepped up to the judge, "Your Honor, knowing that the sentence for the murder is a mandatory life sentence I will not speak long on behalf of the Commonwealth. I would urge the Court to also give a life sentence on the home invasion. It is obvious how this has affected the Barg family, but it also affected many other people. The police officers, only four months on the force, were the first on the scene. These officers needed to take time off the force and receive counseling because of how this murder affected them. Even though they are not direct victims of this heinous crime, the nature of this crime has left the people who live behind the Preston house haunted by the events that took place on October 14th. There was also an assault on Ms. Forte, in her own house, where she was asleep. The defendant had planned this and had taken the key earlier. This merits a life sentence on the lesser charge as well."

Botere interjects: "There is no answer to the impact the death of Mr. Barg had on his family and on the community. I'm not going to even try to respond to that. However, you know from all of the witnesses that testified here that the defendant is not all a bad man. All of his life, up until the morning of October 14th, he served his country, he had a good work ethic, he was a leader at work, he was a father figure to them. What I am asking your Honor is to please take into consideration that the defendant has no criminal record, that he has been a law abiding citizen, that he has made contributions to his community."

Responding, the judge said, "Mr. Cooper, I'm going to sentence you on Indictment 3259 on murder in the first degree, to life imprisonment without parole. On indictments 3260, armed home invasion, for each count of the armed home invasion, twenty to thirty years, to run concurrent with that life sentence and those to run concurrent with each other. Now, our clerk will impose the sentence."

"Jerry Cooper, on indictment Number 95-3259, charging you with murder in the first degree by reason of deliberate premeditated murder, murder by extreme atrocity and cruelty, and felony murder, the jury having returned a verdict of guilty, harken to your sentence as the Court has awarded you. The Court orders you to be imprisoned for life and that the sentence be executed within the precincts of the Massachusetts Correctional Institutional at Cedar Junction, that you stand committed in execution thereof."

The judge's final words, "The court is now adjourned." It was finally over. The courtroom looked as void of emotion as it did when the trial began. My body shivered. Filing out of the courtroom, our hearts were hollow. Our memories of Michael would never cease.

Jacob, my mother and I stood still, embracing each other in a mini circle of sorts. We simply did not move or gravitate to another corner of the courtroom. Our grief was that much more visible as was our relief. We could now go home and attempt to restore our lives. I wondered if that was even possible.

Thanking David and Connie, we left. The girls and I returned to Florida. Jacob flew to New York City. My mother drove back to Upstate, New York. Living again was the goal.

Chapter 48

Almost two years had passed. Routine had established itself. Life in Florida appeared good. Peaceful surroundings abounded. Friends were committed and loyal. Sunny days and temperate nights were plentiful, allowing healing to progress. Still, lingering more than subtly, was a dull ache that had shifted a thousand fold into a spirited pain. How visible it was to me. Getting up everyday was cumbersome. I seemed to have lost my ability to feel anything but a severe cavity in my stomach. This emptiness was taking up more space in me than I would have appreciated. Thoughts of Michael inundated my essence, emphasizing the void already in me. My cries were more frequent and more debilitating.

I was working round the clock, disliking what I was doing. Working to pay my bills and to survive was exhausting. I had scored zero in the romance department, always attracting men who were emotionally unavailable to me. I was a free agent for so long, the desire to have a companion increased. Off and on I had dated, but no one made my heart zing. I could not handle anything complicated. Even if the universe provided me with a suitable companion, I would not have recognized the opportunity, despite my hunger for one. Opportunities were with men who were so needy. Deja-vu was ever present. Once again, my M.O. Thus, I isolated myself more from the opposite sex. I was angry and unforgiving of myself that I would ever bring a man into my life that was unattainable. Surely one would think I would have learned this lesson years ago, after a very painful marriage. Nonetheless, it was quite apparent that I had a long way to go.

Kailee and Emily were doing fine. Despite my hidden suffering, they were not aware of what was going on. My big concern was the lack of financial abundance in my life. After years of supporting my household, I was having a very difficult time making my mortgage payments. This was nothing new as my marriage reflected severe financial strains. When I originally made an offer to buy my home, something inside me said "Take more time." Normally I would have been very attuned to trusting my voice. Yet, somehow, this house offered great possibilities at a time when I could get a mortgage through. Another humbling lesson. Unless you are financially stable with a back-up plan, have a back-up plan for a back-up plan.

My children and I never had the ability to own a house. I desperately wanted to have a home that was ours, one that I could nurture and fix up, not be bound to a landlord would continually benefit from my efforts. However, the bank was doing a fine job owning my house along with accumulations of interest piling up. For two years I was maintaining my mortgage free and clear. Now, I was in debt, skyhigh with this house. Even if I lived long enough to see this mortgage through, I could not enjoy whatever would be left of my years on this earth. Despite my attempts to offer my lender a good amount of money to save my home and putting my faith into a realtor to sell my home, I had to go into foreclosure. Being terribly humbled again, I was equally frustrated at the choices I had made. The fire inside of me was no more. I tried like hell to get it back. I simply could not. As usual, I was forced to look at a visual movie screen of my past decisions.

How would I tell Kailee and Emily that we were going to lose our house, a home that they were comfortable in and felt safe in, where their friends came over for pajama parties, scavenger hunts, dinners and play, a home that symbolized their security? How could I possibly disrupt their lives? What were we going to go? I simply did not have a plan, at least, not this time.

For all the years I committed myself to my visions, I was easily able to manifest them. Now, I felt as powerless as possible, without any motivation to succeed. I felt as though I had failed Kailee, Emily and myself. I was brought down to such a level of submission, I had to face my pain. I could not even find comfort in that.

All my years of passionate living and surviving, continual moves with my family, a horrific car accident at the age of thirteen, the loss of my father, a journey to India at age fifteen, dropping out of college for a year, driving out west when I was a mere nineteen, supposedly to find myself, going back to school and attaining my Masters on my own, witnessing my best friend succumb to cancer, attempting to make a wrong marriage right, raising two children basically by myself, establishing a very lucrative practice as a therapist, watching a loyal ex sister-in-law die way too early in life, helping thousands of others find meaning in their lives, divorcing a man I once loved, but now did not respect, burying my brother at a very untimely age, traveling the world and lecturing throughout, I would have presumed that I could have tackled just about anything. Yet, I was as lost and as confused and as humiliated as I could possibly be. Being told by the bank that all I had was four months to leave and get out and make my life elsewhere, only heightened my anguish and my disappointment in myself.

I was looking back at grief in the mirror. I did not know the person I was staring at. She wore a terribly woeful face. Her eyes reflected a heavy-heartedness, the sparkle shaded by crushing losses of yesteryear. Her fire was out. Her passion blighted by exhaustion and futility. I remembered it was me. Slipping onto my bed at one in the morning, I cried a wail so unbeknown to myself, my body slithered into unconsciousness, my sheets wet from my tears. Hope was no longer an option for me. It use to be my reserve. I could not locate it. Fully submerged in emotional impotence, I was no longer desperate for an answer. Pain completely swallowed me.

Making decision after decision for my children, wanting Kailee and Emily to be happy, supported and confidant, working so hard in my marriage to stay afloat and the drive to keep going, were as familiar to my life as was the blueness to the sky. My steadfast commitment to empower others to help themselves was unconditional. However, I did not take the time to truly acknowledge what I needed to do for myself. Abandoning myself unconsciously played a heavy price on me. I was terribly mentally fatigued and encumbered by this tormenting pain. I was to confront it no matter what, no matter how excruciating the journey. It was now. I was exactly where I was suppose to be. It was not going to go away. This was probably was one of the most courageous things I would ever have to do.

Kailee and Emily would spend a good majority of their summer in Boston with their Dad. Thus, this became a perfect opportunity for me to unclutter the clutter and head back up north. Sharing news with my children about our move was actually very positive. Though they both loved Sarasota, they were quite okay with renewing ties with old friends and family. Kailee would begin eighth grade, Emily fifth. Thus and once again, our new journey would begin.

To add to my grievous state however, I had gotten a call from my mother earlier that day. David Dunn had died instantly from a heart attack he suffered while attending a Patriot's football game in Boston with his son, the day before. I was thoroughly taken aback, beside myself, deeply affected. Although I had only known David shortly, my tie to him was devoted and strong. What he did for my family and for Michael, would never be forgotten. He was our strength at time when we had none. A passionate man dead at the age of forty-six. Again my journey was to begin with a new devastation. I cried myself to sleep like I had never cried before.

Chapter 49

My younger brother flew into Sarasota the evening before I was about to embark on my trek up north. I packed up my entire house efficiently and single-handedly. My friends helped me to pack up my truck. The goodbyes were again, very painful. So many tears shed. Lil, my neighbor across the street, took me out for dinner the night before. Laughter, memories, both solemn and joyous were discussed. I was very blessed. My heart ached for her already.

The next morning, I met with Jacob who was as patient and loving as he could be. Somehow, it was but three years prior that he was down here seeing me off. Now he was helping me home without judgment. There was just enough space for Succi, Stella and Ling right between the driver's seat and the passenger seat. Water was plentiful for them. They were ready to go anywhere we were going.

My home was completely emptied. I sold just about everything, taking only what was needed. Somehow, the need to let go of things that were no longer significant in my life was a huge cleansing. I was never a rug rat. Refined simplicity was refined elegance to me. I did manage however, to place emphasis on my children's possessions, for their security was of great importance to me.

The last few months provided me with distraction of mega dimensions. I had a job offer at a hospice outside New York City. Given the opportunity to store my belongings in my mother's home, while I worked in the city, allowed me to get my feet planted, secure money in my pocket and bring my children from Boston to begin school somewhere. I was contemplating moving all of us outside of Manhattan, I was not sure just where that would be yet. Although I had all of Kailee's and Emily's school papers and health records, only six weeks were available to me to tie up loose ends. My interest was presently was for my dogs. They too were my everything. Their unspoken devotion to my pain and my humanness brought me tremendous moments of solace. People I hardly knew told me to give them up. Never.

In the midst of my struggle to properly house them, at least temporarily, my mother had a friend who would take them in upstate, while I began work in the city. What a crushing blow to me. Simultaneously, I was somewhat relieved. Yet, how could I possibly abandon these dogs? They were always there for me. Another gripping reality forced me to let go, trust and reason that all would work out for the highest good. I was so tired believing that this day. Yet, I had nothing more to hold on to. I would at least in the moment, be only responsible for myself. I was not even sure what that meant.

Jacob and I began our long pilgrimage home. We talked, laughed and ate on the road. Pit stops were few, merely to walk the dogs and to refresh our legs from getting stiff. The anxiety that was mounting in my chest wall was huge. I had never endured bouts of anxiety in the proportions I was presently experiencing them and I did not relay this to Jacob. My heart would pound so greatly, I would have to catch my breath. I never wanted to leave Florida. I was so unprepared as to my next step or where I was going to live, my body was taking the opportunity to soak it all in. I was terrified. Not of change, but of fearing that I was making another mistake. Nighttime in the truck became my friend. Jacob and I had found a station that carried the oldest love songs known to my generation. I was soothed merely by their melodies.

When we stopped at a Kentucky Fried Chicken fast food joint, Jacob looked at me rather teasingly and said, "Hmm, this must be a challenge for you." Laughter broke between us. True to organic foods and prodding myself on eating well, living well, was blown to bits that evening. However, it tasted great. This time, I was not going to be hard on myself. We ate, we drove, we shared our tidbits with Succi, Stella and Ling. We drove some more, well into the wee hours of the morning, making only one overnight stay at a motel. Twenty-seven and a half hours later, we parked in front of my mother's home in upstate, New York, mid morning, ready to unpack a moving truck. Our adrenaline was in tact, thus, it was best we stayed with the flow. Two hours and counting, the truck was unloaded. I was heading to New York City with Jacob to begin my job and to hopefully find housing for Kailee, Emily and my dogs. Kissing my mother goodbye, Jacob and I took my car which was attached to the moving truck. We then began our way toward to the Big Apple.

I did not have anytime to acclimate to life up north. I was already freezing, although it was barely the end of July. I had yet to see my kids in over two months, though my contact with them via the phone and letters were often. The welling inside of me was so abundant, wailing late into the morning hours again predominated my sleep. I could not make peace with this emptiness residing inside of me. Yet, I had to succumb to its power of me, because I had so little fight left inside my bones. Tomorrow was my first day commencing at hospice. There was no breaks, no time to grieve what I had just left behind. Arriving at Jacob's pad, one and a half rooms later, we ate, he left to meet some friends and I fell into a sound sleep until the next morning.

Chapter 50

The traffic. I was to be outside of Queens in less than an hour. Rather, it took me two hours and fifteen minutes to forge my way through up town streets, one way here, the other way there, over a bridge, dead locked at more than one red light. When I finally found my work building, in a not so nice neighborhood, parking was impossible. Determined to walk inside, refreshed, unaffected, I finally made my way to the main entrance only to discover that I was not able to get inside. It was a secured entrance. Adjusting my eyes on the plaque on the side wall, adjacent to the door, I found Hospice, 6th floor. Buzzing, without a voice to respond back, the door magically opened. How safe could that be? Dressed business-like, but casual, I entered into a massive room filled with cubicles, a conference room and some people busily talking on phones. I approached the front desk asking for the man who hired me in Florida via interviews over the phone. He was not coming in today. An enormous red flag, frenetically sweeping, appeared in my mind. I insisted that I was to work today, my starting date being July 26th. He forgot to come in to meet me. He was tied up at a meeting across what seemed like another continent, New Jersey. My frustration was mounting. They directed me to another woman, Claire whom I would be working with. She was delightful, highly apologetic and spent hours sacrificing time to accommodate me. We hit it off without a glitch.

The majority of the day was spent on the road, in Claire's car, constant traffic abounding. Despite the appointments Claire had made, she never made them on time. Not a fault of hers, simply the fault of the big city and its surrounding suburbs. Red flag number two. My job description was to publicly speak about hospice, offering my counseling expertise, $50,000 dollars per year. Now, my objective was to encourage more hospitals and more doctors to accept hospice into their environments. In other words, I was a salesperson, convincing others to basically try hospice. Red flag number three. Everything I was interviewed for was the antithesis of what I was told. What I was promised was entirely different from what I would be doing. My unseen boss had good reason not to want to meet with me.

I rationalized many thoughts. Kailee and Emily did not have to begin school until the second week in September. I had roughly one month and so many weeks to bank a portion of a fifty-thousand dollar salary, work to my capacity, with very little direction. Though I was a single mother, I would enter into the worst neighborhoods of burroughs at ungodly times. Getting my mind focused, I decided to tough it out, while looking for a place to live.

One month past. Grueling, and still without a secure place to live, time was running thin. Not only could I not locate a decent apartment that would accept my dogs, I could not find one that would accept my children. The salary I was making was barely enough to cover any acceptable living space. I ate meagerly, simply because my appetite had waned. Spending outrageous hours in a car only to make it three miles, still far away from my designated work site, surpassed my desire to feed myself. Weight was dropping off me like flies.

That movie screen appeared in front of me again. How many more mistakes could I possibly make? No apartments manifested themselves. No new changes in my job situation were coming to fruition. I was juggling living at my brother's in Manhattan and my mother's cousins' home on the Island, most likely outdoing my stay. I was definitely not being able to utilize my talents. What was worse, I was working in an organization that constantly reflected grief of unlimited magnitude. New York City offered very little warmth and closeness. I have always adored the energy from New York. However, I was a very small peon in a huge metropolis that was distant, fast, and sometimes indifferent. Not the environment in which to help me heal. My grief was always there, heavy on my heart. I finally had to ask myself why I would want to work in an environment that spoke only of bereavement and distress. Finally, I went to a warm and extremely, compassionate individual within the organization whom I trusted. She took me in, validating everything I felt. She offered me comfort and wisdom, reassuring me that my talents would not be recognized here. She confirmed my suspicions about the lack of integrity within the infrastructure of the organization. In essence, she gave me permission to move forward, away from more pain, more isolation and more turmoil.

As usual, my boss was nowhere to be seen. I left a long note, explaining my dissatisfaction. Within two days I headed back upstate nearer to my mother. No job, no place to stay. Kailee and Emily would be starting school in two weeks. Quickly and readily I enrolled them in their perspective schools. My mother was kind enough to take the girls, my dogs and me in, while I secured any type of employment and hopefully a place to live.

Somehow, I just could not accept the fact that I was returning home. I came to this little town when I was twelve years old, ready to begin the seventh grade. Seeing the world through very young eyes afforded me an unblemished outlook. The homes were settled, some big, oversized and snuggly, surrounded by porches and enormous maple trees. I was an excellent student, I made friends easily and I felt safe. A year later, we were in our car accident. Despite our tragedy, I had a very warm and loving upbringing, with many successes to speak of in my high school years. I was different though. What was important to me before our accident, changed drastically after our accident, though I would have hardly been cognizant of such insight then. Experiencing death in a hospital ward, day after day changes you. Beginning high school late, due to innumerable, life-threatening injuries changes you. I was still free spirited and fun loving, but my world and how I saw it was very different from the basic teenager. My last four months in that hospital became privy to daily deaths of children, with audible sobs of parents in the background.

My friends though few, were from different groups. Not groups that would be considered popular. If I was popular, it was unbeknown to me. Still, I was a teenager and fitting in was not always that easy. The community was quite conservative in nature. Not much had changed in twenty-six years, somewhat disconcerting. The winters were gruesome, long and dormancy was familiar. Everybody hibernated. Being single afforded little opportunity to make connections. If you were born here, it was much easier to break in. Industry was so sparse, finding decent employment to maintain a healthy lifestyle was difficult, especially for a single mom.

As an outsider, looking back and one who was gone for a long time, the struggle to stay put here became insurmountable. I felt broken for having to have gone full circle. I reprimanded myself for having to return to a place I simply had outgrown. I also could not appreciate anything under seventy degrees. I dreaded the winter. Fresh, progressive blood was not readily understood. The energy was depressed, unchallenging and I felt a thousand more times trampled on emotionally. Again, the more I resisted, the more resistance was available to me. I had nowhere to go but here. I was begging the universe to assure me that a divine plan was in the making. I bit my lip, found an apartment and a landlord that would accept my entire clan. Prodding ever so slowly, I began my life over again, with my children and my dogs.

Chapter 51

Another two years passing, I was finally able to immerse myself in reflection and who I had become. Very, very slowly, I accepted the pilgrimage of my former forty- three years. Though the pain within me still subsided, I acquired a quiet resolve.

My first year in upstate was long, ferociously painful, with soulful cries at night that left me too empty to feel anything but the cold. The grief I was so expert at stuffing down became at the foremost of my responsibilities. I had to finally acknowledge it. Plugging through had always been my survival. Not this time.

The rage I had at my ex-husband was beyond what I could possibly describe in words. My soul experienced a deep, deep hurt. It simply was there. Kailee and Emily were quite little when I divorced. I did not have time to consciously dwell on the anguish I experienced in my marriage. Still, I was relieved that I left a union that was terribly isolating. For years, everything I did, I did for my children. I would never take that back. Sacrifice was a priority. Struggling financially without my ex was easier than struggling with him. Now, and after all of the years of working constantly, paying bills, providing my children with clothes on their back, food in their bellies, affording them limitless opportunities to pursue their interests regardless, I was outraged and sorrowed beyond reproach at their father. I had more time to think about the neglect we all endured.

Before returning north, I promised myself I would downsize my life. My responsibilities were already gigantic. I was beginning to know my limitations. I wanted to be there even more for my children. That would require me to cut down on work time. In turn, this would be also mean less income. In the process of making that decision, the time I had to participate in my children's lives also gave me more time to think and more time to struggle. Feelings of hurt, disappointment and the recognition of the delinquency from my ex had come full circle. I spent ten years with an individual who simply was not awake. Those hopes and dreams I once had, somehow, become muffled in the throes of raising children, working and surviving. I was not even sure if those dreams could ever manifest. That grief was facing me right inside my heart and right between my eyes. It was as bold and as enormous as ever, I had to tend to it. My grace in doing as such was hardly savvy. I cried. I screamed. I coiled. I resisted with all my might and it just would not go away. Then, I finally acquiesced to my broken state. I was as powerless as a new born baby, dependent on something much bigger than myself. For the years I stuffed my pain inward, I also built a huge pit of sadness in my soul, tearing at my heart. My life would not progress until I acknowledged that chasm getting bigger and bigger inside of me.

This time, letting go appeared so terribly unsettling. I was no longer in control of what I had always been in control of, merely surviving. Searching for an outcome to my pain, made me miss the most important aspect of living, staying in the moment of where I was to be, regardless of how painful a place it was. A Sufi Master once told me that the only time we are truly ever awake is when we die. I did not want to wait until that moment in my life to fully awaken.

My pain literally cracked me open. It also fully awakened me. Though my will was determined, my heart loving and generous and my disposition usually positive, somewhere along the way I lost in touch with me. It was so difficult for me to receive. I often chose relationships where I would inevitably be the ultimate caretaker. I did not consciously play this scenario out. It was merely what I attracted. What I attracted was what I needed to learn nonetheless. Though my social life with the opposite sex was not expansive by any means, I was becoming more and more aware of what I would no longer accept. If a man said he would call and he did not follow through, I was not interested. If a man would make plans with me and cancel them at the last minute more than once, I was no longer available. I needed to be a priority for someone. I needed to be special to someone. I needed them to honor me and also respect my time. I accepted who they may have been, but at a distance. I simply did not want to get involved with another individual who made excuses as to why he could not be available. Though I would adore a very loving and mutually reciprocal relationship, I was okay if one was not materializing. If it meant not having a partner, if those were in my cards, then I would have to be okay with that. If I was blessed enough to meet a loving man, then I would have to trust that I would recognize him.

I was working on finding balance in my life and allowing individuals into my life who were one hundred percent supportive of me, without censorship. Rediscovering myself, setting boundaries and honoring my essence, as well as continuing my love of mothering with my children was a lovely invitation into living once more.

So much of my first year back was understanding the many losses in my life: Continual moves with my family beginning at an early age, the uprooting and the inability to establish lifelong friends; the car accident when I was thirteen, forcing me to grow up well beyond my years obliterating a good portion of my childhood; my father's untimely death leaving me cut off from watching a sound and healthy relationship between partners develop in the natural course of events; the loss of my respected friend, Laura at the age of twenty-six, opening more sorrow in my heart; the tumultuous breakup of my marriage, leaving wounds inside my soul untended to; my former sister-in-law's death from brain cancer, reminding me to love that much more; the many dogs I gently laid to rest, searing my insides with more aches; the loss of my house in Florida, exasperating the awareness of my mistakes; the unsuccessful attempts at having loving relationships, forcing me to question if I was even lovable; and my brother's vicious and abominable murder which finally broke me. Michael's death opened up my past. Michael's leaving made me question everything I thought I knew. His death marked an insurmountable crossroad in my life.

My brother's passing compelled me to make peace with my grief, but not without a great struggle. The gaping hole that already existed in my womb came to my highest place, my consciousness. It hurt like no other hell I have experienced. The deepest gut cries I had, tore at me nightly for hours on end. I simply could not stop. They kept coming. I implored God to please take away my pain. I argued with God. I bargained, I did everything humanely possible so I would not have to have this pain. My requests were not altered in any way, shape or form. Every waking hour I experienced, I berated myself for coming back up north. My soul felt so heavy, because I simply could not forgive the mistakes I had made. Isolation bore through me ripping me to emotional shreds. Anything I managed to do was for the sake of Kailee and Emily. I realized that any love I was going to know and hold on to would be for and about my children. It was the three of us. I would have to sustain myself honoring that fact. Whatever I was releasing, was from a place that no longer could house my meticulous stuffing.

Through two, extremely, bitter cold winters, Springs that never were and partially rainy summers, I began to end my torture of myself. Every disappointment I endured, every mistake that had I had made was slowly disintegrating. Slowly. I began to open to my inner voice again, trusting it, knowing that whatever I chose I would be fully supported by the universe. My free will became choosier. Though segregated by some of my decisions, I remained true to them. Some days were good. Other days still brought tremendous pain. This panoramic view of all of yesteryear released me to my greatest challenge into living life again: Hope. Somehow, what I once knew was resurfacing.

Chapter 52

There is nothing etched in stone that tells you how to deal with grief and loss. There is no written manual that states how one loss outweighs another loss. There is no written manual that declares that your grief is less or more than another person's grief. Still, there is no written manual on how to survive this earthly plane. Loss, pain, grief. It hurts so much. There is really never getting over it. There is however, getting on with it.

My reclamation into living again was my pain. Despite the years I was brilliant at stuffing my pain inward, the universe provided me with brilliant opportunities to seize it. Yet, I was just not cognizant of taking the opportunity. Allowing myself to finally succumb to my innermost pain, also allowed me to understand it. That was harrowing in itself. No matter how unwilling I was, hope ultimately became my savior.

Such mini optimism came out of sheer, unrelenting pain. I could not go any lower than I had already gone. Through the wear and tear of being so frustrated with myself, the energy I spent silently criticizing myself kept me exhausted. Exhausted emotionally and disappointed with not allowing myself to move forward, I ultimately had to choose acceptance. Surrendering myself to acceptance opened me to more tolerance of my past mistakes and of myself. With this gentle understanding, though sometimes with not always knowing why, a definitive purpose of what I had gone through became clearer to me. Redefining my relationship with life and humanity was a priority. Regardless of how horrifically in pain I was in, I was finally able to stretch myself beyond any usual limitation I may have held. Once my recognition came to fruition, all I could do was accept the inevitable, my pain. The grief so outweighed the happiness in my life at that point, I was exactly where I was suppose to be, in it. In many respects, stepping in became my gift.

I was not asking myself not to feel sadness and happiness concurrently. I was not asking myself not to have expectations that were unreasonable. I was not asking myself not to sometimes feel discouragement and a sense of helplessness. What I was able to do however, was to eventually take all that mass confusion, that disappointment and that pain and manifest it into a more generous and more loving gesture. Otherwise, I would have desecrated myself even more. If I did not allow myself a crevice of light, I would never be able to reclaim and reestablish my deep and loving connection to myself and to others. I did not think I could live without that connection. That was one of my biggest lessons, finding the connection. Thus, began my journey back to myself.

This kindling of spirit gave me a wonderful opportunity to share again. Without that rekindling, I would have been denied what I fully know is deeply fundamental to me; living a more human centered way of living, a way that touches the very springs of my soul, regardless of what I would wake up to and face each day. Living my life fully and being touched by it always made my heart sing. I just could not find the song anymore. There was simply too much hurt. In the midst of my survival, doing, making everyone else's life manageable, I forgot my own. Then the tragedies, the losses and the disappointments, how neatly packed away in me they were. Eventually, survival became a deadening and a disquieting process.

As I awakened and as I am still waking up and in that process, and it is sometimes a painful one, I have learned that letting go is acceptance in disguise, despite what I may encounter. As my daily pulse of living and trusting becomes more vivid to me, I attempt to rally with myself as opposed to rallying against myself. My pain can now be dispersed into a gentle faith. How, I do not always know. All I do know is that I need to do it.

Everyday, I attempt to live a quiet harmony. Such harmony allows me seek a higher order that does not need to be so questioned so much. Surviving and reasoning, surviving and reasoning, and more surviving and more reasoning alone led me to despair. I will never be able to bring my father back. In the past, I have wondered what my life would have been like if I did not lose my father at an early age. Would my choices be different? Would I have married the man that is my children's father? Would I have chosen a different career path? What if? I will not know and now it is not important that I seek answers to those questions. Yet, I will always quietly yearn for my father.

I will never be able to tangibly nurture my friendship with Laura. That friendship meant everything to me. She never had the ability to live the life she so wanted to have. A brilliant artist laid to rest at twenty-six years of age. My heart will never cease to pine for her.

I will never be able to understand why my former sister-in-law was plagued with a tumor that literally ravaged her life and at a time when she had so much to look forward to. Kelly's loves were her children and her family. Her youngest daughter never really knew her. Perhaps, it is not important to understand why she died so young. What is important, is to have experienced Kelly's essence, her love of giving. Her death intensely tore at my heart. I will always ache for her presence and I will continue to cry for her family and especially for her children.

I will never be able to snuggle with those canine friends who have since left me. These beautiful creatures have sustained me through my darkest times. They have also lightened my life with supreme joy. They have been a tremendous source of insight into loving unconditionally. I so respect their beings. Their life spans are much too short. The thought of one day saying goodbye to yet another one of my loyal friends, hysterically breaks me open.

I may not have that loving union I have longed for. I quietly grieve what I have yet to manifest. That grief is what never was. It is a mourning that comes and goes. I sometimes fear that the love I have inside of me will never be shared with someone who too understands that kind of love. So, I cry and I accept. I cry and I accept. Finally, I will never, ever get over losing Michael and the vicious way in which he left this earth. Those wounds are huge and full of a pain that comes and goes without warning and will continue to for the rest of my life. I still have haunting visions of his barbaric death. I still feel a deep searing in the pit of my stomach. I cannot imagine what he must have experienced moments before his death. Just the mention of his name swallows me to unremitting tears.

Life has not always provided the answers or the journey I thought I should have had. Looking outside of myself only lead me to more distress. I now understand that all of my answers lie within me. I have laid many of my shoulds, my woulds and my coulds to rest. I have forgiven my ex-husband because it is much more painful not to. I can only answer to myself and be liable for my choices. I now recognize my choices, not shun them. I now acknowledge the gift in my experiences, not stuff them away. Still, I feel the pain nonetheless.

No matter how I walk on my path, no matter how variegated everybody's human experience is, no matter how different, how excruciatingly agonizing, no matter how complicated, life, somehow goes on. Getting on with it, that is the hard part. Letting go and trusting can be even harder. Yet, the surrender of it all brings a resplendent peace, even if it is for the moment I am in. Such a peace is not to be questioned. It is there and it offered me a glimmer of hope when my life appeared to be tortuous. It is what I choose to do with that pain that makes all the difference in the world. Sometimes, I simply do not always know the correct choice, if there is indeed one. Instead, I try to embrace where I am and simply be.

For me to fully open again is to ripen to myself, committing to the knowledge that I must participate with life and all that comes with it without crucifying my soul. Life's hits, already defy my ability to remain consistently loving. That is challenging enough.

To love is to hope. To live is to hope. My tenacity of spirit has been marred by excruciatingly hard challenges. It is not as necessary for me to choose the road less traveled anymore. My children are healthy and thriving. They have been my guiding lights even when they are so unaware of their gifts to me. My practice is still growing. My commitment to fully and wholly help others help themselves is passionate. My involvement in facing life's crushing blows is now done with a gentle eye, not a harsh one.

Jacob is happily married and was given a beautiful, brand new son. One life is taken, another is given. He holds this supremely perfect, little human being in the crux of his palms. I watch as Jacob restrains his inner anguish inside. Michael can never hold Jacob's son. Thus, Jacob's agony becomes a visible reminder of what he cannot share with Michael.

My mother walks on attempting to remain focused. She still tries to make sense of it all, even when no sense is to be made of it. She is a member of a support group known as POM, Parents of Murdered Children; a very high price to pay to be a member. To lose a child is a horrific tragedy. I do not think it is genuinely possible to even suggest that my mother will ever be the same. Sometimes she smiles though, despite the emptiness she is always reminded of having. That is grace.

My heart is consciously open, though my hurt is far from being mended. It may never really be. I am still Michael's sibling and I still feel the anguish. I still cry. That is okay. I have loving friends in my life that are there for me without condition. I have come to realize all too well that I have this inherent ability to commit to the openness of my heart, despite my pain. Such a choice enables me to live on purpose.

Like pain, hope is boundless. I can affirm from my soul a sense of great empowerment to embrace my pain and now participate in it with without harsh criticism. Ultimately, I can feel more integrated, my supported and more constructive. Pain has brought me far. It has given me faith, trust and hope. Pain has also reminded me that being vulnerable lets me see that I am still alive.

But the heavens never cried. The day we lay Michael to rest, the heavens never did cry. My mother so wanted the heavens to bellow with storm and with a ferocity of wind to reflect her torment. Instead the sun shone brilliantly. The irony of it. Perhaps that was hope.

I will always cry for anyone who has suffered, regardless of their circumstance. There is no reason to justify pain of any kind. It merely comes with living as does hope. I have hope for the human spirit. I will never underestimate the power of it. The greatest thing we have is life, and where there is life, there is always hope. As I stand alone with myself I can share the sunlight as much as I can share the rain. I can share the contradictions of life as much as I can share the splendor of it. In my worst nightmare, I can easily be enveloped by my losses. Yet, in my sweetest dream, I am blessed by the gifts of them. My suffering has been agonizing. However, in order for me to live again, I have to risk the pain. I know, how difficult. As I woke up, I have prayed that you too, will gently awake and grasp and gather the threads of your own life with a dignified hope.

About The Author

Cindy E. Barg, M.Ed. is a highly respected public speaker, psychotherapist & educator whose expertise lies in the arena of, but is not limited to: death & dying, self-empowerment, relationships, grief, loss and getting beyond "life's stuff." In 1971, Ms. Barg was told she would never walk again or be able to have children. To date, she has conducted over five hundred workshops at retreat centers, wellness facilities, corporations, universities and primary and secondary school settings. Cindy has operated a private practice for sixteen years on Cape Cod, Florida and New York and she has lectured extensively throughout the northeast and the south. Most recognized for her unique and gifted approach to healing, Cindy continues to teach others to tap into their personal power, grasping and gathering the threads of their lives, no matter how profoundly tragic or joyful their circumstances.

Cindy presently lives in Upstate, NY as a single mother of two extraordinary girls and two wonderful canines who have taught her much about life and living. As she continues on her journey, she serves humanity utilizing love as the basis for living on purpose and reestablishing a deep and loving connection to our hearts.

CPSIA information can be obtained
at www.ICGtesting.com
Printed in the USA
BVHW071659090620
581035BV00001B/70